3 9047 00013986 1

D1092253

mill
fan.

Unabridged repub... ....gi... ...) book. Pu
vii + 134pp. 6½ x 9¼. 23210

Barnaby and Mr O'Malley

CROCKETT JOHNSON

DOVER PUBLICATIONS INC., NEW YORK

6614

PUBLIC LIBRARY SAN MATEO CALIFORNIA

817.02
J

Copyright © 1975 by Dover Publications, Inc.
Copyright © 1943, 1944 by Field Publications.
Copyright © renewed 1972 by Crockett Johnson.
All rights reserved under Pan American and International Copyright Conventions.

Published in Canada by General Publishing Company, Ltd., 30 Lesmill Road, Don Mills, Toronto, Ontario.
Published in the United Kingdom by Constable and Company, Ltd., 10 Orange Street, London WC 2.

This Dover edition, first published in 1975, is an unabridged republication of the work originally published by Henry Holt and Company, N.Y. (n.d.) . A new Publisher's Note has been written specially for the present edition.

International Standard Book Number: 0-486-23210-7
Library of Congress Catalog Card Number: 75-16604

Manufactured in the United States of America
Dover Publications, Inc.
180 Varick Street
New York, N.Y. 10014

CONTENTS

PUBLISHER'S NOTE

All the material in this volume originally appeared in *PM* (and by syndication in many other newspapers in the United States) in the years 1943 and 1944. Barnaby, his parents, his human girl friend Jane and his supernatural friends (his fairy godfather Mr. O'Malley, Gus the Ghost, McSnoyd the invisible leprechaun and the talking dog Gorgon) had already been introduced in the earliest strips beginning in 1942 (reprinted in the Dover volume *Barnaby*).

Though the humor of this comic strip is timeless, a few of the topics naturally reflect the days of World War II when the strip was created, and younger readers may welcome some elucidation.

Families were encouraged to grow vegetables at home in so-called Victory Gardens, so that more farm produce would be available for the troops. Even many urban elementary schools had small plots of ground to which the pupils were marched out periodically to plant corn or other easy-to-grow foods.

Air Wardens were civilians who patrolled their neighborhoods during practice air raid alerts, making sure no lights were visible and looking out for possible enemy aircraft.

The gentleman named Mr. Anthony to whom Mr. O'Malley boasts he has given advice was a radio performer who gave people advice on all subjects over the air.

Food rationing was in force during the war, and stamps out of ration books had to be presented when making purchases.

The OPA (Office of Price Administration) combated inflation and profiteering by fixing prices. Hoarding and black-marketing were evils that required constant vigilance.

James Caesar Petrillo was a fiery musicians' union leader who fought for a share of the profits from the performance of recorded music.

EPISODE ONE
Barnaby's Garden

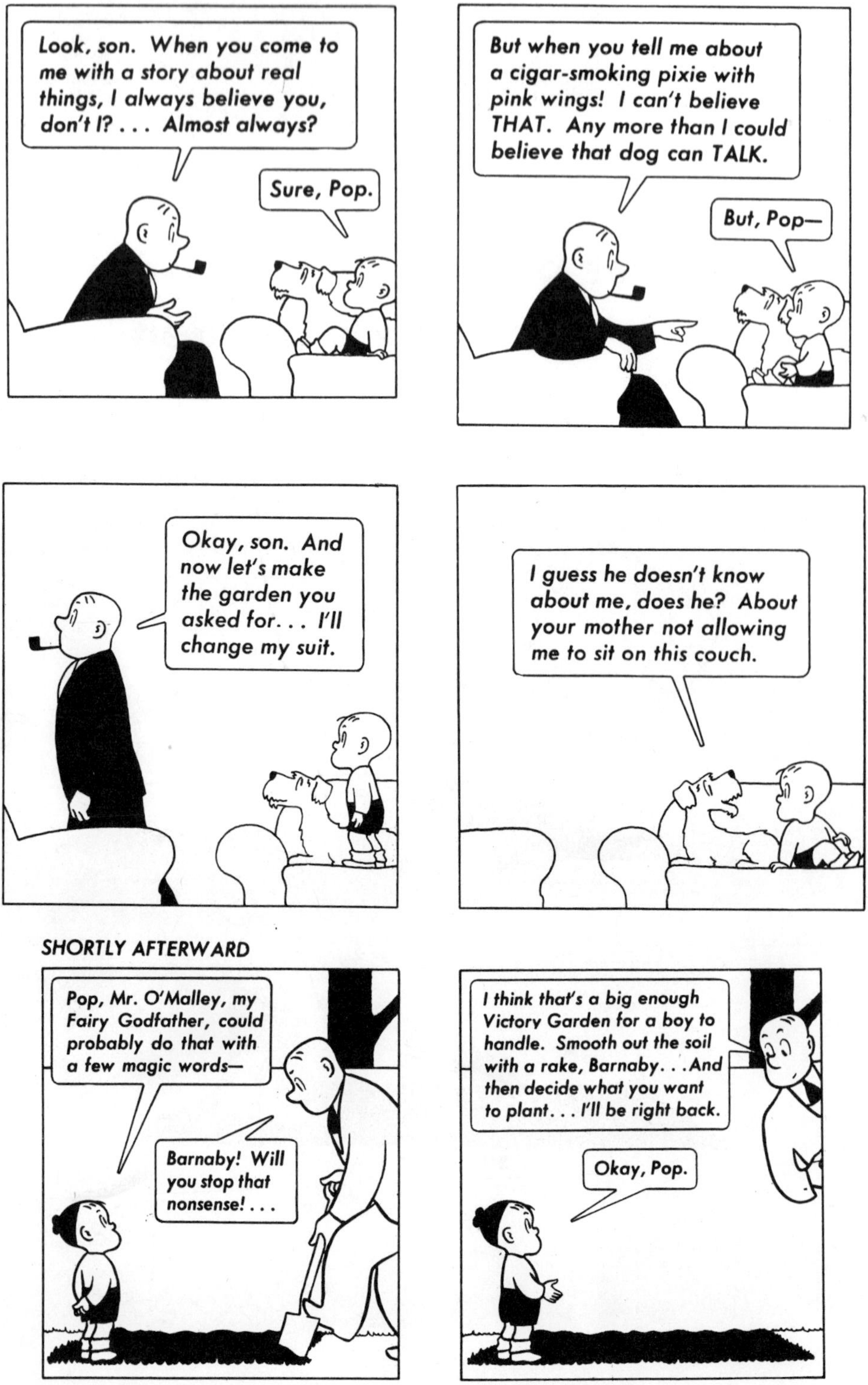
Look, son. When you come to me with a story about real things, I always believe you, don't I? . . . Almost always?
Sure, Pop.
But when you tell me about a cigar-smoking pixie with pink wings! I can't believe THAT. Any more than I could believe that dog can TALK.
But, Pop—
Okay, son. And now let's make the garden you asked for. . . I'll change my suit.
I guess he doesn't know about me, does he? About your mother not allowing me to sit on this couch.
SHORTLY AFTERWARD
Pop, Mr. O'Malley, my Fairy Godfather, could probably do that with a few magic words—
Barnaby! Will you stop that nonsense! . . .
I think that's a big enough Victory Garden for a boy to handle. Smooth out the soil with a rake, Barnaby. . . And then decide what you want to plant. . . I'll be right back.
Okay, Pop.

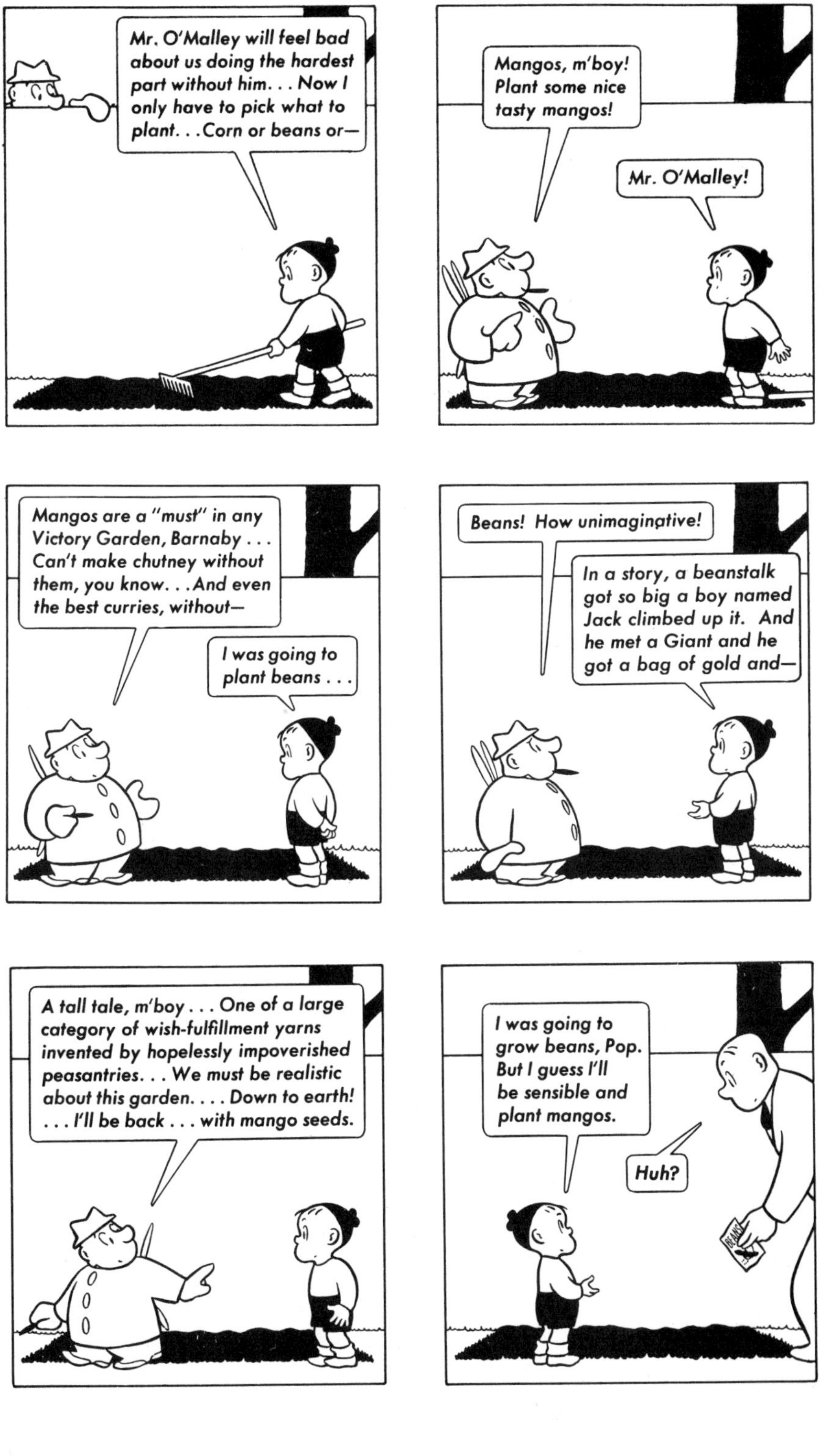

Mr. O'Malley will feel bad about us doing the hardest part without him. . . Now I only have to pick what to plant. . .Corn or beans or—
Mangos, m'boy! Plant some nice tasty mangos!
Mr. O'Malley!
Mangos are a "must" in any Victory Garden, Barnaby . . . Can't make chutney without them, you know. . .And even the best curries, without—
I was going to plant beans . . .
Beans! How unimaginative!
In a story, a beanstalk got so big a boy named Jack climbed up it. And he met a Giant and he got a bag of gold and—
A tall tale, m'boy . . . One of a large category of wish-fulfillment yarns invented by hopelessly impoverished peasantries. . . We must be realistic about this garden. . . . Down to earth! . . . I'll be back . . . with mango seeds.
I was going to grow beans, Pop. But I guess I'll be sensible and plant mangos.
Huh?

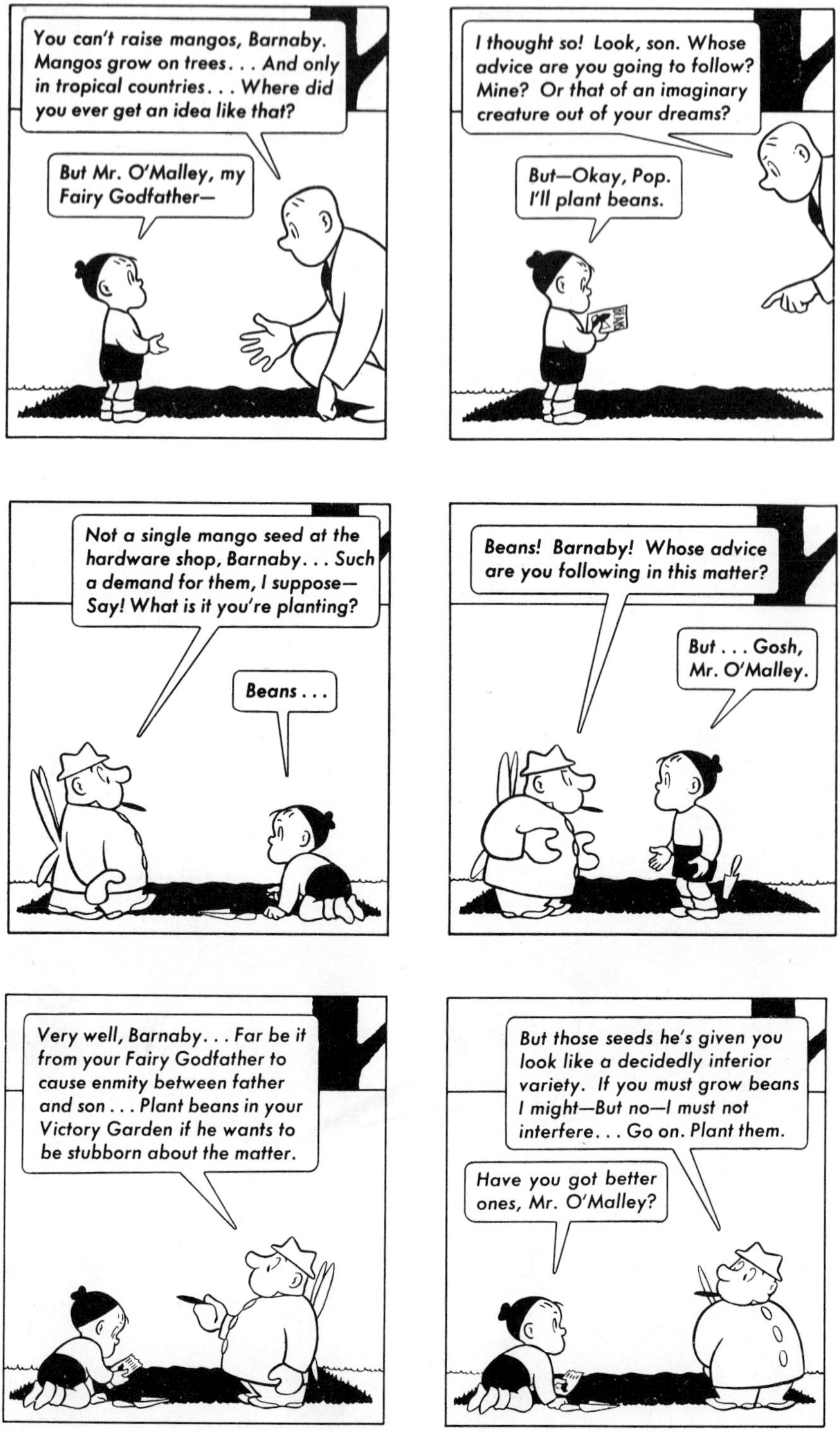
You can't raise mangos, Barnaby. Mangos grow on trees. . . And only in tropical countries. . . Where did you ever get an idea like that?
But Mr. O'Malley, my Fairy Godfather—
I thought so! Look, son. Whose advice are you going to follow? Mine? Or that of an imaginary creature out of your dreams?
But—Okay, Pop. I'll plant beans.
Not a single mango seed at the hardware shop, Barnaby. . . Such a demand for them, I suppose— Say! What is it you're planting?
Beans . . .
Beans! Barnaby! Whose advice are you following in this matter?
But . . . Gosh, Mr. O'Malley.
Very well, Barnaby. . . Far be it from your Fairy Godfather to cause enmity between father and son . . . Plant beans in your Victory Garden if he wants to be stubborn about the matter.
But those seeds he's given you look like a decidedly inferior variety. If you must grow beans I might—But no—I must not interfere. . . Go on. Plant them.
Have you got better ones, Mr. O'Malley?

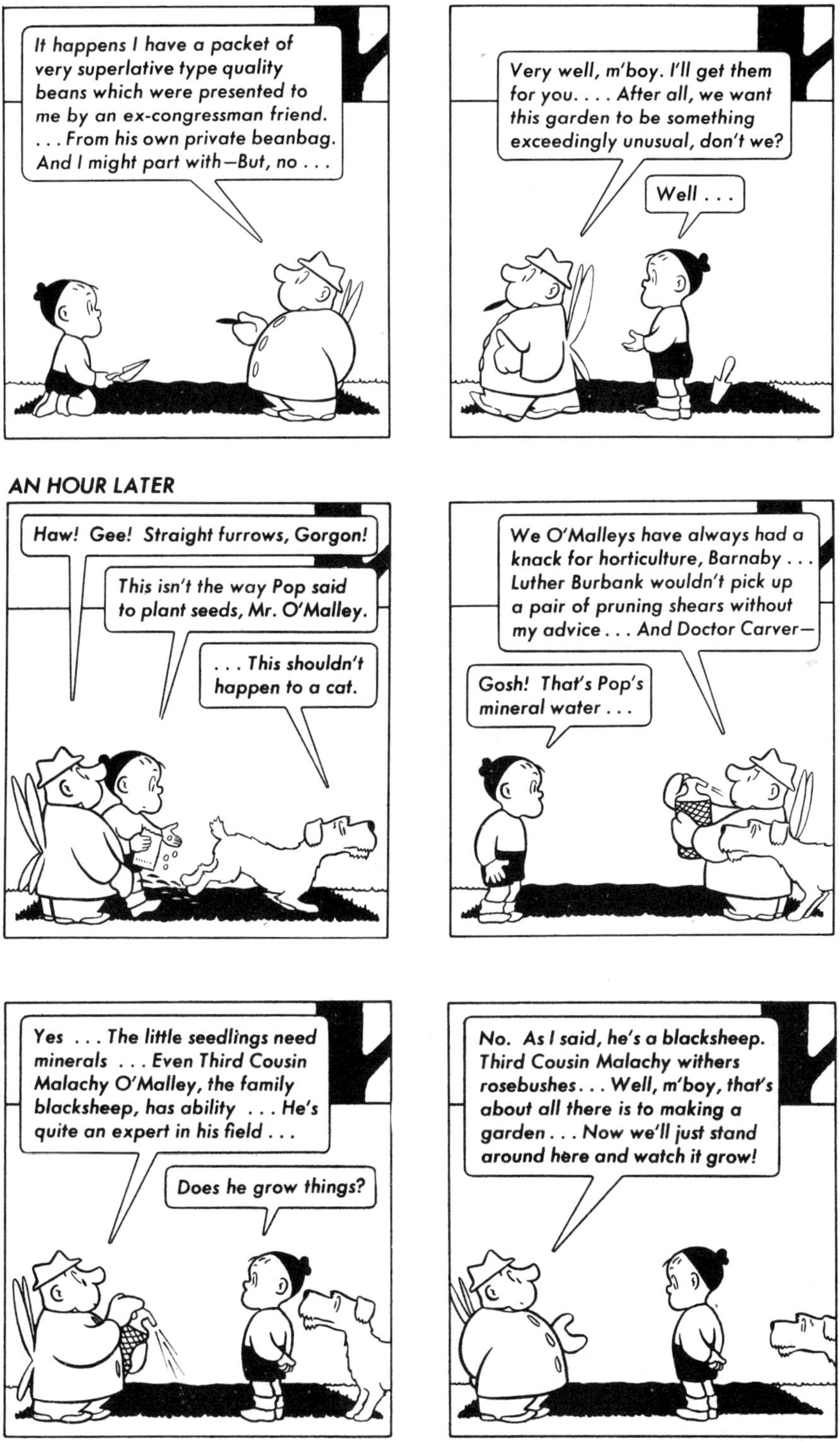
It happens I have a packet of very superlative type quality beans which were presented to me by an ex-congressman friend. . . . From his own private beanbag. And I might part with—But, no . . .
Very well, m'boy. I'll get them for you. . . . After all, we want this garden to be something exceedingly unusual, don't we?
Well . . .
AN HOUR LATER
Haw! Gee! Straight furrows, Gorgon!
This isn't the way Pop said to plant seeds, Mr. O'Malley.
. . . This shouldn't happen to a cat.
We O'Malleys have always had a knack for horticulture, Barnaby . . . Luther Burbank wouldn't pick up a pair of pruning shears without my advice . . . And Doctor Carver—
Gosh! That's Pop's mineral water . . .
Yes . . . The little seedlings need minerals . . . Even Third Cousin Malachy O'Malley, the family blacksheep, has ability . . . He's quite an expert in his field . . .
Does he grow things?
No. As I said, he's a blacksheep. Third Cousin Malachy withers rosebushes . . . Well, m'boy, that's about all there is to making a garden . . . Now we'll just stand around here and watch it grow!

EARLY NEXT MORNING

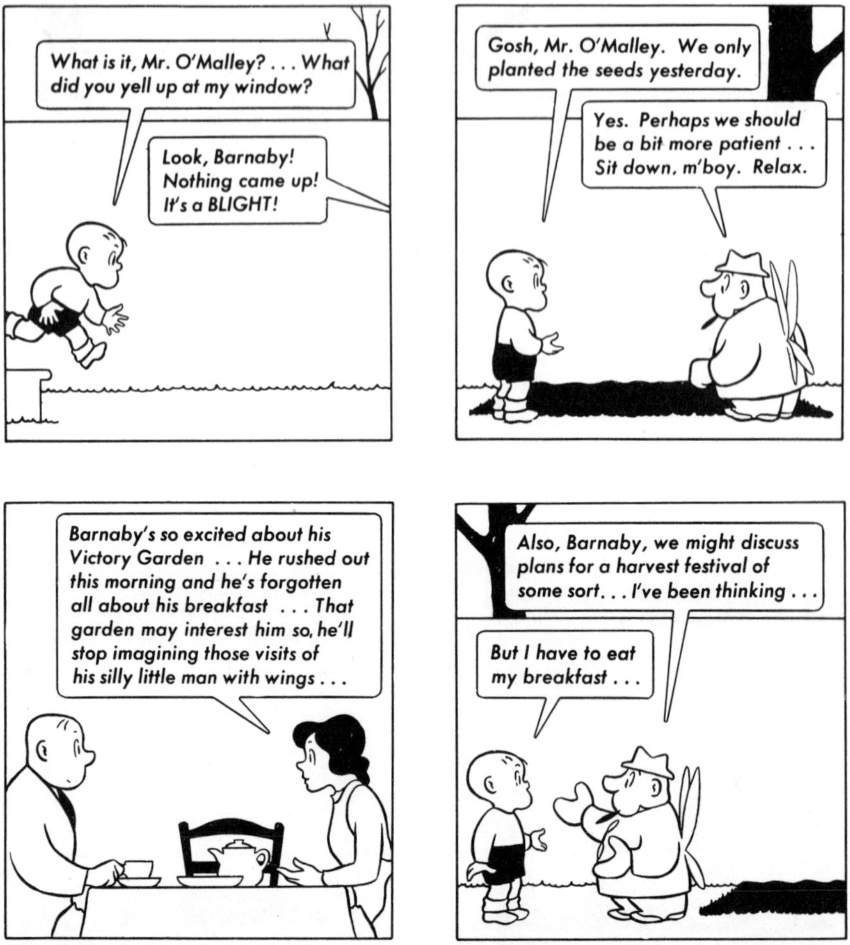
What is it, Mr. O'Malley? . . . What did you yell up at my window?
Look, Barnaby! Nothing came up! It's a BLIGHT!
Gosh, Mr. O'Malley. We only planted the seeds yesterday.
Yes. Perhaps we should be a bit more patient . . . Sit down, m'boy. Relax.
Barnaby's so excited about his Victory Garden . . . He rushed out this morning and he's forgotten all about his breakfast . . . That garden may interest him so, he'll stop imagining those visits of his silly little man with wings . . .
Also, Barnaby, we might discuss plans for a harvest festival of some sort. . . I've been thinking . . .
But I have to eat my breakfast . . .

LATER THAT DAY

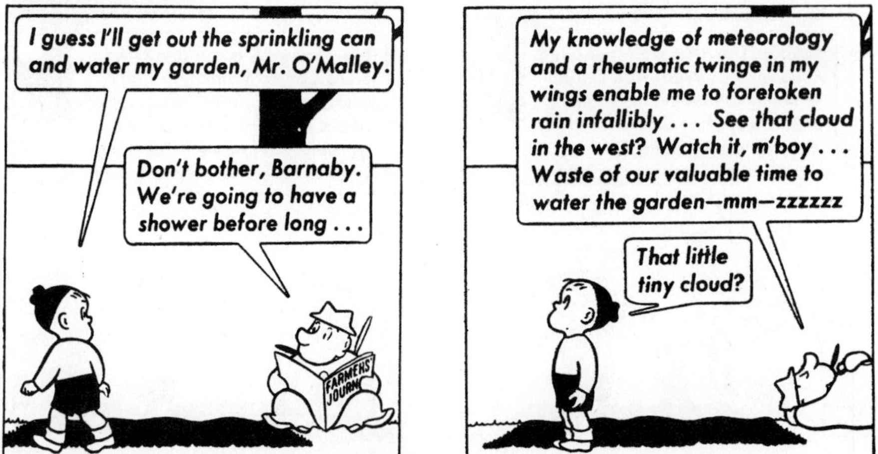
I guess I'll get out the sprinkling can and water my garden, Mr. O'Malley.
Don't bother, Barnaby. We're going to have a shower before long . . .
FARMERS' JOURN
My knowledge of meteorology and a rheumatic twinge in my wings enable me to foretoken rain infallibly . . . See that cloud in the west? Watch it, m'boy . . . Waste of our valuable time to water the garden—mm—zzzzzz
That little tiny cloud?

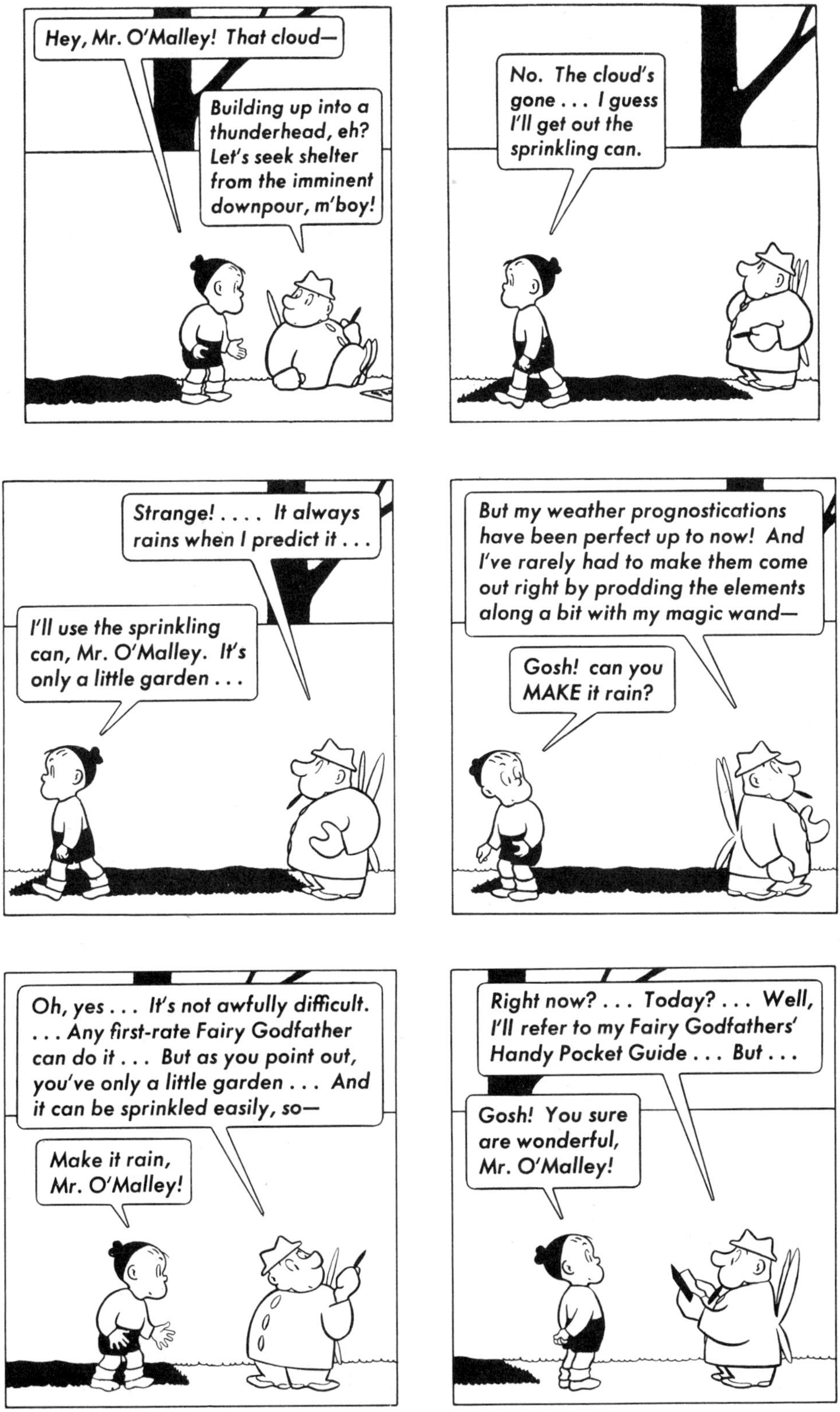
Hey, Mr. O'Malley! That cloud—
Building up into a thunderhead, eh? Let's seek shelter from the imminent downpour, m'boy!
No. The cloud's gone . . . I guess I'll get out the sprinkling can.
Strange! . . . . It always rains when I predict it . . .
I'll use the sprinkling can, Mr. O'Malley. It's only a little garden . . .
But my weather prognostications have been perfect up to now! And I've rarely had to make them come out right by prodding the elements along a bit with my magic wand—
Gosh! can you MAKE it rain?
Oh, yes . . . It's not awfully difficult. . . . Any first-rate Fairy Godfather can do it . . . But as you point out, you've only a little garden . . . And it can be sprinkled easily, so—
Make it rain, Mr. O'Malley!
Right now? . . . Today? . . . Well, I'll refer to my Fairy Godfathers' Handy Pocket Guide . . . But . . .
Gosh! You sure are wonderful, Mr. O'Malley!

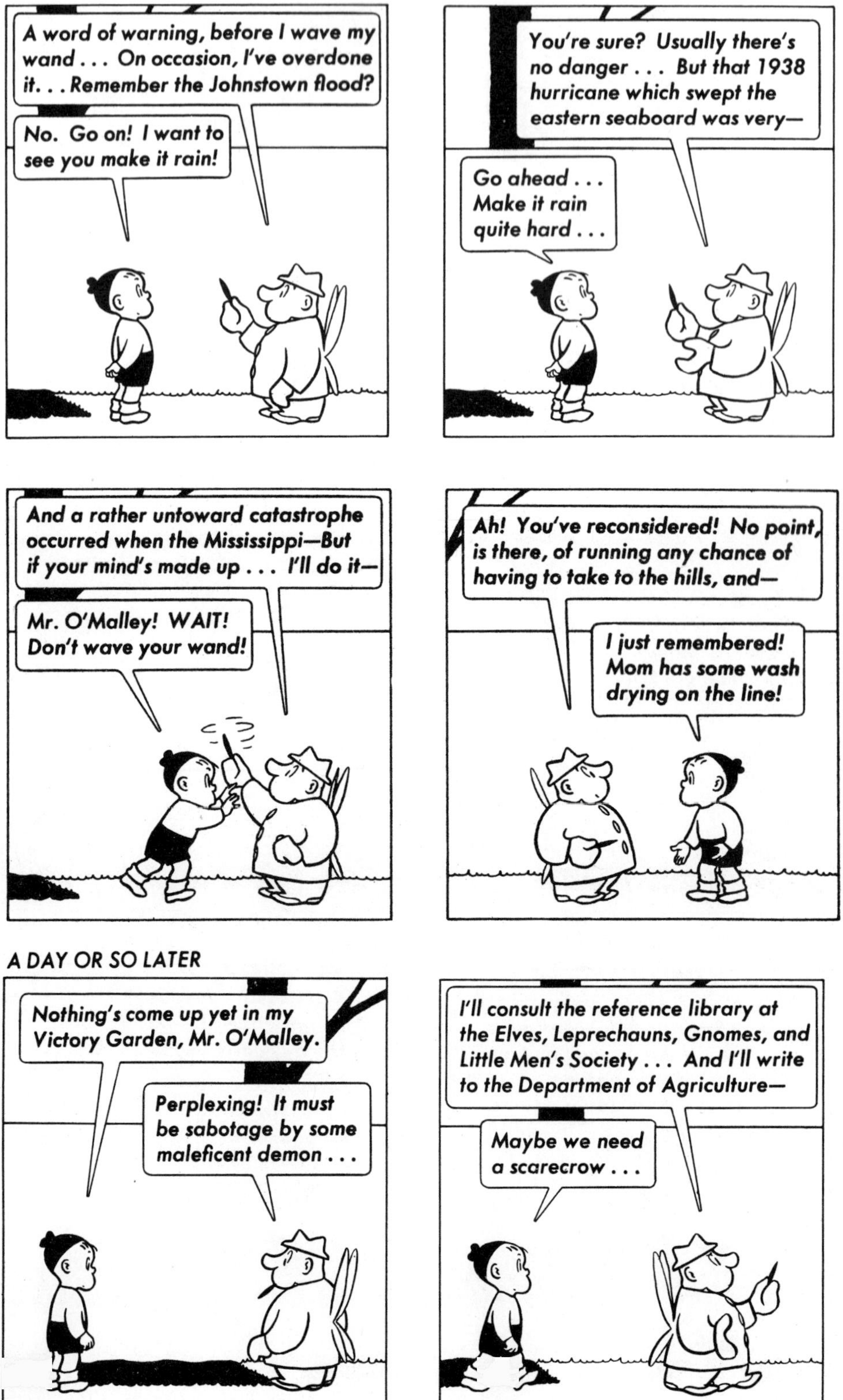
A word of warning, before I wave my wand . . . On occasion, I've overdone it. . . Remember the Johnstown flood?
No. Go on! I want to see you make it rain!
You're sure? Usually there's no danger . . . But that 1938 hurricane which swept the eastern seaboard was very—
Go ahead . . . Make it rain quite hard . . .
And a rather untoward catastrophe occurred when the Mississippi—But if your mind's made up . . . I'll do it—
Mr. O'Malley! WAIT! Don't wave your wand!
Ah! You've reconsidered! No point, is there, of running any chance of having to take to the hills, and—
I just remembered! Mom has some wash drying on the line!
A DAY OR SO LATER
Nothing's come up yet in my Victory Garden, Mr. O'Malley.
Perplexing! It must be sabotage by some maleficent demon . . .
I'll consult the reference library at the Elves, Leprechauns, Gnomes, and Little Men's Society . . . And I'll write to the Department of Agriculture—
Maybe we need a scarecrow . . .

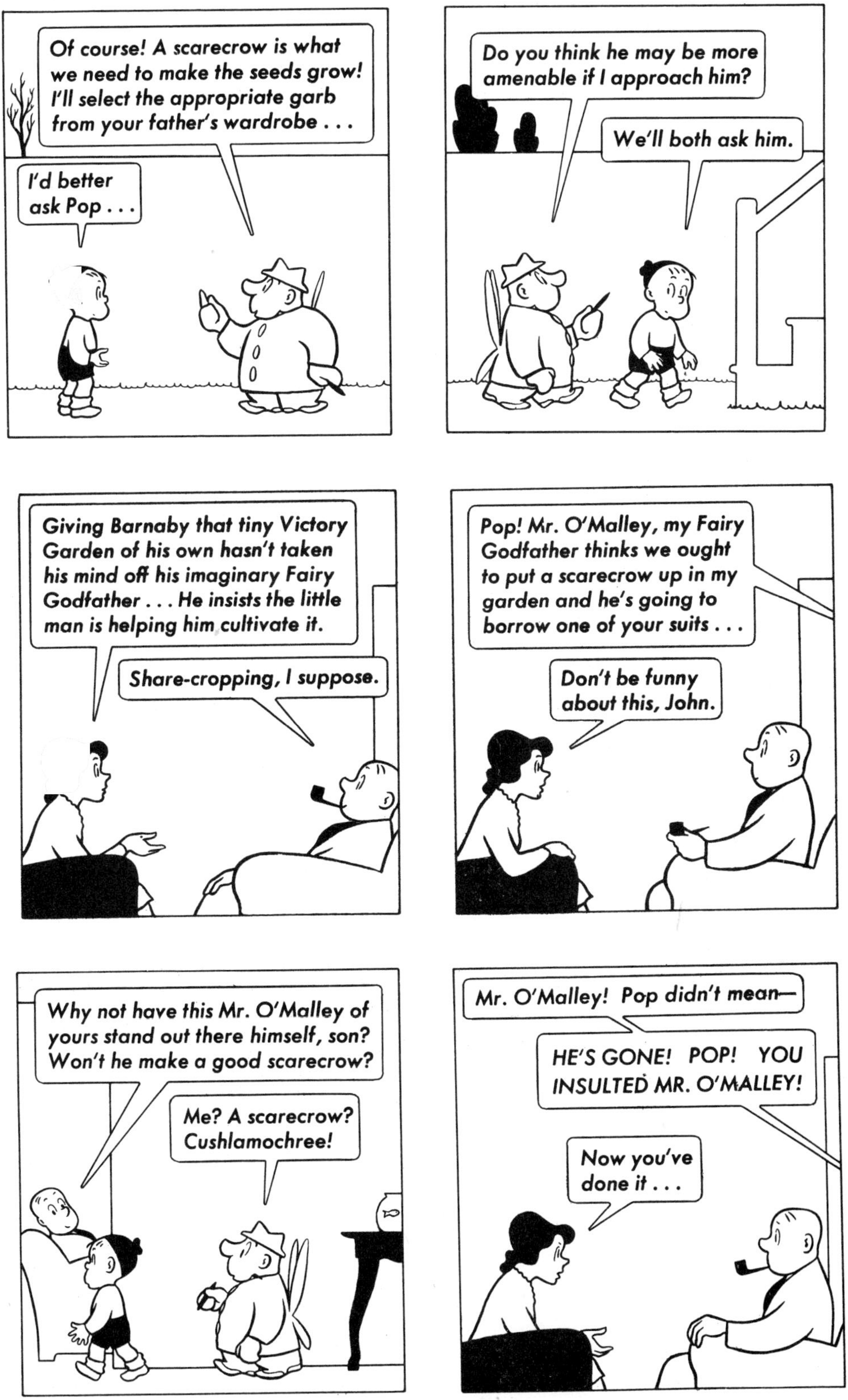

Of course! A scarecrow is what we need to make the seeds grow! I'll select the appropriate garb from your father's wardrobe . . .
I'd better ask Pop . . .
Do you think he may be more amenable if I approach him?
We'll both ask him.
Giving Barnaby that tiny Victory Garden of his own hasn't taken his mind off his imaginary Fairy Godfather . . . He insists the little man is helping him cultivate it.
Share-cropping, I suppose.
Pop! Mr. O'Malley, my Fairy Godfather thinks we ought to put a scarecrow up in my garden and he's going to borrow one of your suits . . .
Don't be funny about this, John.
Why not have this Mr. O'Malley of yours stand out there himself, son? Won't he make a good scarecrow?
Me? A scarecrow? Cushlamochree!
Mr. O'Malley! Pop didn't mean—
HE'S GONE! POP! YOU INSULTED MR. O'MALLEY!
Now you've done it . . .

EPISODE TWO

O'Malley and the Lion

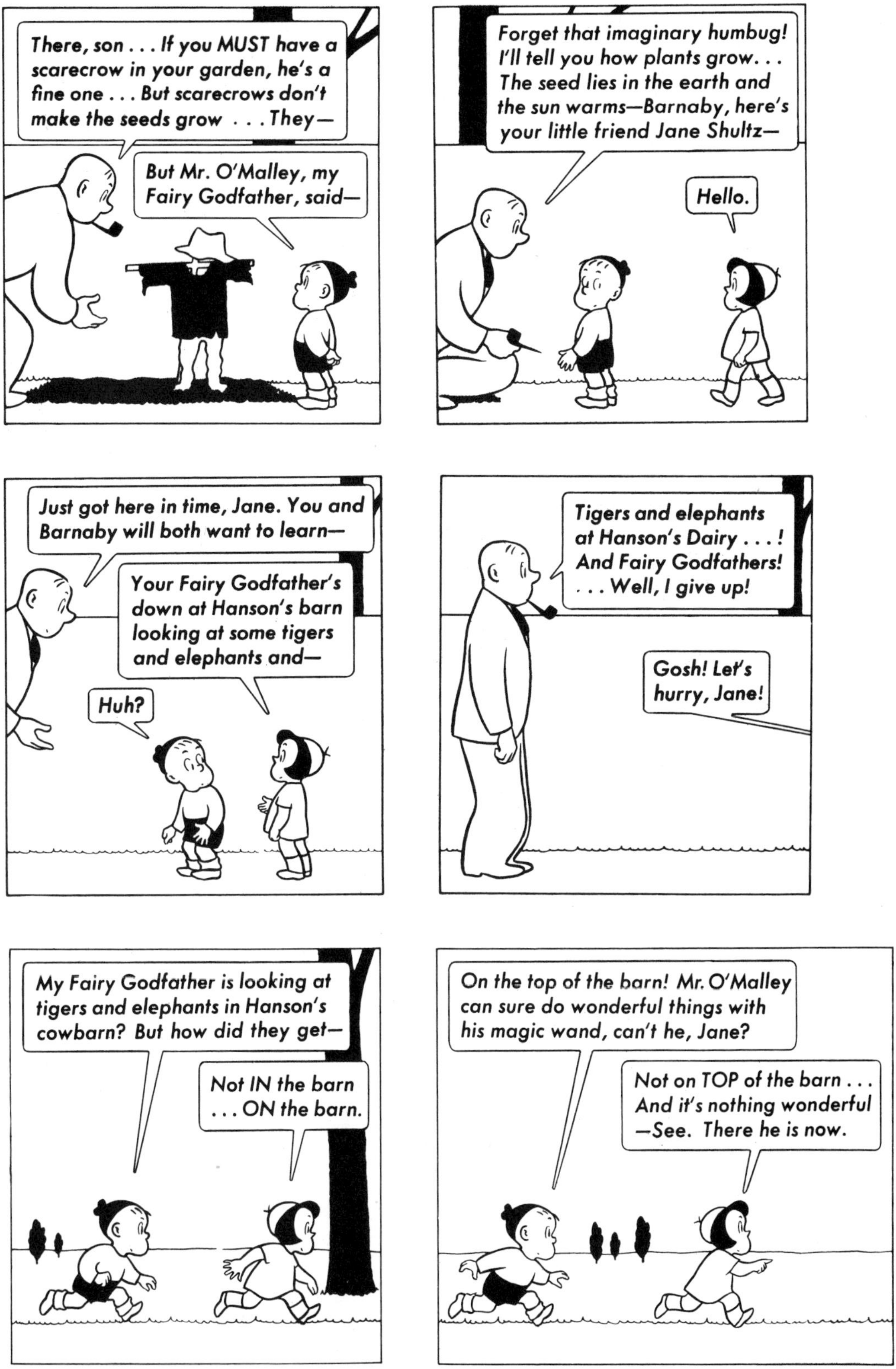
There, son . . . If you MUST have a scarecrow in your garden, he's a fine one . . . But scarecrows don't make the seeds grow . . . They—
But Mr. O'Malley, my Fairy Godfather, said—
Forget that imaginary humbug! I'll tell you how plants grow. . . The seed lies in the earth and the sun warms—Barnaby, here's your little friend Jane Shultz—
Hello.
Just got here in time, Jane. You and Barnaby will both want to learn—
Your Fairy Godfather's down at Hanson's barn looking at some tigers and elephants and—
Huh?
Tigers and elephants at Hanson's Dairy . . . ! And Fairy Godfathers! . . . Well, I give up!
Gosh! Let's hurry, Jane!
My Fairy Godfather is looking at tigers and elephants in Hanson's cowbarn? But how did they get—
Not IN the barn . . . ON the barn.
On the top of the barn! Mr. O'Malley can sure do wonderful things with his magic wand, can't he, Jane?
Not on TOP of the barn . . . And it's nothing wonderful —See. There he is now.

CIRCUS
Wonderful.
COMING!

CIRCUS
A circus! Coming to our town! . . . You're not insulted anymore, are you, Mr. O'Malley? You won't go away now! And miss the circus!
Probably only a two-ring circus.
COMING!

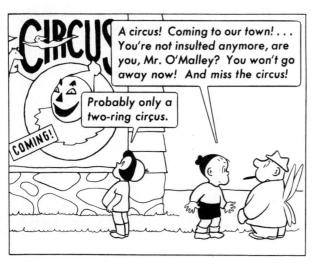

I won't miss the circus, m'boy. I'm not leaving until it departs . . . I am JOINING the circus . . . Severing our very fine relationship is painful, but the attitude of your relatives and friends—

But nobody meant to insult you, Mr. O'Malley! And what about our Victory Garden? And if you go—
Barnaby, you shouldn't stand in the way of your Fairy Godfather getting a good job as a freak—

FREAK! Cushlamachree! See, m'boy? That's the sort of thing I won't stand for any longer!

Me! In a side show! . . . With my ability to turn a quadruple off the springboard and my agility on a high wire! Absurd! Years ago a circus owner insulted me by proposing that idea . . . Fellow named Phineas Taylor Barnum.

Maybe the circus man thought people would pay lots of money just to look at you . . . Even if you didn't turn somersaults . . .

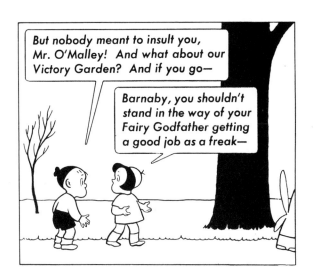

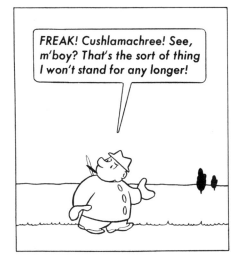

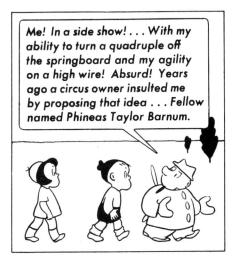

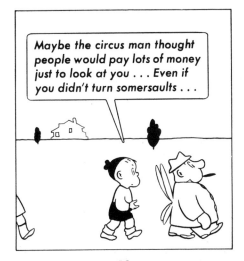

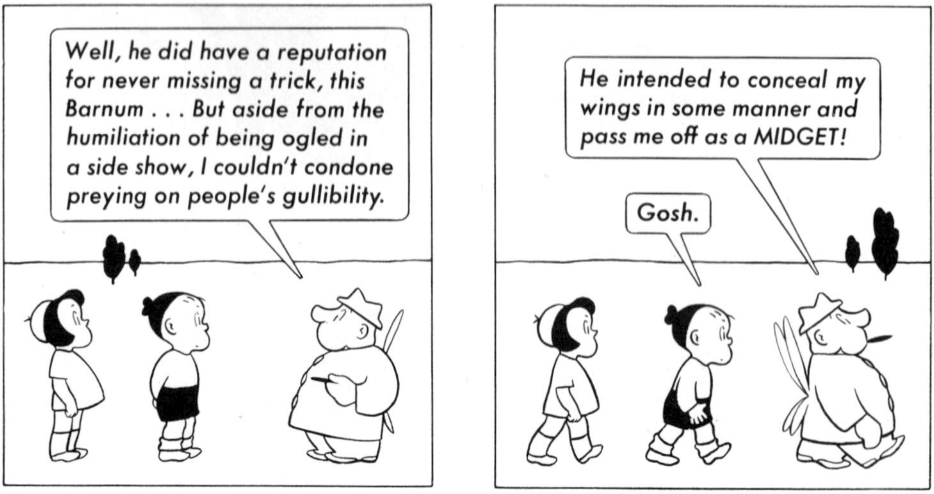
Well, he did have a reputation for never missing a trick, this Barnum . . . But aside from the humiliation of being ogled in a side show, I couldn't condone preying on people's gullibility.
He intended to conceal my wings in some manner and pass me off as a MIDGET!
Gosh.

THE NEXT DAY

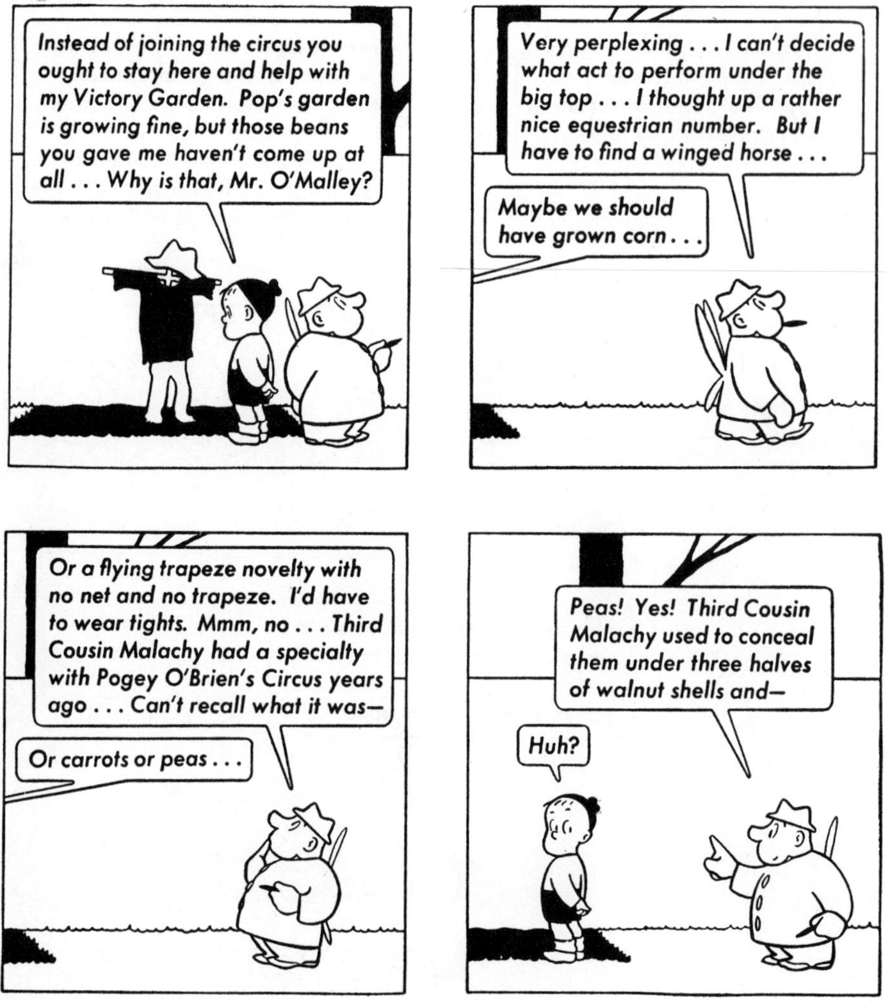
Instead of joining the circus you ought to stay here and help with my Victory Garden. Pop's garden is growing fine, but those beans you gave me haven't come up at all . . . Why is that, Mr. O'Malley?
Very perplexing . . . I can't decide what act to perform under the big top . . . I thought up a rather nice equestrian number. But I have to find a winged horse . . .
Maybe we should have grown corn . . .
Or a flying trapeze novelty with no net and no trapeze. I'd have to wear tights. Mmm, no . . . Third Cousin Malachy had a specialty with Pogey O'Brien's Circus years ago . . . Can't recall what it was—
Or carrots or peas . . .
Peas! Yes! Third Cousin Malachy used to conceal them under three halves of walnut shells and—
Huh?

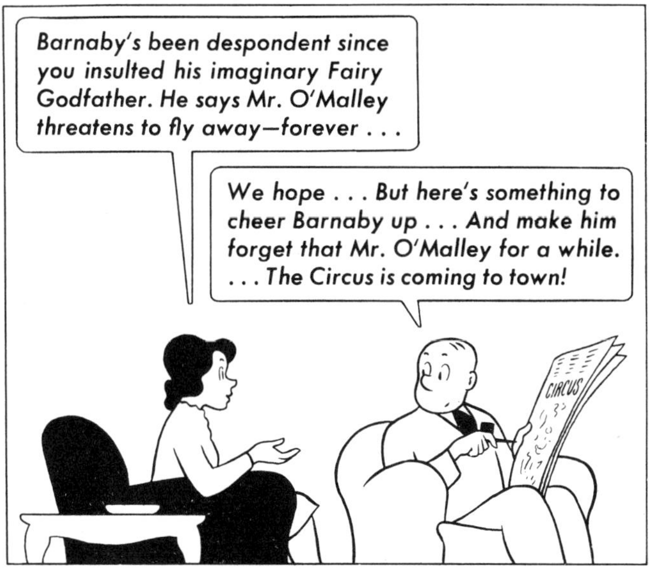
Barnaby's been despondent since you insulted his imaginary Fairy Godfather. He says Mr. O'Malley threatens to fly away—forever . . .
We hope . . . But here's something to cheer Barnaby up . . . And make him forget that Mr. O'Malley for a while. . . . The Circus is coming to town!
CIRCUS

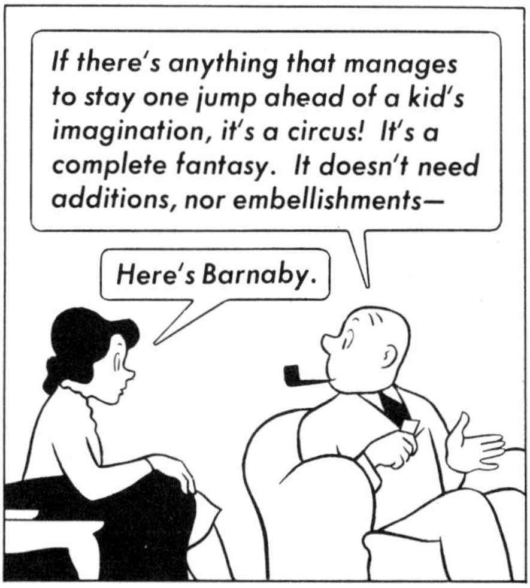
If there's anything that manages to stay one jump ahead of a kid's imagination, it's a circus! It's a complete fantasy. It doesn't need additions, nor embellishments—
Here's Barnaby.

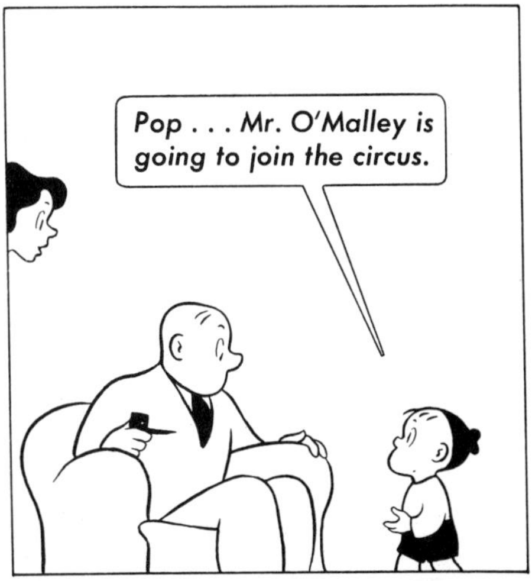
Pop . . . Mr. O'Malley is going to join the circus.

THAT NIGHT

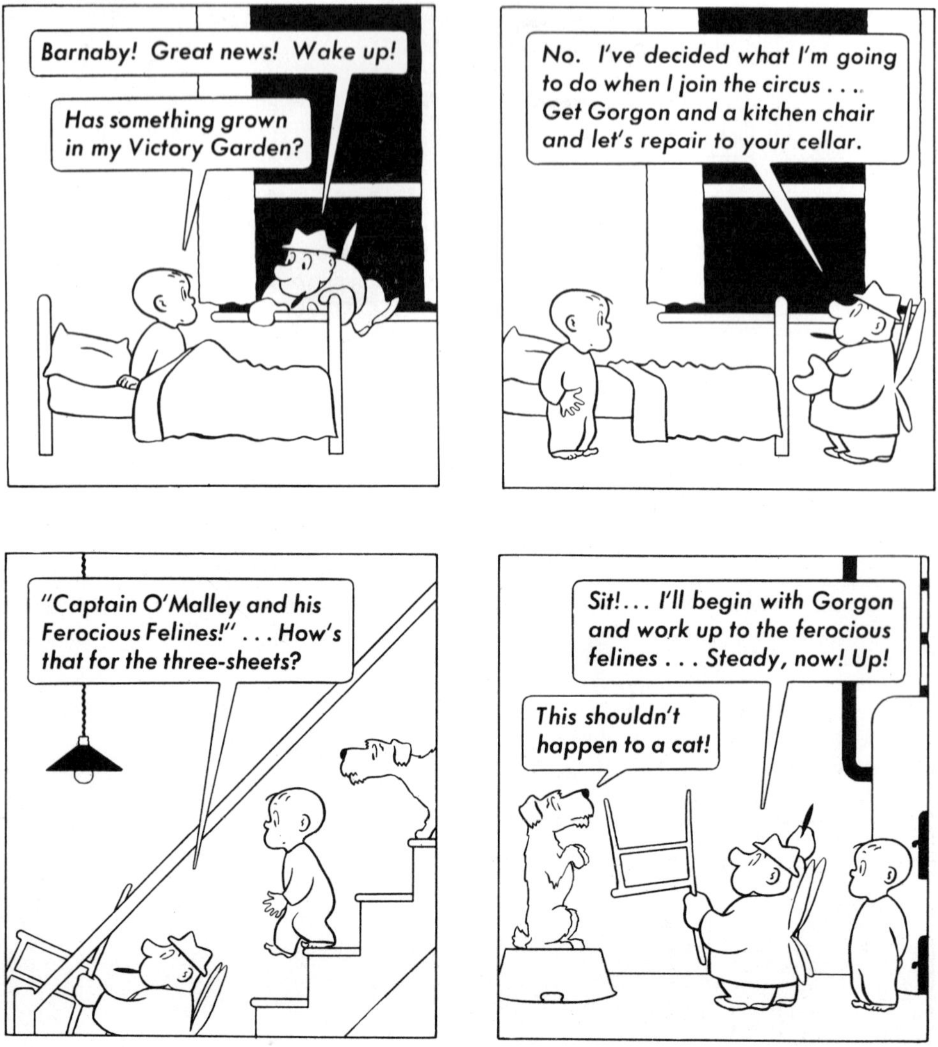

Barnaby! Great news! Wake up!
Has something grown in my Victory Garden?
No. I've decided what I'm going to do when I join the circus . . . Get Gorgon and a kitchen chair and let's repair to your cellar.
"Captain O'Malley and his Ferocious Felines!" . . . How's that for the three-sheets?
Sit!. . . I'll begin with Gorgon and work up to the ferocious felines . . . Steady, now! Up!
This shouldn't happen to a cat!

AND THE NEXT DAY

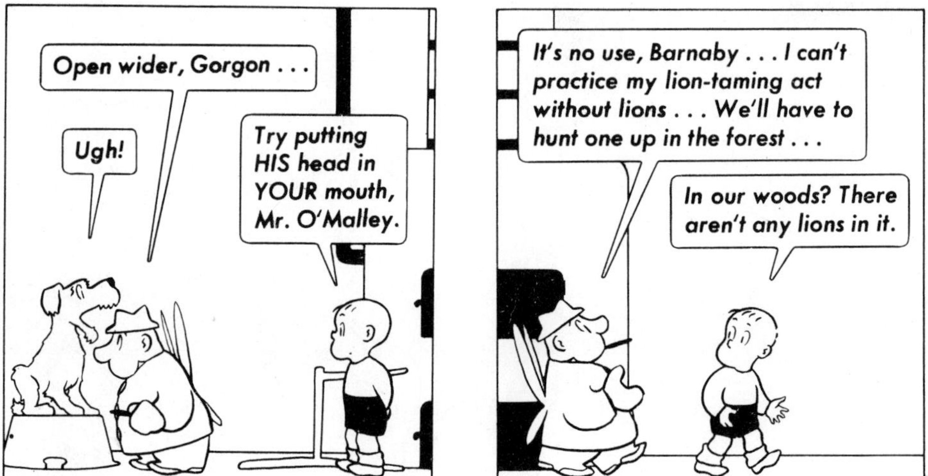

Open wider, Gorgon . . .
Ugh!
Try putting HIS head in YOUR mouth, Mr. O'Malley.
It's no use, Barnaby . . . I can't practice my lion-taming act without lions . . . We'll have to hunt one up in the forest . . .
In our woods? There aren't any lions in it.

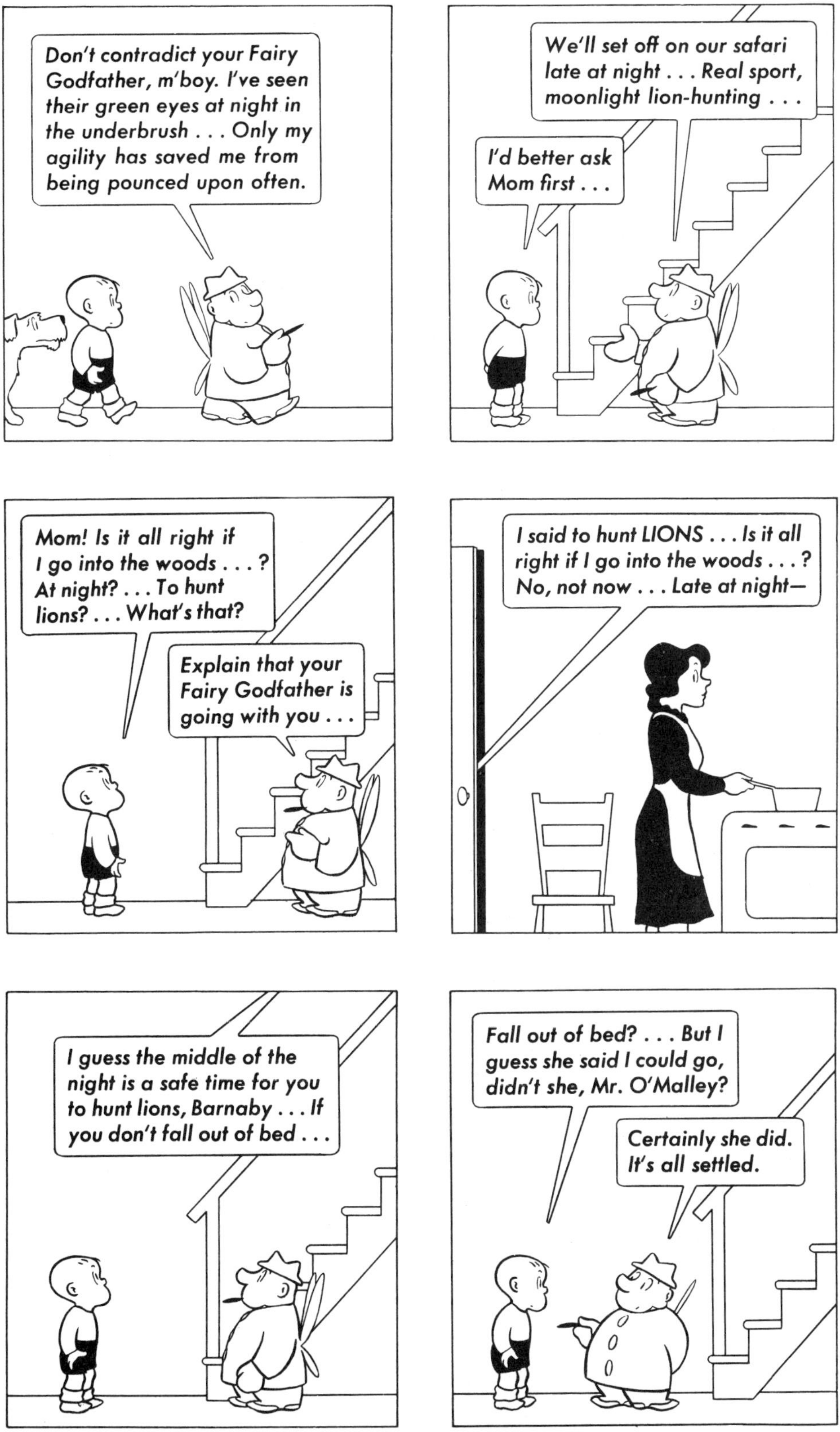
Don't contradict your Fairy Godfather, m'boy. I've seen their green eyes at night in the underbrush . . . Only my agility has saved me from being pounced upon often.
We'll set off on our safari late at night . . . Real sport, moonlight lion-hunting . . .
I'd better ask Mom first . . .
Mom! Is it all right if I go into the woods . . . ? At night? . . . To hunt lions? . . . What's that?
Explain that your Fairy Godfather is going with you . . .
I said to hunt LIONS . . . Is it all right if I go into the woods . . . ? No, not now . . . Late at night—
I guess the middle of the night is a safe time for you to hunt lions, Barnaby . . . If you don't fall out of bed . . .
Fall out of bed? . . . But I guess she said I could go, didn't she, Mr. O'Malley?
Certainly she did. It's all settled.

LATE THAT EVENING

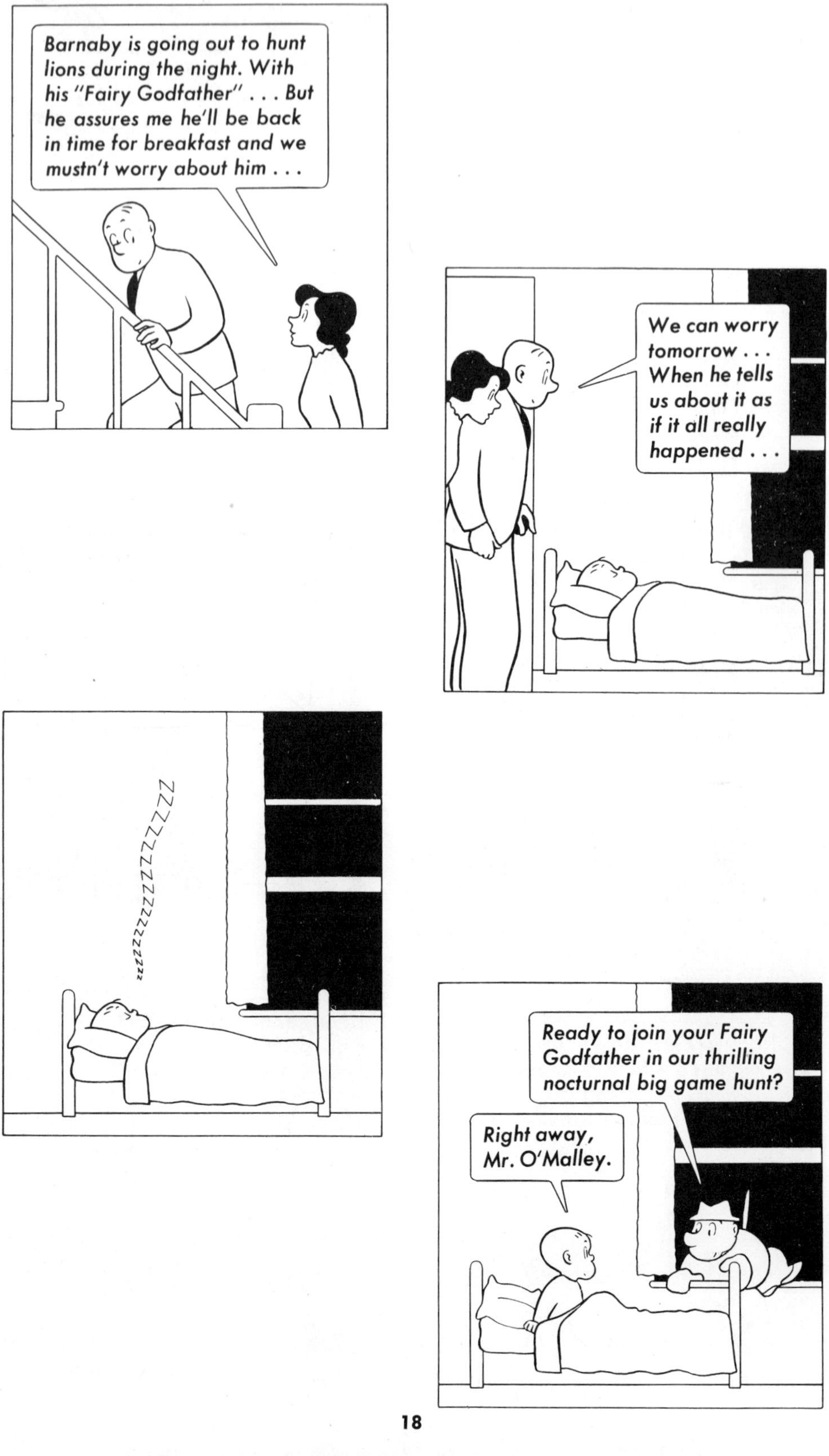
Barnaby is going out to hunt lions during the night. With his "Fairy Godfather" . . . But he assures me he'll be back in time for breakfast and we mustn't worry about him . . .
We can worry tomorrow . . . When he tells us about it as if it all really happened . . .
Ready to join your Fairy Godfather in our thrilling nocturnal big game hunt?
Right away, Mr. O'Malley.

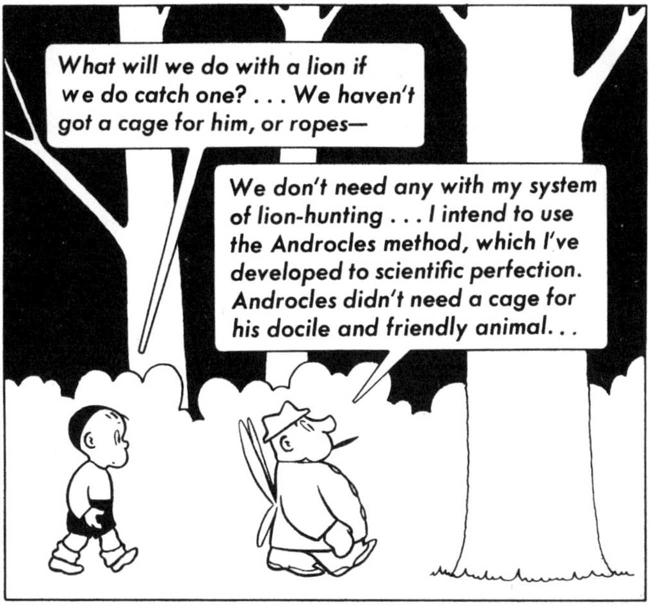
What will we do with a lion if we do catch one? . . . We haven't got a cage for him, or ropes—
We don't need any with my system of lion-hunting . . . I intend to use the Androcles method, which I've developed to scientific perfection. Androcles didn't need a cage for his docile and friendly animal. . .

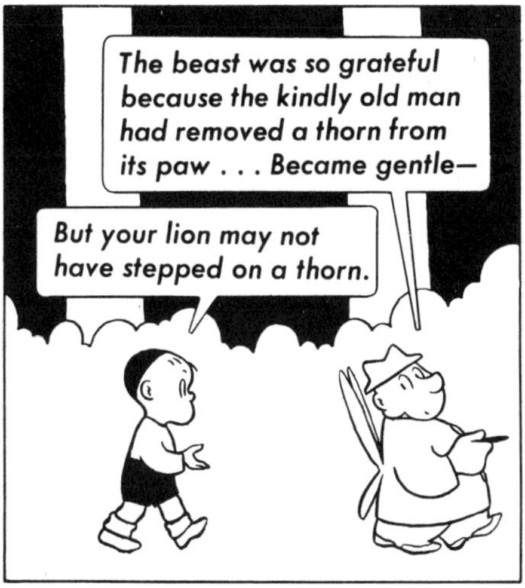
The beast was so grateful because the kindly old man had removed a thorn from its paw . . . Became gentle—
But your lion may not have stepped on a thorn.

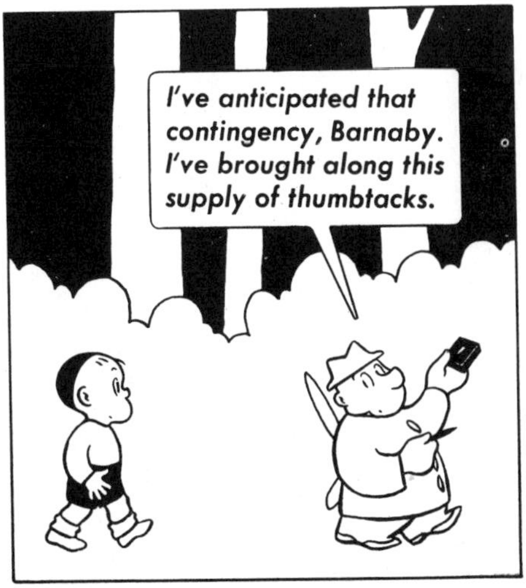
I've anticipated that contingency, Barnaby. I've brought along this supply of thumbtacks.

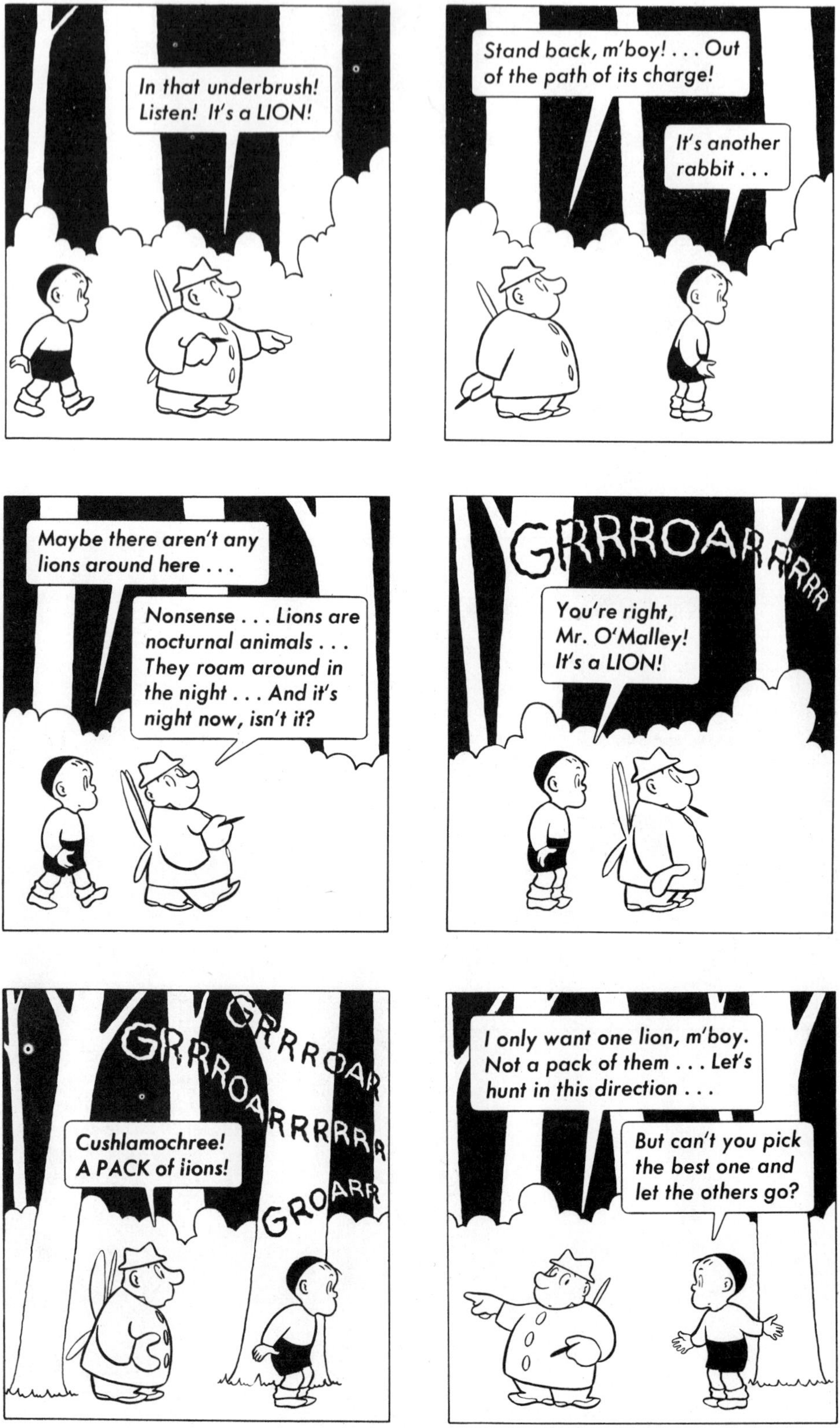
In that underbrush! Listen! It's a LION!
Stand back, m'boy! . . . Out of the path of its charge!
It's another rabbit . . .
Maybe there aren't any lions around here . . .
Nonsense . . . Lions are nocturnal animals . . . They roam around in the night . . . And it's night now, isn't it?
GRRROARRRRR
You're right, Mr. O'Malley! It's a LION!
GRRROAR
GRRROARRRRRRR
GROARR
Cushlamochree! A PACK of iions!
I only want one lion, m'boy. Not a pack of them . . . Let's hunt in this direction . . .
But can't you pick the best one and let the others go?

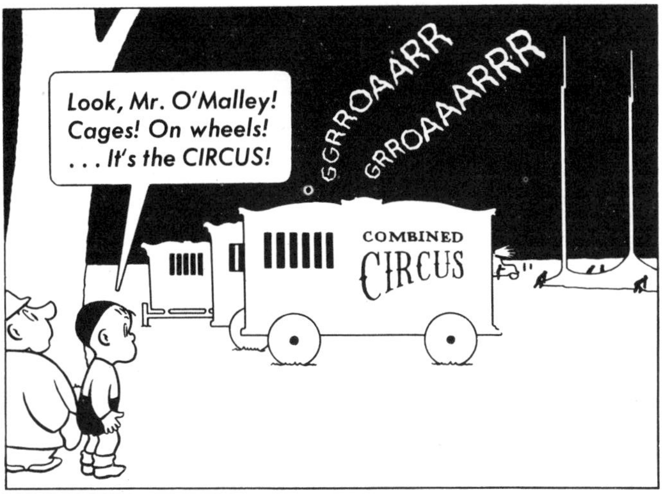
Look, Mr. O'Malley! Cages! On wheels! . . . It's the CIRCUS!
GGRROAARR
GRROAAARRR
COMBINED CIRCUS

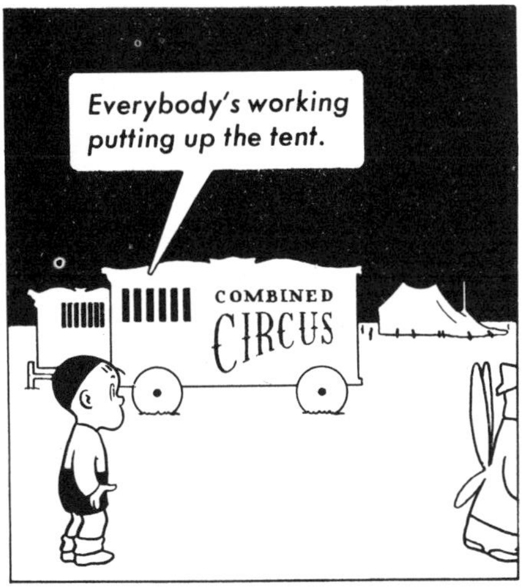
Everybody's working putting up the tent.
COMBINED CIRCUS

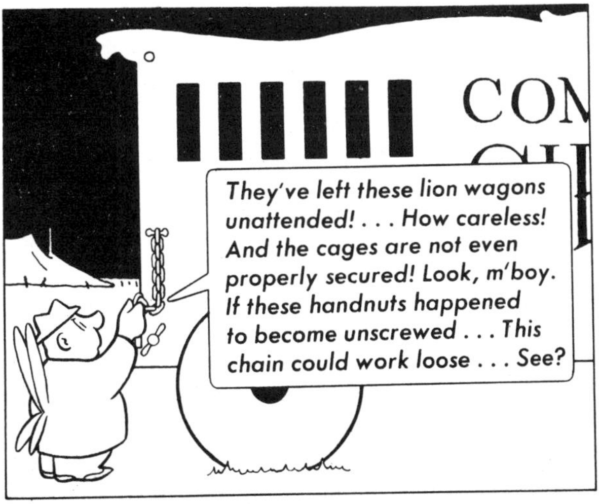
They've left these lion wagons unattended! . . . How careless! And the cages are not even properly secured! Look, m'boy. If these handnuts happened to become unscrewed . . . This chain could work loose . . . See?

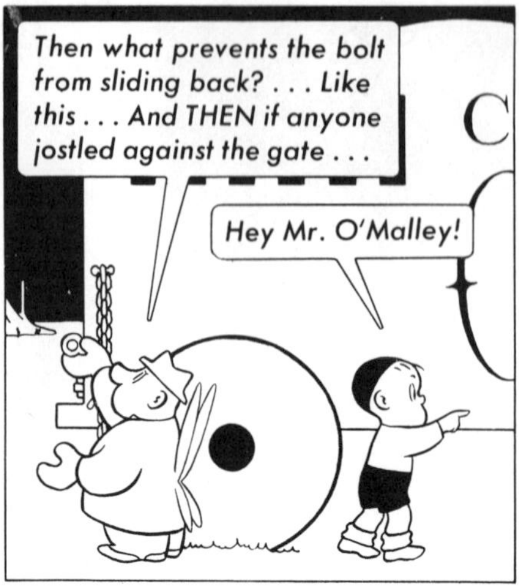
Then what prevents the bolt from sliding back? . . . Like this . . . And THEN if anyone jostled against the gate . . .
Hey Mr. O'Malley!

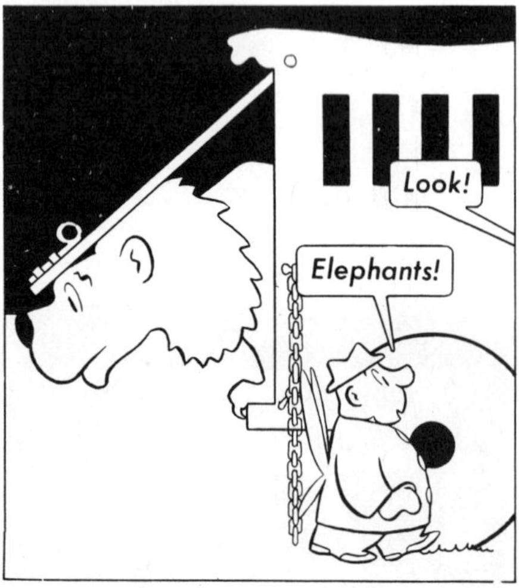
Look!
Elephants!

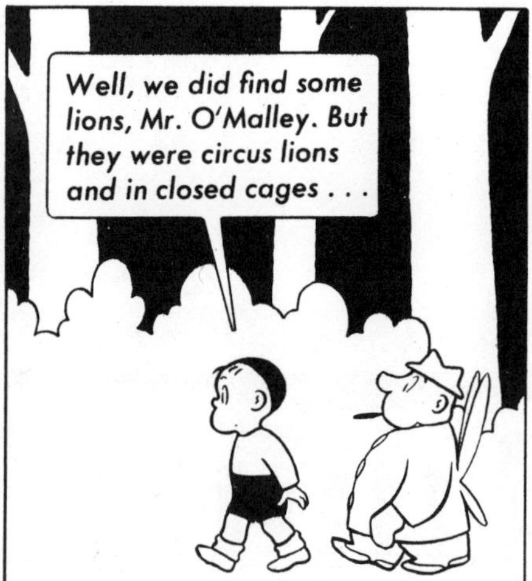
Well, we did find some lions, Mr. O'Malley. But they were circus lions and in closed cages . . .

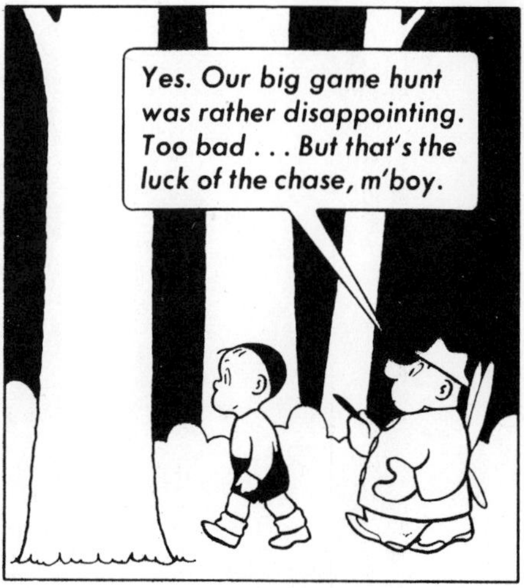
Yes. Our big game hunt was rather disappointing. Too bad . . . But that's the luck of the chase, m'boy.

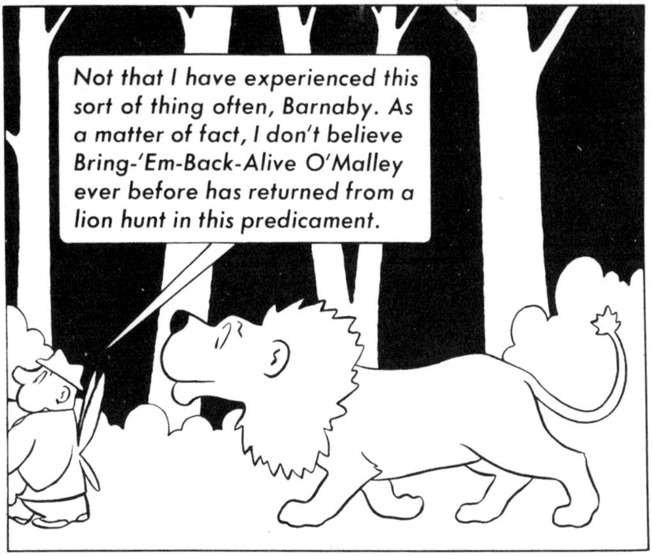
Not that I have experienced this sort of thing often, Barnaby. As a matter of fact, I don't believe Bring-'Em-Back-Alive O'Malley ever before has returned from a lion hunt in this predicament.

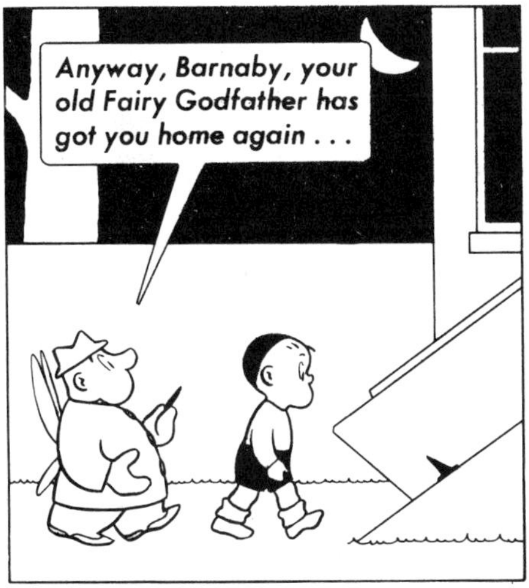
Anyway, Barnaby, your old Fairy Godfather has got you home again . . .

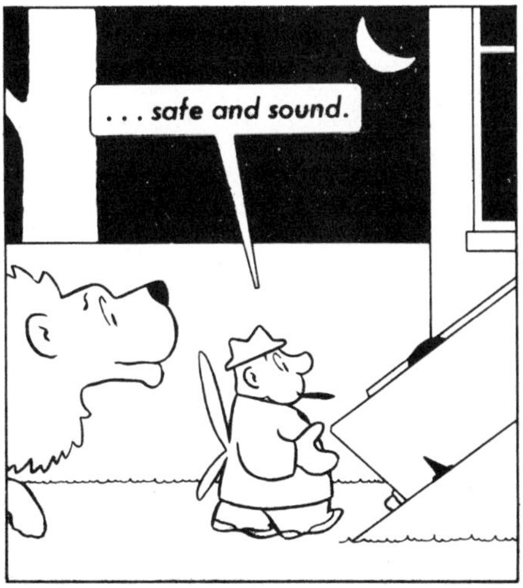
. . . safe and sound.

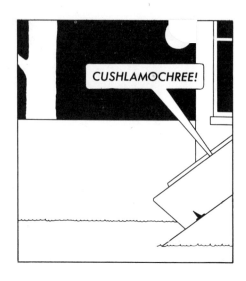

CUSHLAMOCHREE!

Cushlamochree! I'd tame this monster in short order . . . But I haven't got a chair.

A lion-tamer has to have a chair . . . It's his badge of office —Look, m'boy! He's leaving! . . . At last!

He's coming back again . . . Shall I holler for Gorgon? He chases cats . . .

He brought you a chair! . . . I think he's tame already!

ALL THAT NIGHT

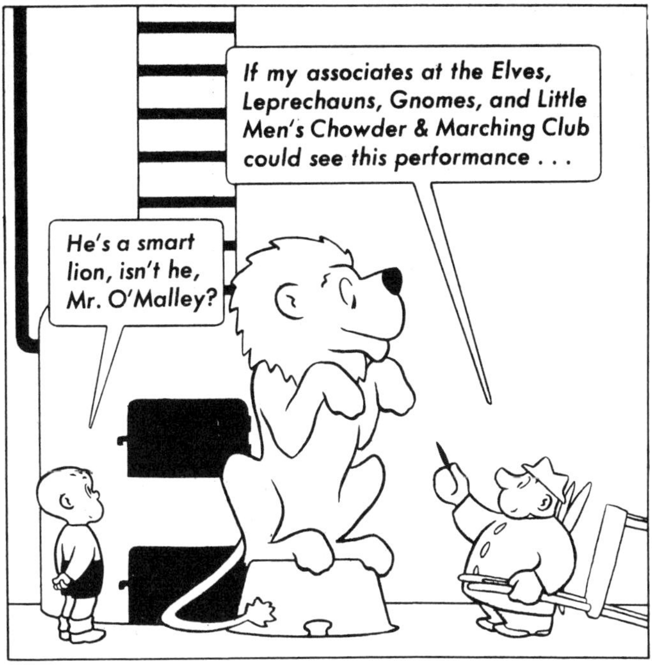
He's a smart lion, isn't he, Mr. O'Malley?
If my associates at the Elves, Leprechauns, Gnomes, and Little Men's Chowder & Marching Club could see this performance . . .

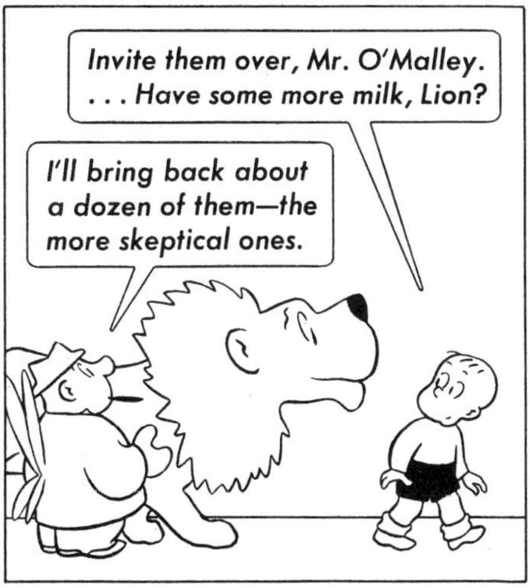
I'll bring back about a dozen of them—the more skeptical ones.
Invite them over, Mr. O'Malley. . . . Have some more milk, Lion?

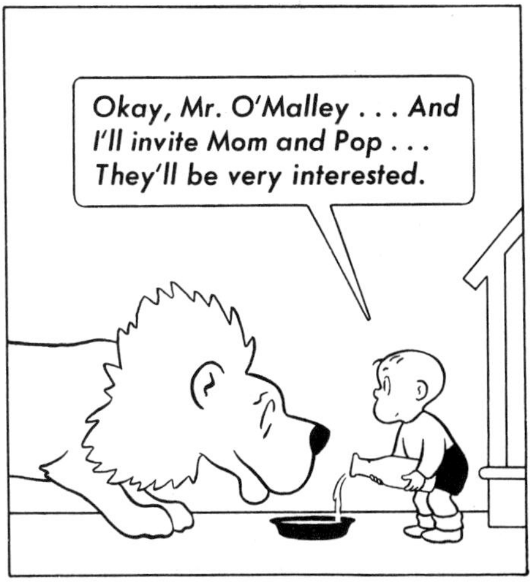
Okay, Mr. O'Malley . . . And I'll invite Mom and Pop . . . They'll be very interested.

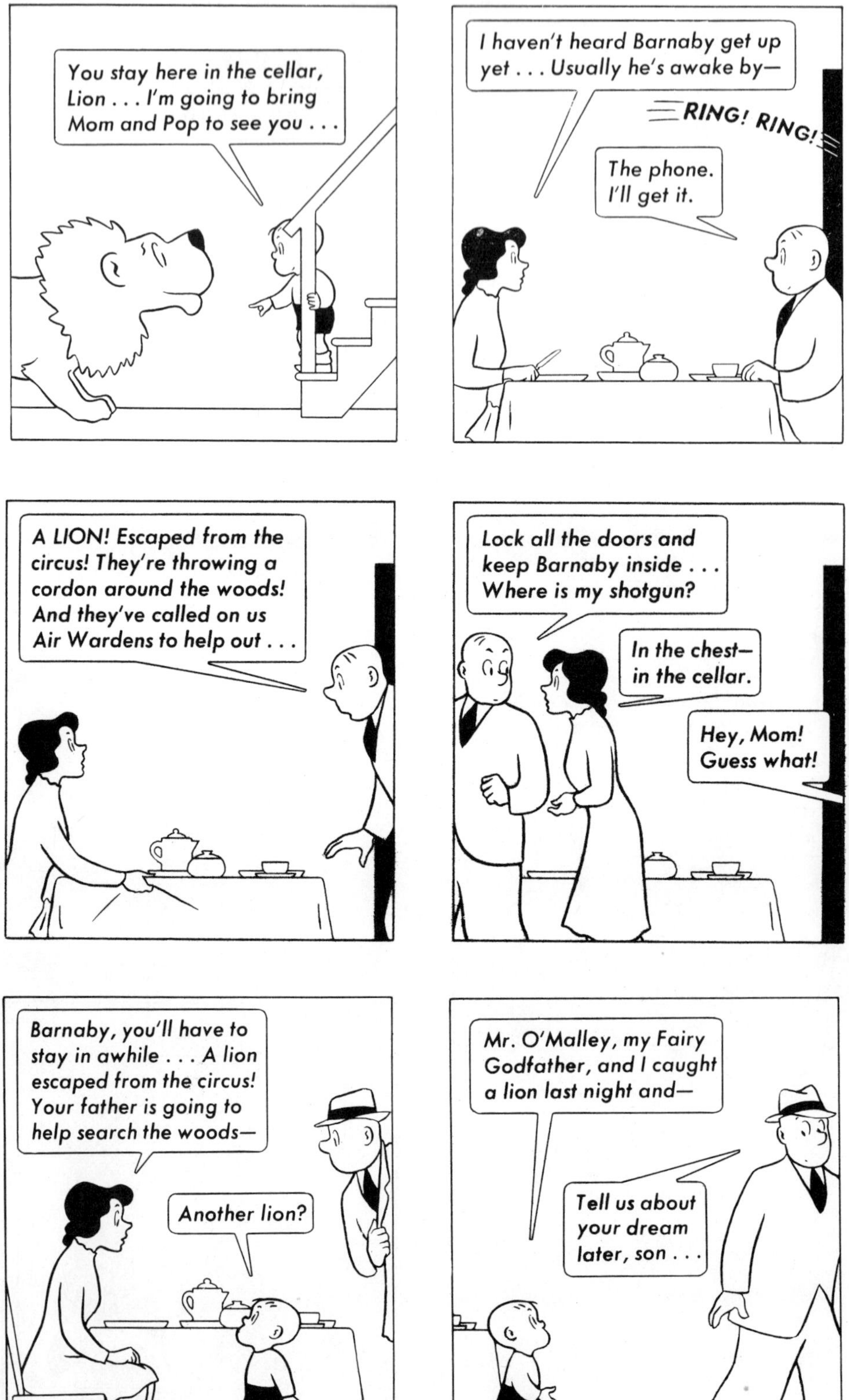
You stay here in the cellar, Lion . . . I'm going to bring Mom and Pop to see you . . .
I haven't heard Barnaby get up yet . . . Usually he's awake by—
RING! RING!
The phone. I'll get it.
A LION! Escaped from the circus! They're throwing a cordon around the woods! And they've called on us Air Wardens to help out . . .
Lock all the doors and keep Barnaby inside . . . Where is my shotgun?
In the chest— in the cellar.
Hey, Mom! Guess what!
Barnaby, you'll have to stay in awhile . . . A lion escaped from the circus! Your father is going to help search the woods—
Another lion?
Mr. O'Malley, my Fairy Godfather, and I caught a lion last night and—
Tell us about your dream later, son . . .

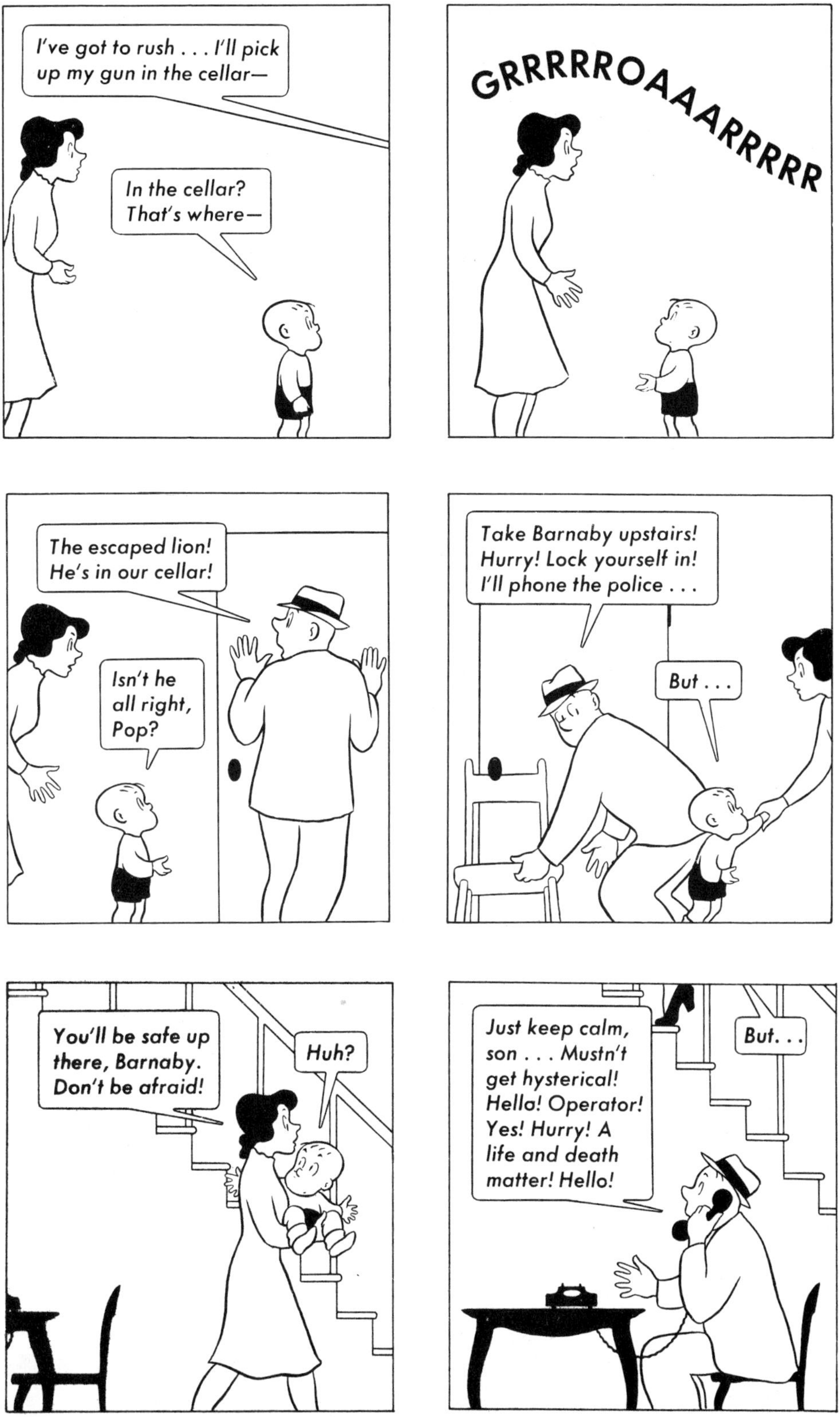
I've got to rush . . . I'll pick up my gun in the cellar—
In the cellar? That's where—
GRRRRROAAAARRRRR
The escaped lion! He's in our cellar!
Isn't he all right, Pop?
Take Barnaby upstairs! Hurry! Lock yourself in! I'll phone the police . . .
But . . .
You'll be safe up there, Barnaby. Don't be afraid!
Huh?
Just keep calm, son . . . Mustn't get hysterical! Hello! Operator! Yes! Hurry! A life and death matter! Hello!
But. . .

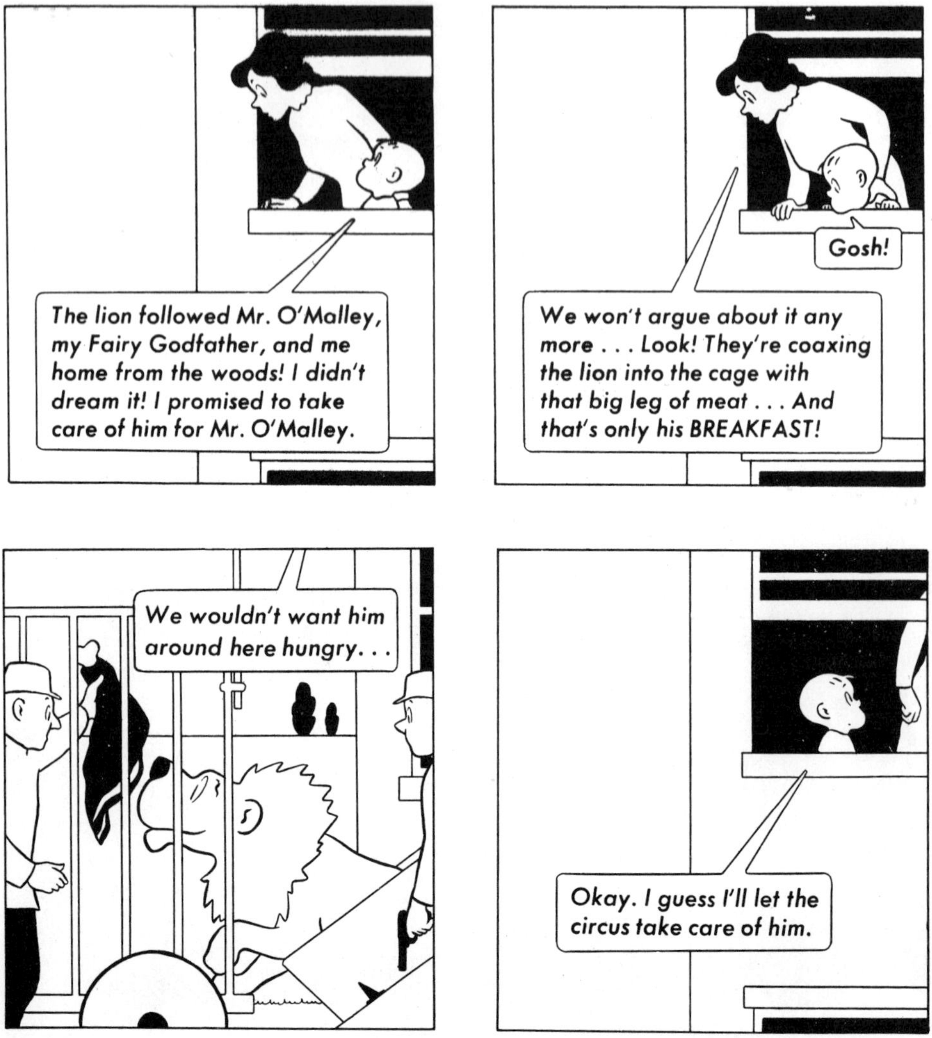
The lion followed Mr. O'Malley, my Fairy Godfather, and me home from the woods! I didn't dream it! I promised to take care of him for Mr. O'Malley.
We won't argue about it any more . . . Look! They're coaxing the lion into the cage with that big leg of meat . . . And that's only his BREAKFAST!
Gosh!
We wouldn't want him around here hungry. . .
Okay. I guess I'll let the circus take care of him.

THIRTY MINUTES LATER

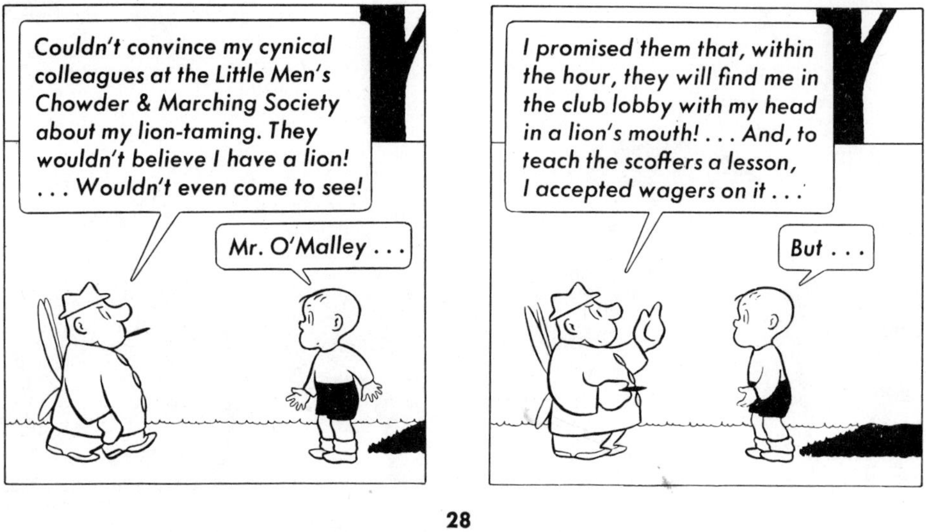
Couldn't convince my cynical colleagues at the Little Men's Chowder & Marching Society about my lion-taming. They wouldn't believe I have a lion! . . . Wouldn't even come to see!
Mr. O'Malley . . .
I promised them that, within the hour, they will find me in the club lobby with my head in a lion's mouth! . . . And, to teach the scoffers a lesson, I accepted wagers on it . . .
But . . .

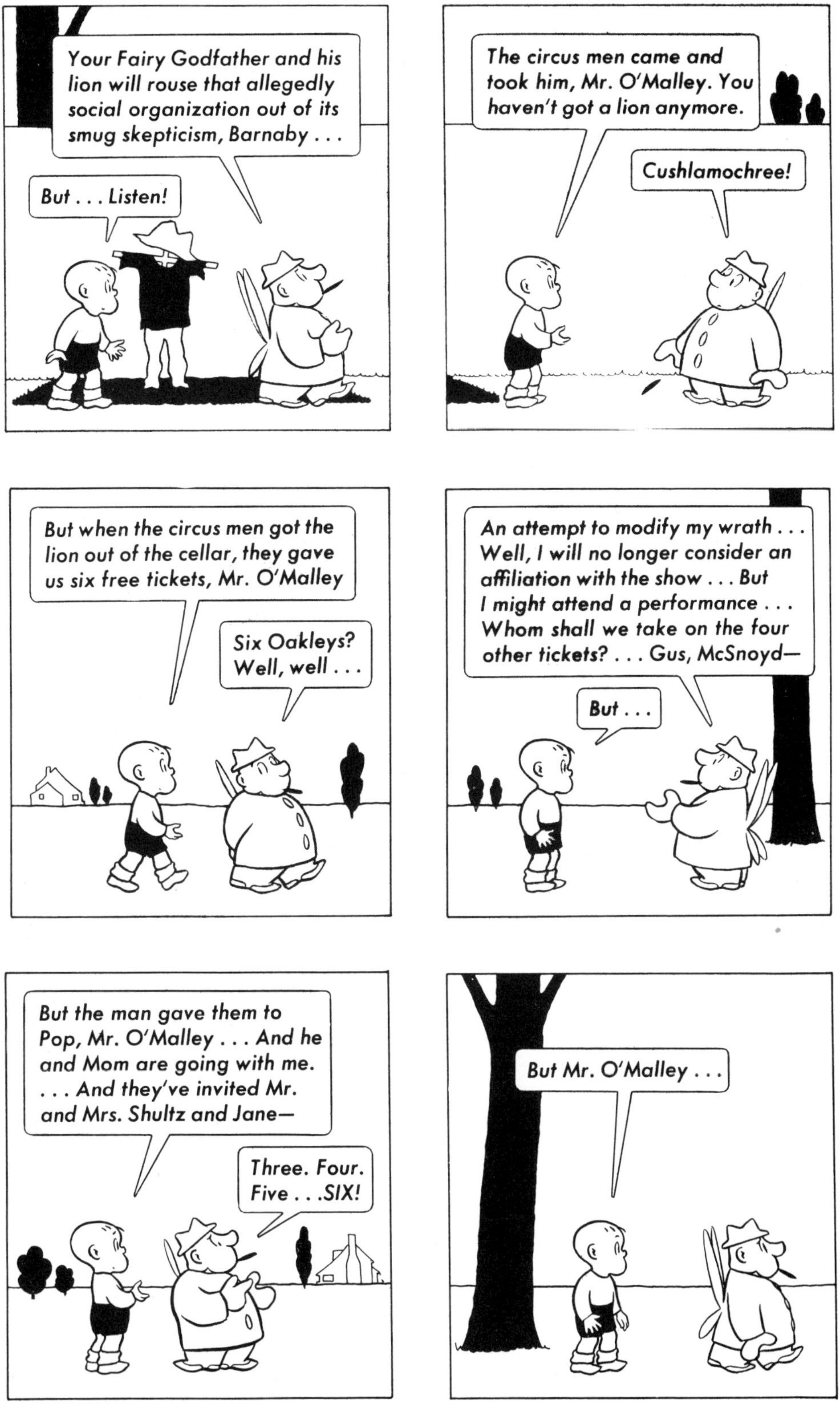
Your Fairy Godfather and his lion will rouse that allegedly social organization out of its smug skepticism, Barnaby . . .
But . . . Listen!
The circus men came and took him, Mr. O'Malley. You haven't got a lion anymore.
Cushlamochree!
But when the circus men got the lion out of the cellar, they gave us six free tickets, Mr. O'Malley
Six Oakleys? Well, well . . .
An attempt to modify my wrath . . . Well, I will no longer consider an affiliation with the show . . . But I might attend a performance . . . Whom shall we take on the four other tickets? . . . Gus, McSnoyd—
But . . .
But the man gave them to Pop, Mr. O'Malley . . . And he and Mom are going with me. . . . And they've invited Mr. and Mrs. Shultz and Jane—
Three. Four. Five . . .SIX!
But Mr. O'Malley . . .

Isn't it marvelous, son?—Why, Barnaby! What is the matter?

I wonder what Mr. O'Malley, my Fairy Godfather, is doing now . . .

NEXT MORNING

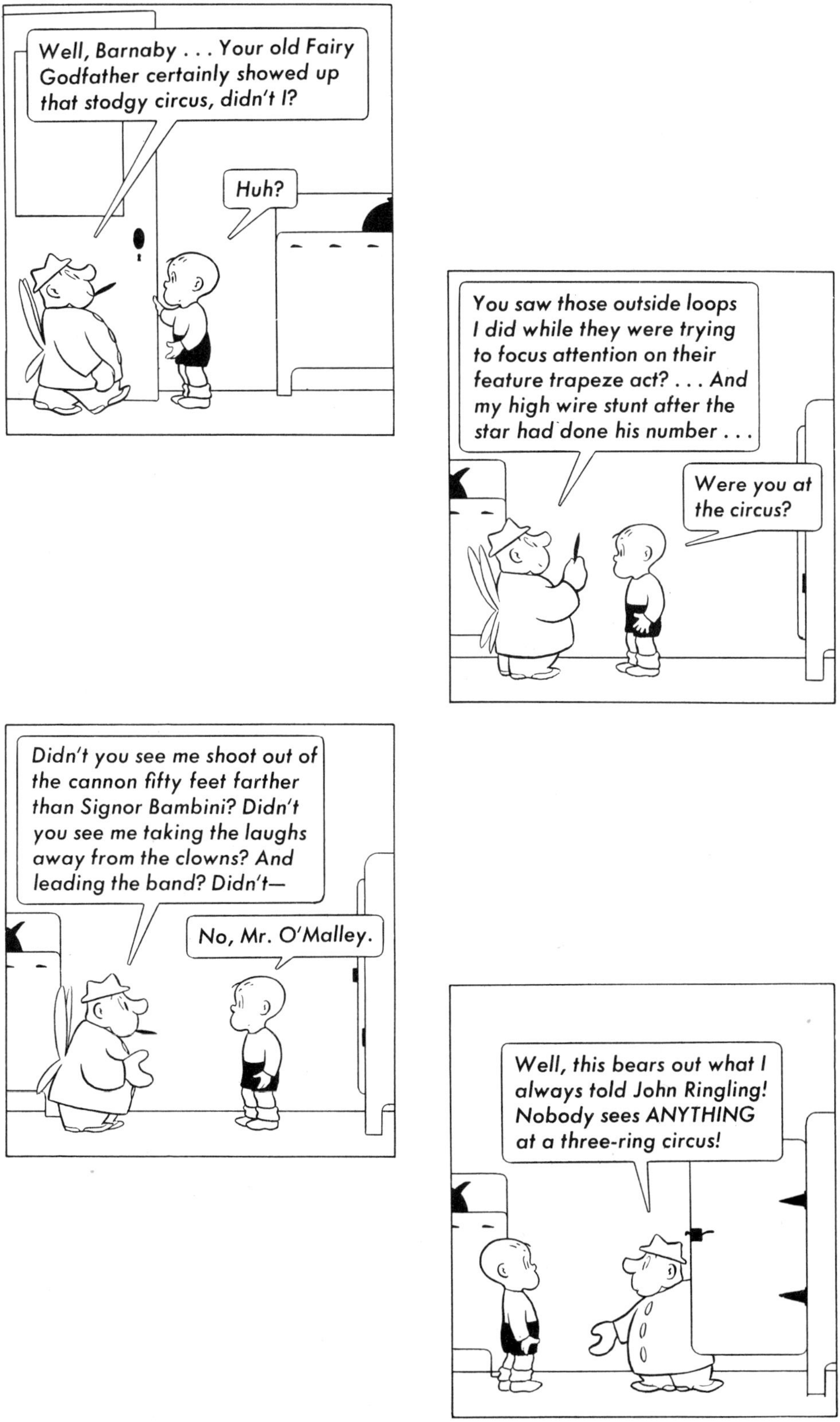
Well, Barnaby . . . Your old Fairy Godfather certainly showed up that stodgy circus, didn't I?
Huh?
You saw those outside loops I did while they were trying to focus attention on their feature trapeze act? . . . And my high wire stunt after the star had done his number . . .
Were you at the circus?
Didn't you see me shoot out of the cannon fifty feet farther than Signor Bambini? Didn't you see me taking the laughs away from the clowns? And leading the band? Didn't—
No, Mr. O'Malley.
Well, this bears out what I always told John Ringling! Nobody sees ANYTHING at a three-ring circus!

EPISODE THREE

Atlas, the Giant

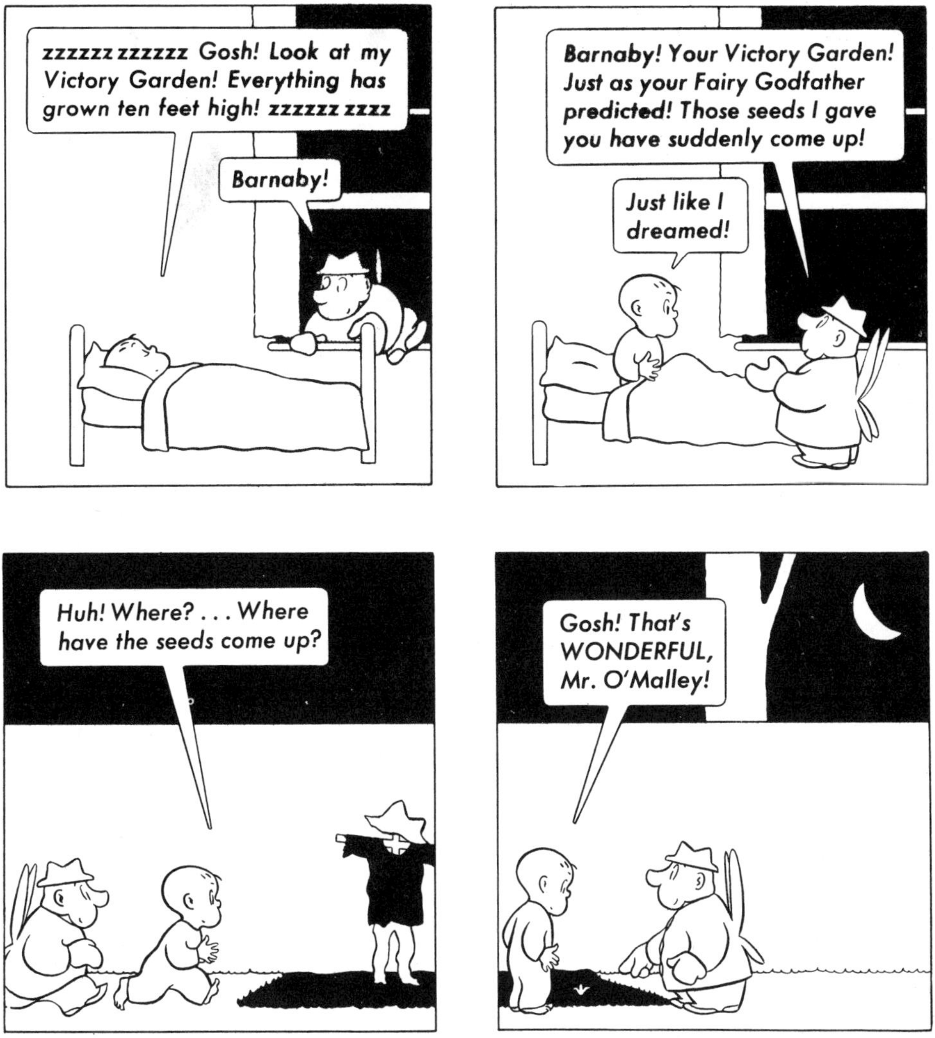
zzzzzz zzzzzz Gosh! Look at my Victory Garden! Everything has grown ten feet high! zzzzzz zzzz
Barnaby!
Barnaby! Your Victory Garden! Just as your Fairy Godfather predicted! Those seeds I gave you have suddenly come up!
Just like I dreamed!
Huh! Where? . . . Where have the seeds come up?
Gosh! That's WONDERFUL, Mr. O'Malley!

NEXT MORNING

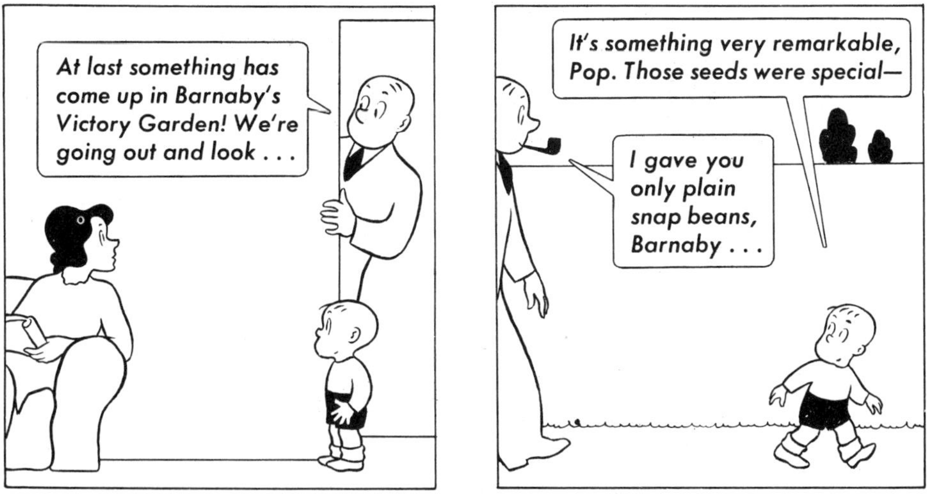
At last something has come up in Barnaby's Victory Garden! We're going out and look . . .
It's something very remarkable, Pop. Those seeds were special—
I gave you only plain snap beans, Barnaby . . .

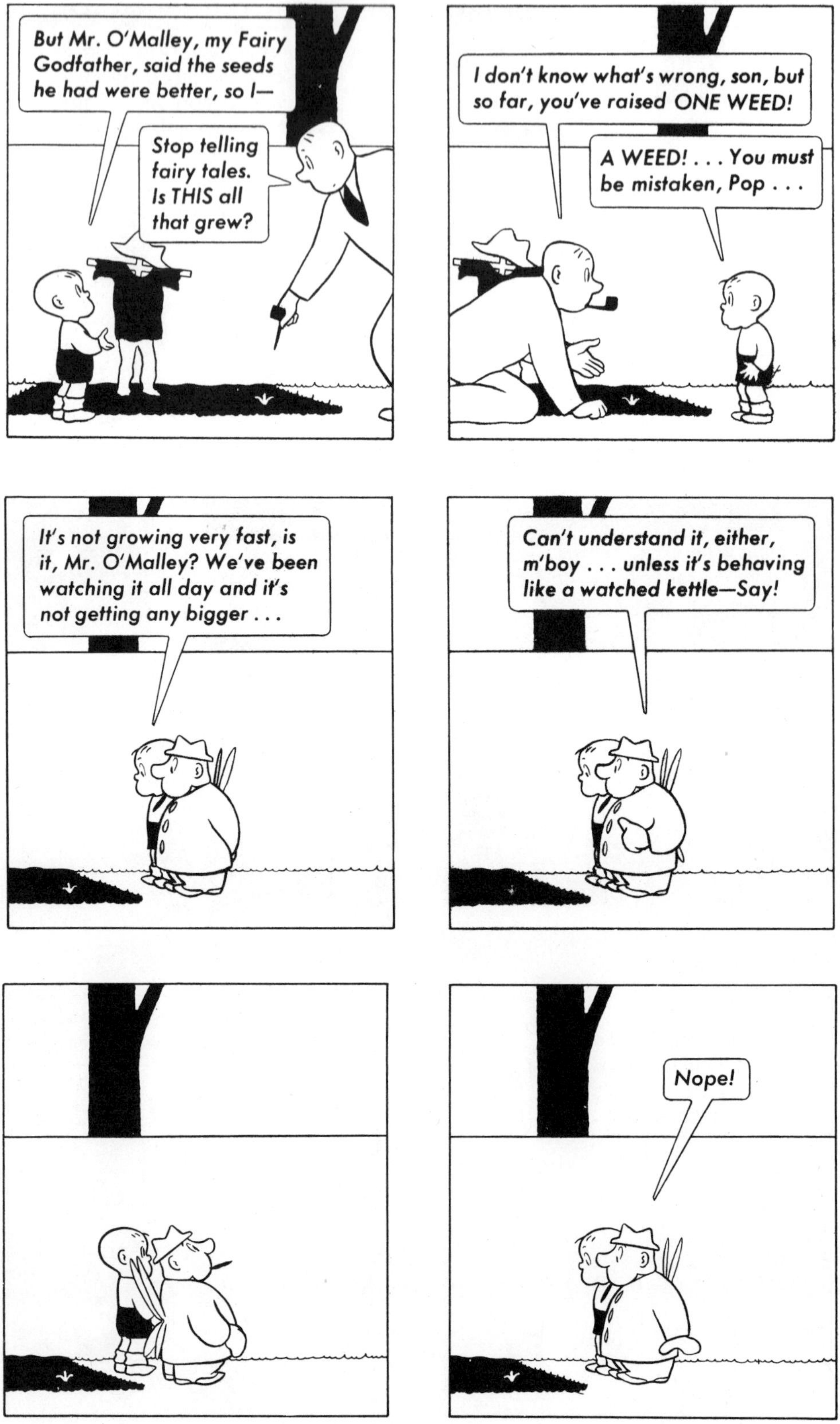
But Mr. O'Malley, my Fairy Godfather, said the seeds he had were better, so I—
Stop telling fairy tales. Is THIS all that grew?
I don't know what's wrong, son, but so far, you've raised ONE WEED!
A WEED! . . . You must be mistaken, Pop . . .
It's not growing very fast, is it, Mr. O'Malley? We've been watching it all day and it's not getting any bigger . . .
Can't understand it, either, m'boy . . . unless it's behaving like a watched kettle—Say!
Nope!

THAT EVENING

Barnaby believes that little weed in his garden is going to grow up into a marvelous bean plant . . . I hope it doesn't die from the care he's giving it . . . It will break his heart.
Barnaby! Prepare yourself for terrible news! Torn up by the roots! The beanstalk!

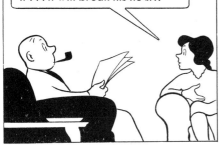

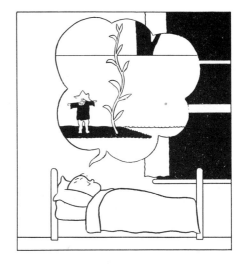

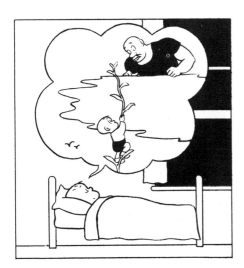

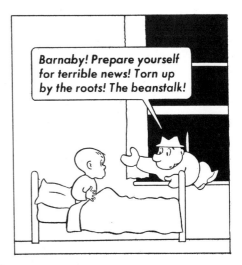

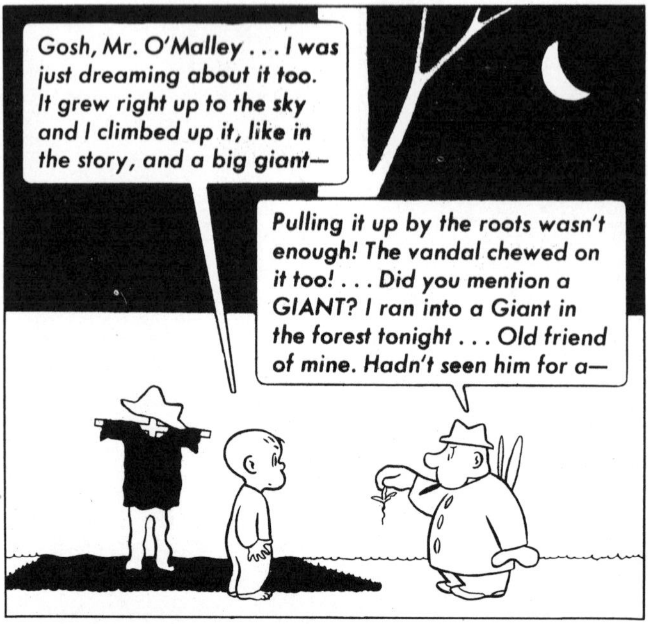
Gosh, Mr. O'Malley . . . I was just dreaming about it too. It grew right up to the sky and I climbed up it, like in the story, and a big giant—
Pulling it up by the roots wasn't enough! The vandal chewed on it too! . . . Did you mention a GIANT? I ran into a Giant in the forest tonight . . . Old friend of mine. Hadn't seen him for a—

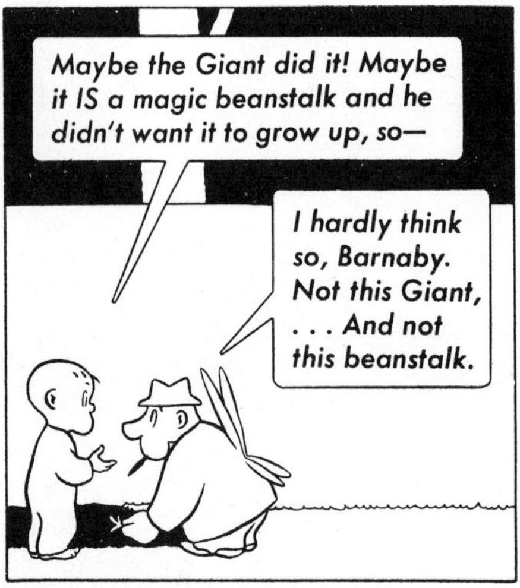
Maybe the Giant did it! Maybe it IS a magic beanstalk and he didn't want it to grow up, so—
I hardly think so, Barnaby. Not this Giant, . . . And not this beanstalk.

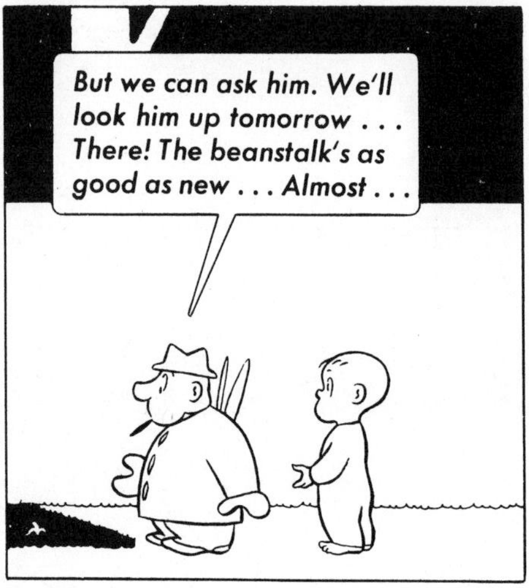
But we can ask him. We'll look him up tomorrow . . . There! The beanstalk's as good as new . . . Almost . . .

THE FOLLOWING MORNING

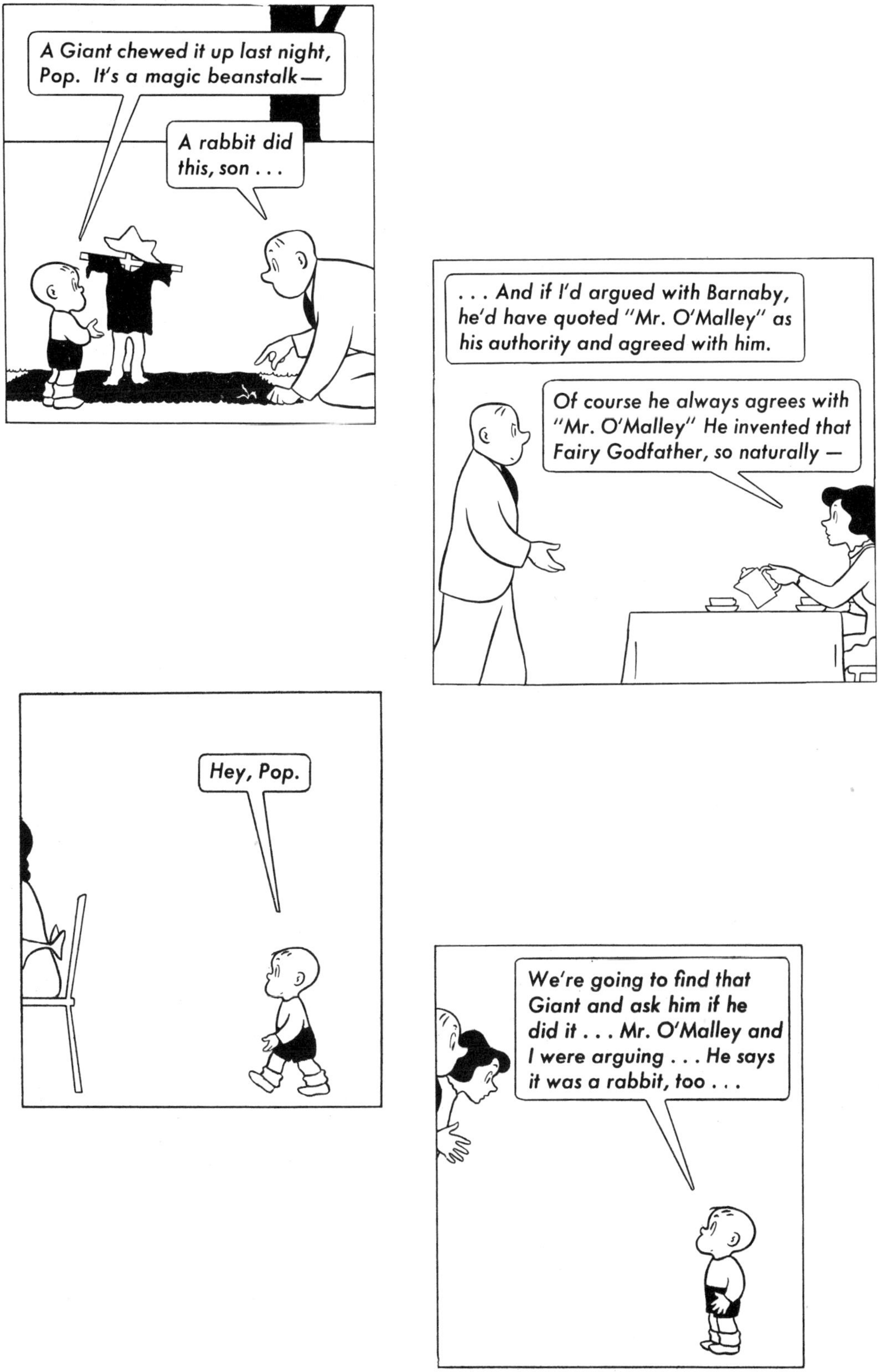
A Giant chewed it up last night, Pop. It's a magic beanstalk—
A rabbit did this, son . . .
. . . And if I'd argued with Barnaby, he'd have quoted "Mr. O'Malley" as his authority and agreed with him.
Of course he always agrees with "Mr. O'Malley" He invented that Fairy Godfather, so naturally —
Hey, Pop.
We're going to find that Giant and ask him if he did it . . . Mr. O'Malley and I were arguing . . . He says it was a rabbit, too . . .

IN THE AFTERNOON

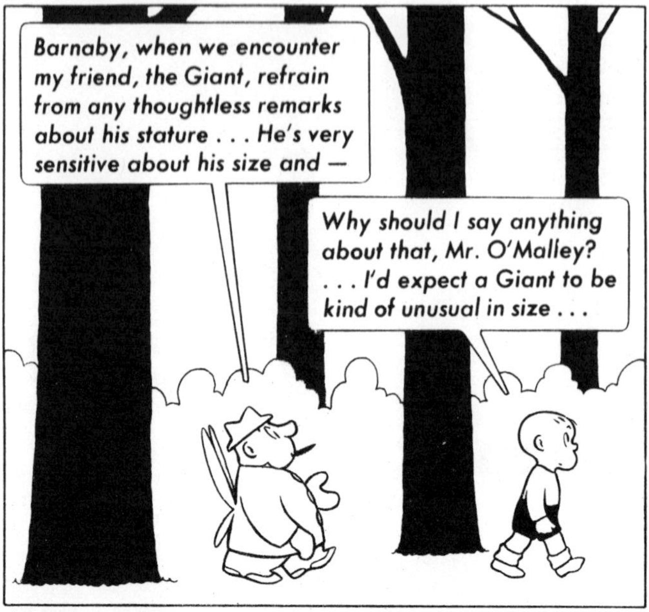
Barnaby, when we encounter my friend, the Giant, refrain from any thoughtless remarks about his stature . . . He's very sensitive about his size and —
Why should I say anything about that, Mr. O'Malley? . . . I'd expect a Giant to be kind of unusual in size . . .

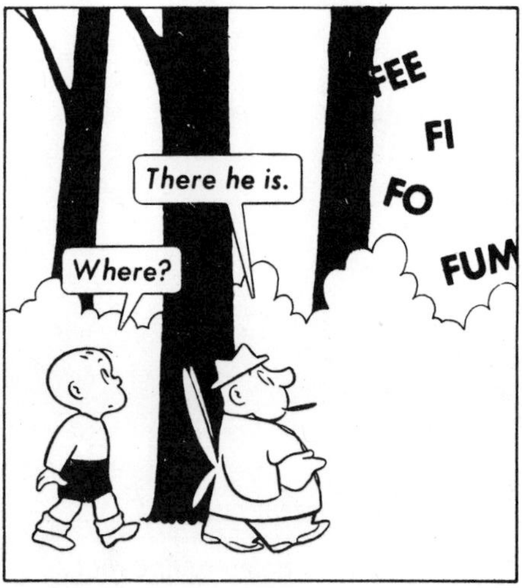
FEE
FI
FO
FUM
There he is.
Where?

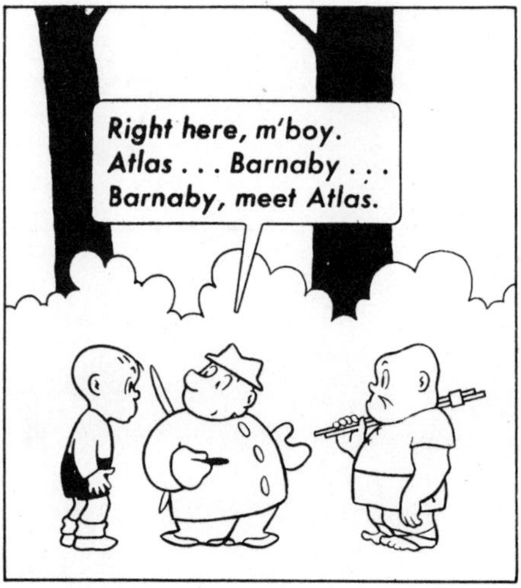
Right here, m'boy. Atlas . . . Barnaby . . . Barnaby, meet Atlas.

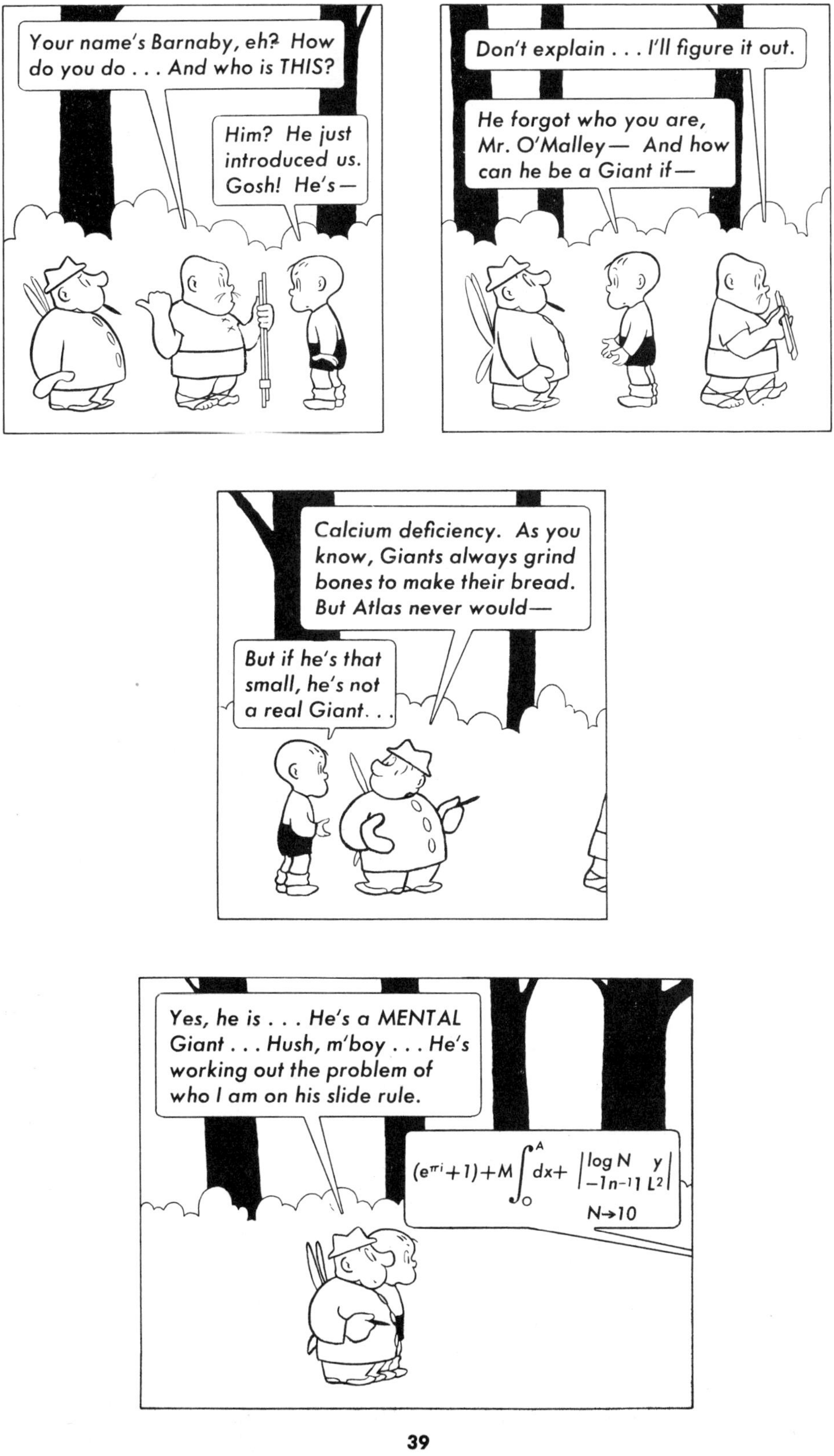
Your name's Barnaby, eh? How do you do . . . And who is THIS?
Him? He just introduced us. Gosh! He's—
Don't explain . . . I'll figure it out.
He forgot who you are, Mr. O'Malley— And how can he be a Giant if—
Calcium deficiency. As you know, Giants always grind bones to make their bread. But Atlas never would—
But if he's that small, he's not a real Giant. . .
Yes, he is . . . He's a MENTAL Giant . . . Hush, m'boy . . . He's working out the problem of who I am on his slide rule.
$(e^{\pi i}+1)+M\int_0^A dx+\begin{vmatrix}\log N & y\\ -1n^{-1}1 & L^2\end{vmatrix}_{N\to 10}$

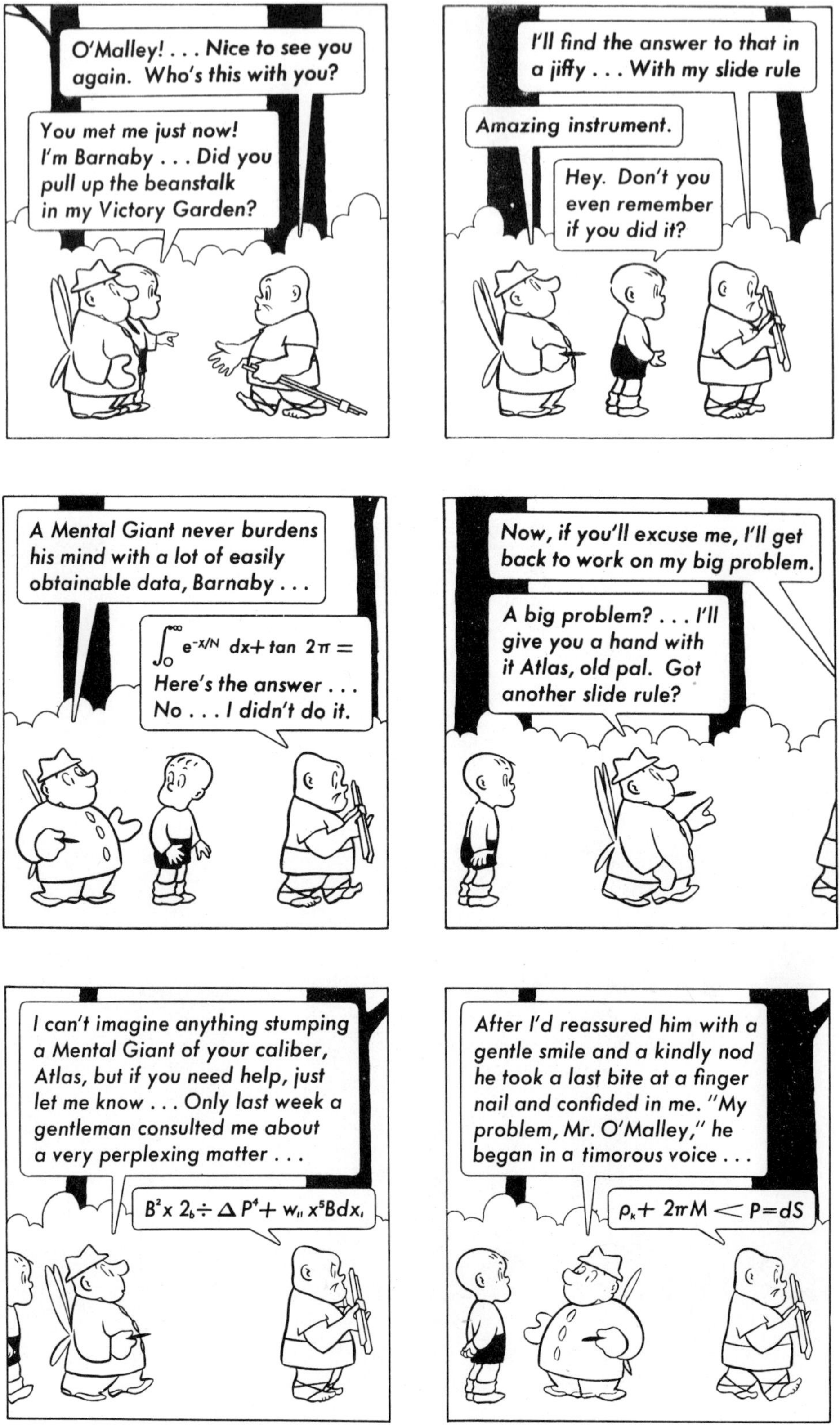
O'Malley! . . . Nice to see you again. Who's this with you?
You met me just now! I'm Barnaby . . . Did you pull up the beanstalk in my Victory Garden?
I'll find the answer to that in a jiffy . . . With my slide rule
Amazing instrument.
Hey. Don't you even remember if you did it?
A Mental Giant never burdens his mind with a lot of easily obtainable data, Barnaby . . .
$\int_0^\infty e^{-x/N}\,dx + \tan 2\pi =$
Here's the answer . . . No . . . I didn't do it.
Now, if you'll excuse me, I'll get back to work on my big problem.
A big problem? . . . I'll give you a hand with it Atlas, old pal. Got another slide rule?
I can't imagine anything stumping a Mental Giant of your caliber, Atlas, but if you need help, just let me know . . . Only last week a gentleman consulted me about a very perplexing matter . . .
$B^2 x\, 2_b \div \Delta P^4 + w_{11}\, x^5 B dx_1$
After I'd reassured him with a gentle smile and a kindly nod he took a last bite at a finger nail and confided in me. "My problem, Mr. O'Malley," he began in a timorous voice . . .
$\rho_x + 2\pi M < P = dS$

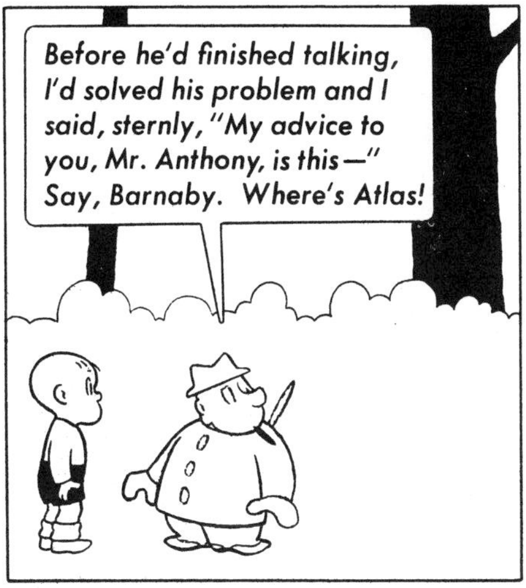
Before he'd finished talking, I'd solved his problem and I said, sternly, "My advice to you, Mr. Anthony, is this—" Say, Barnaby. Where's Atlas!

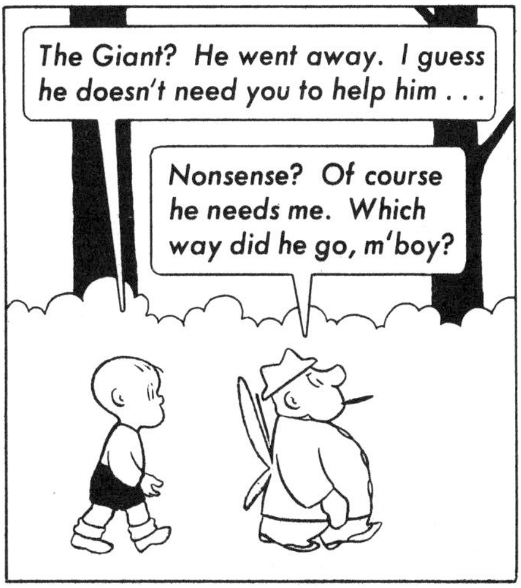
The Giant? He went away. I guess he doesn't need you to help him . . .
Nonsense? Of course he needs me. Which way did he go, m'boy?

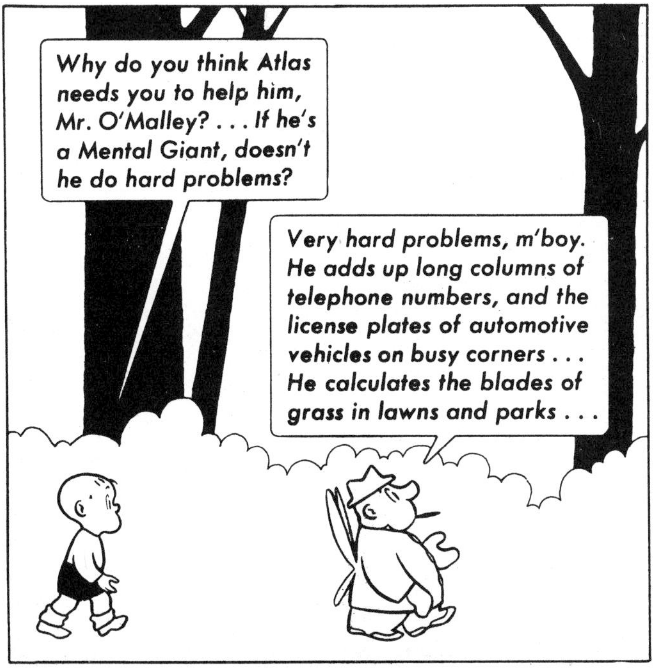
Why do you think Atlas needs you to help him, Mr. O'Malley? . . . If he's a Mental Giant, doesn't he do hard problems?
Very hard problems, m'boy. He adds up long columns of telephone numbers, and the license plates of automotive vehicles on busy corners . . . He calculates the blades of grass in lawns and parks . . .

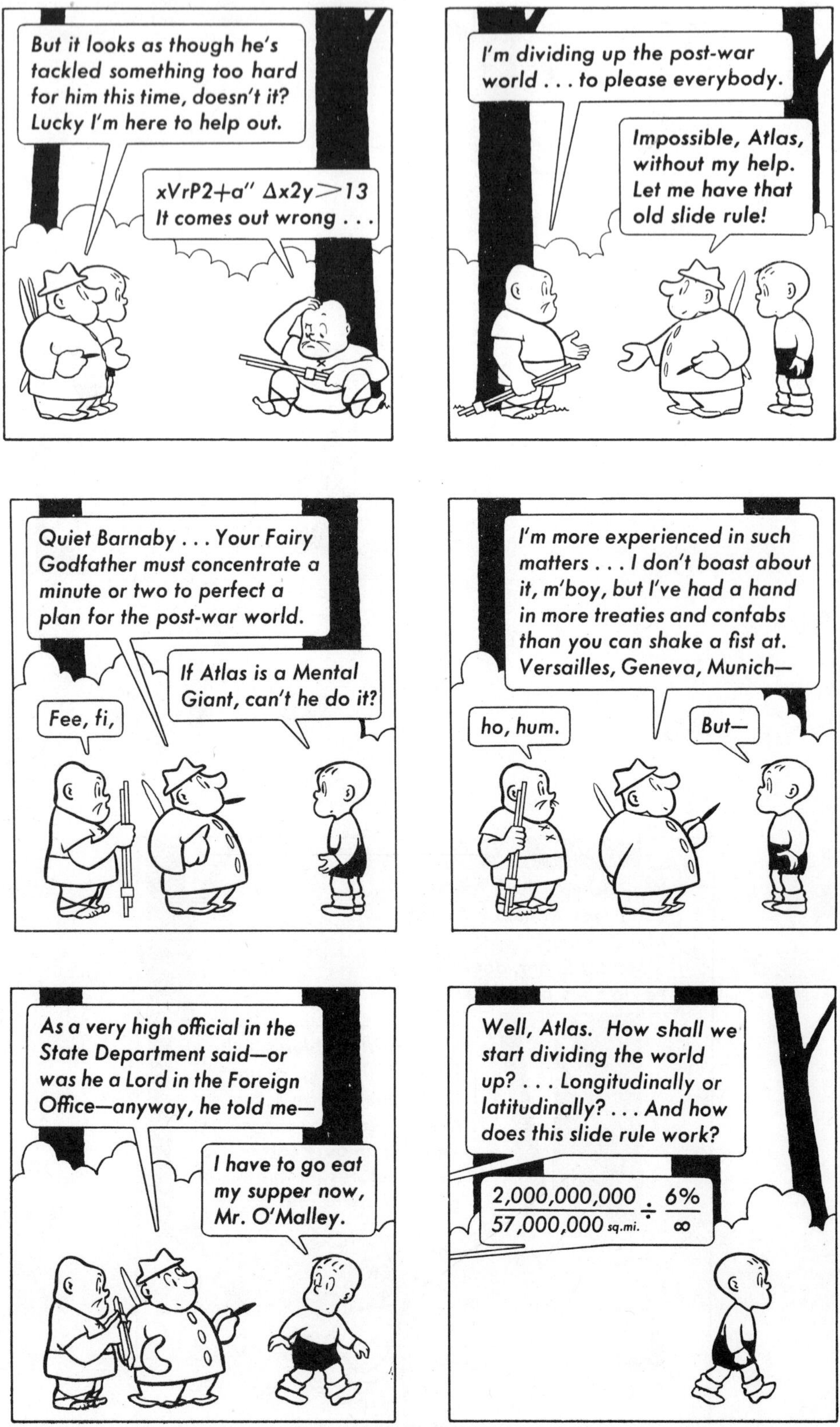
But it looks as though he's tackled something too hard for him this time, doesn't it? Lucky I'm here to help out.
xVrP2+a" Δx2y>13 It comes out wrong . . .
I'm dividing up the post-war world . . . to please everybody.
Impossible, Atlas, without my help. Let me have that old slide rule!
Quiet Barnaby . . . Your Fairy Godfather must concentrate a minute or two to perfect a plan for the post-war world.
If Atlas is a Mental Giant, can't he do it?
Fee, fi,
I'm more experienced in such matters . . . I don't boast about it, m'boy, but I've had a hand in more treaties and confabs than you can shake a fist at. Versailles, Geneva, Munich—
ho, hum.
But—
As a very high official in the State Department said—or was he a Lord in the Foreign Office—anyway, he told me—
I have to go eat my supper now, Mr. O'Malley.
Well, Atlas. How shall we start dividing the world up? . . . Longitudinally or latitudinally? . . . And how does this slide rule work?
2,000,000,000 / 57,000,000 sq.mi. ÷ 6% / ∞

LATE AT NIGHT

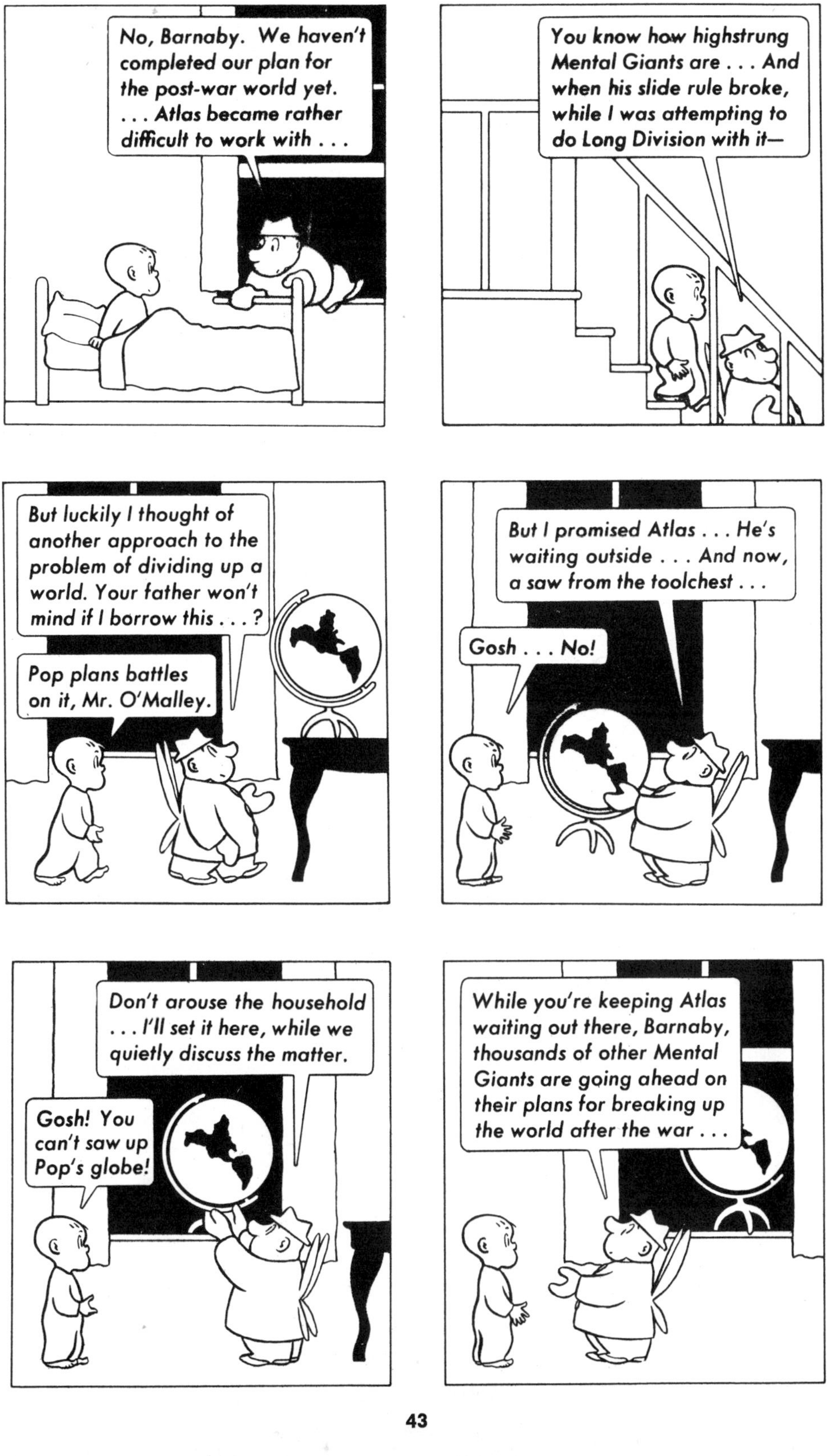
No, Barnaby. We haven't completed our plan for the post-war world yet. . . . Atlas became rather difficult to work with . . .
You know how highstrung Mental Giants are . . . And when his slide rule broke, while I was attempting to do Long Division with it—
But luckily I thought of another approach to the problem of dividing up a world. Your father won't mind if I borrow this . . . ?
Pop plans battles on it, Mr. O'Malley.
But I promised Atlas . . . He's waiting outside . . . And now, a saw from the toolchest . . .
Gosh . . . No!
Don't arouse the household . . . I'll set it here, while we quietly discuss the matter.
Gosh! You can't saw up Pop's globe!
While you're keeping Atlas waiting out there, Barnaby, thousands of other Mental Giants are going ahead on their plans for breaking up the world after the war . . .

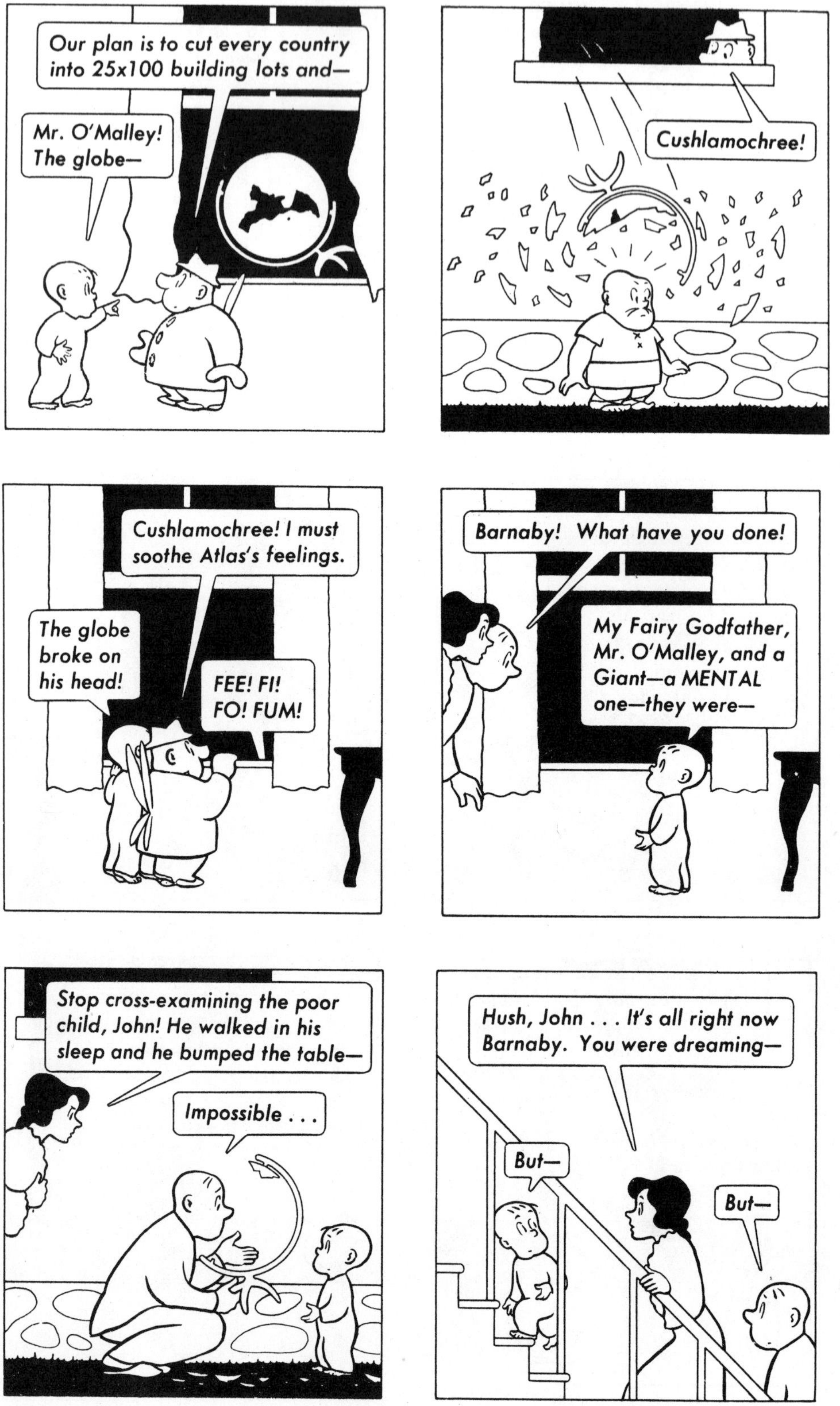
Our plan is to cut every country into 25x100 building lots and—
Mr. O'Malley! The globe—
Cushlamochree!
Cushlamochree! I must soothe Atlas's feelings.
The globe broke on his head!
FEE! FI! FO! FUM!
Barnaby! What have you done!
My Fairy Godfather, Mr. O'Malley, and a Giant—a MENTAL one—they were—
Stop cross-examining the poor child, John! He walked in his sleep and he bumped the table—
Impossible . . .
Hush, John . . . It's all right now Barnaby. You were dreaming—
But—
But—

EPISODE FOUR
Gorgon's Father

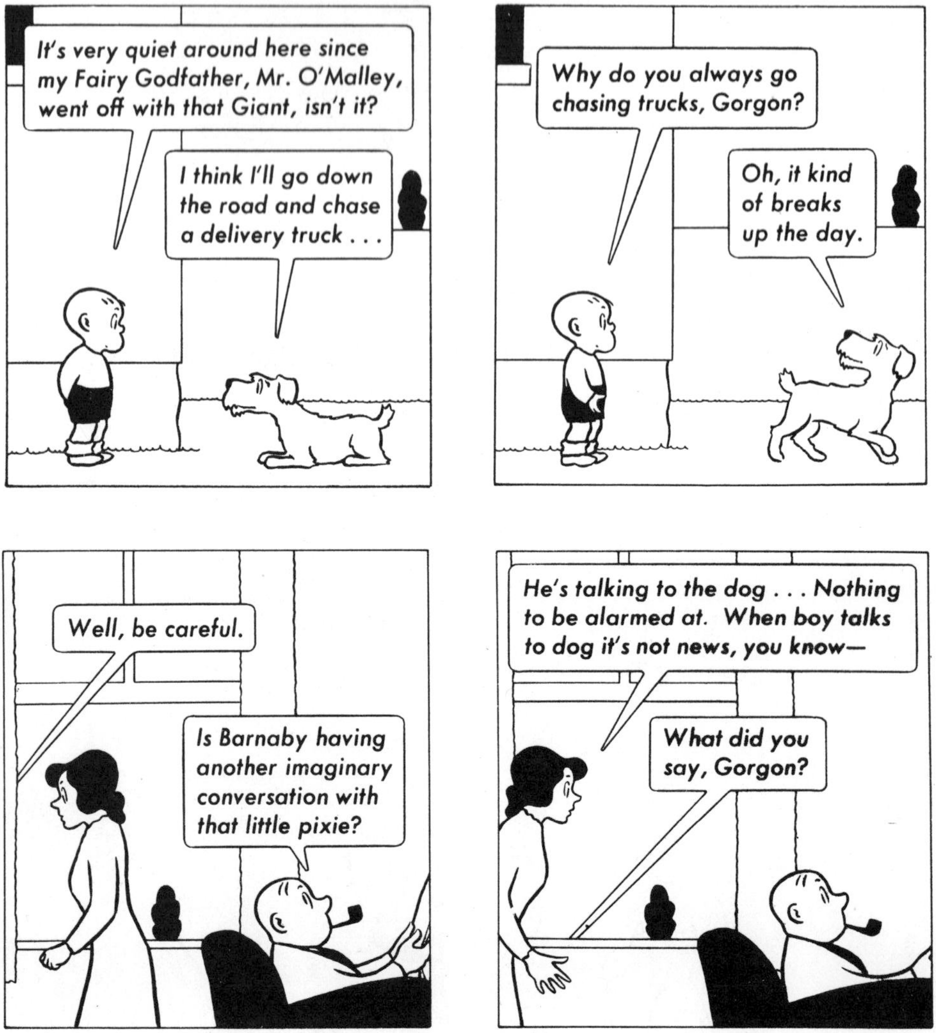
It's very quiet around here since my Fairy Godfather, Mr. O'Malley, went off with that Giant, isn't it?
I think I'll go down the road and chase a delivery truck . . .
Why do you always go chasing trucks, Gorgon?
Oh, it kind of breaks up the day.
Well, be careful.
Is Barnaby having another imaginary conversation with that little pixie?
He's talking to the dog . . . Nothing to be alarmed at. When boy talks to dog it's not news, you know—
What did you say, Gorgon?

THE NEXT DAY

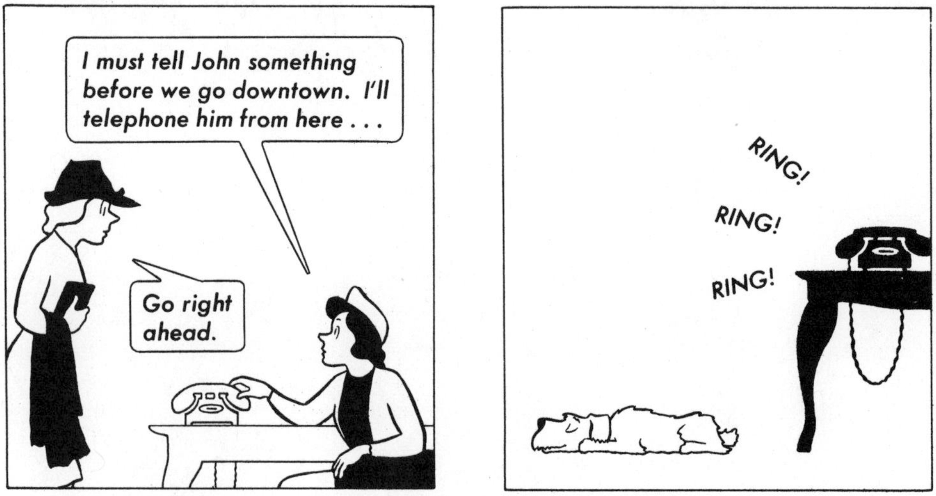
I must tell John something before we go downtown. I'll telephone him from here . . .
Go right ahead.
RING!
RING!
RING!

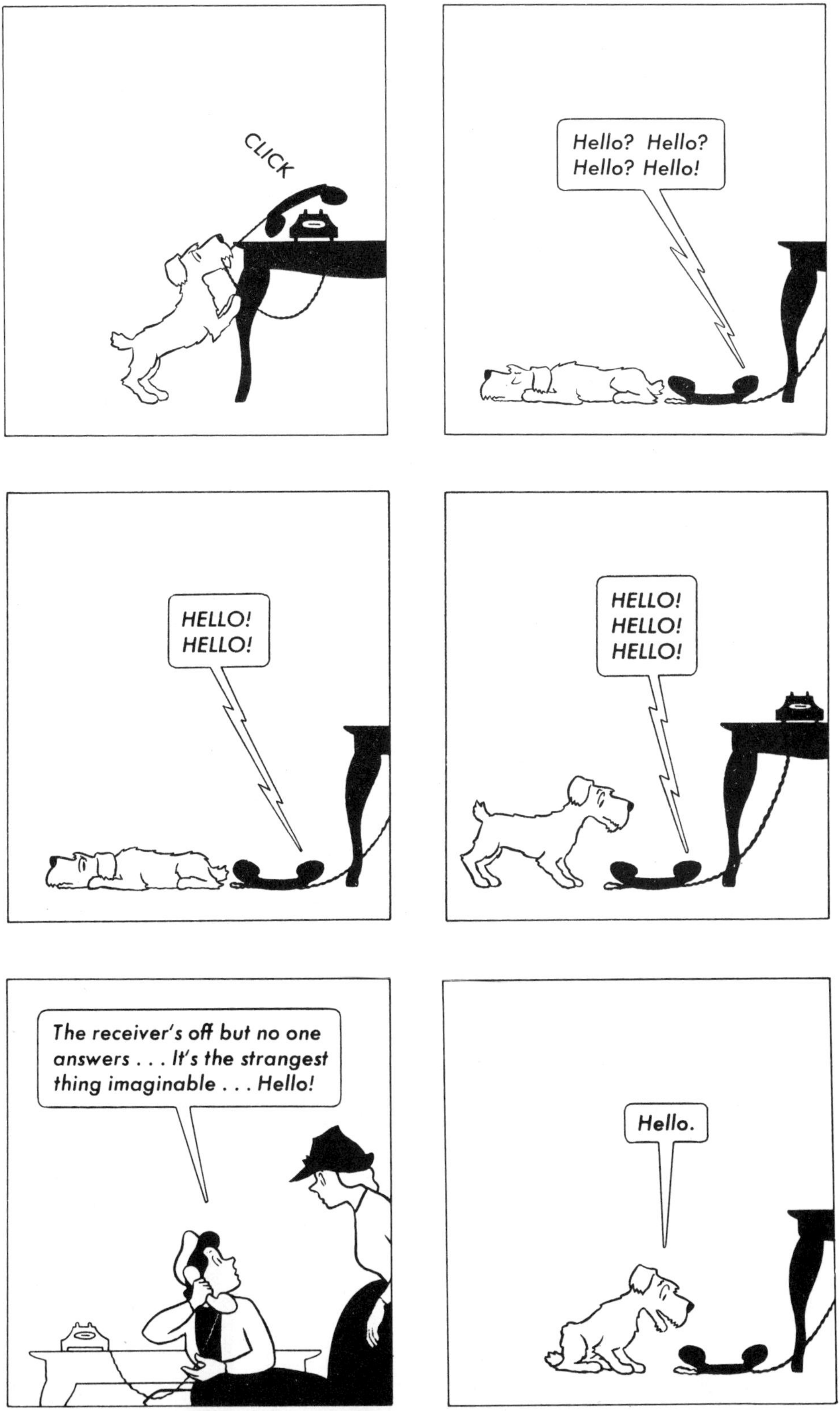
CLICK
Hello? Hello? Hello? Hello!
HELLO! HELLO!
HELLO! HELLO! HELLO!
The receiver's off but no one answers . . . It's the strangest thing imaginable . . . Hello!
Hello.

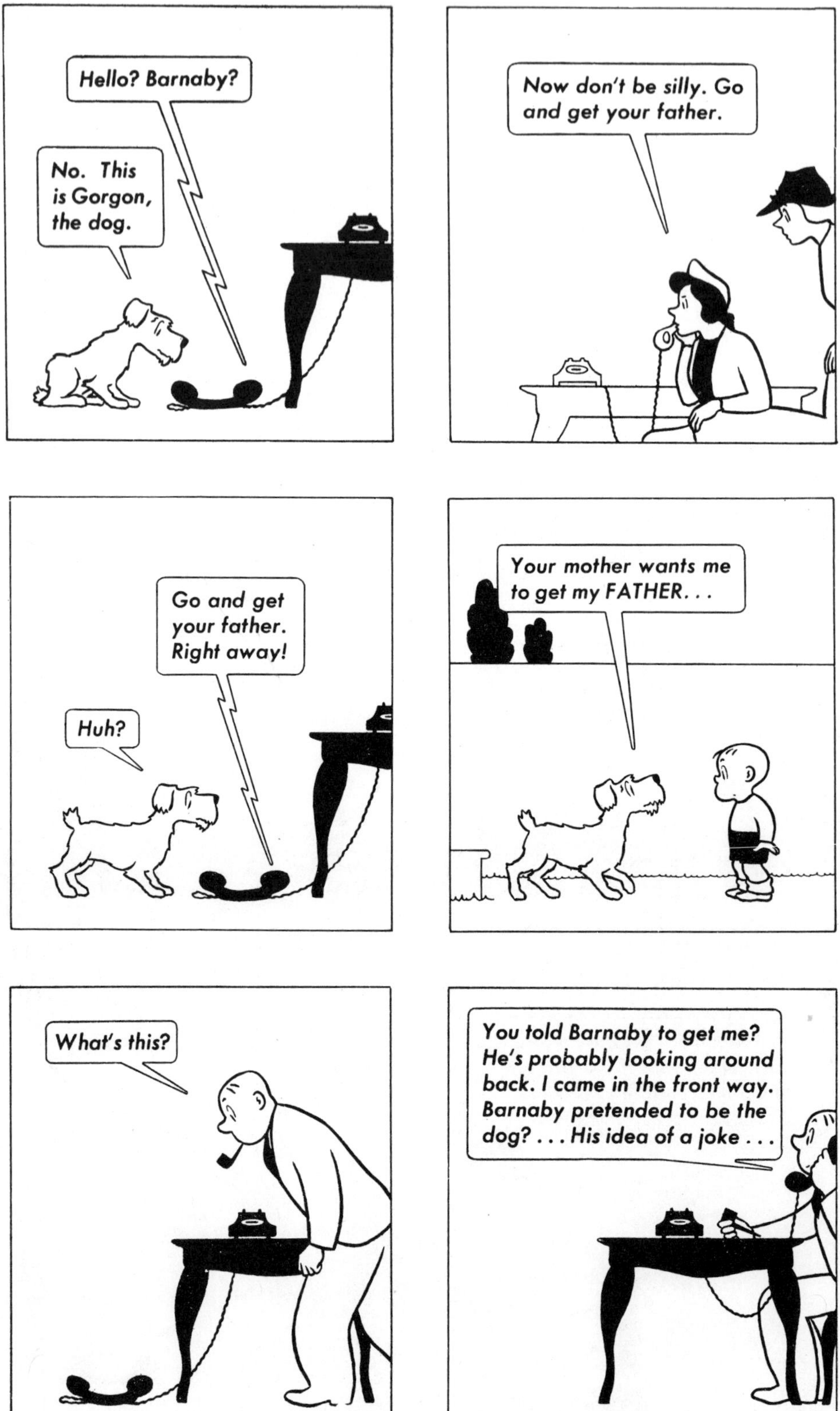
Hello? Barnaby?
No. This is Gorgon, the dog.
Now don't be silly. Go and get your father.
Go and get your father. Right away!
Huh?
Your mother wants me to get my FATHER. . .
What's this?
You told Barnaby to get me? He's probably looking around back. I came in the front way. Barnaby pretended to be the dog? . . . His idea of a joke . . .

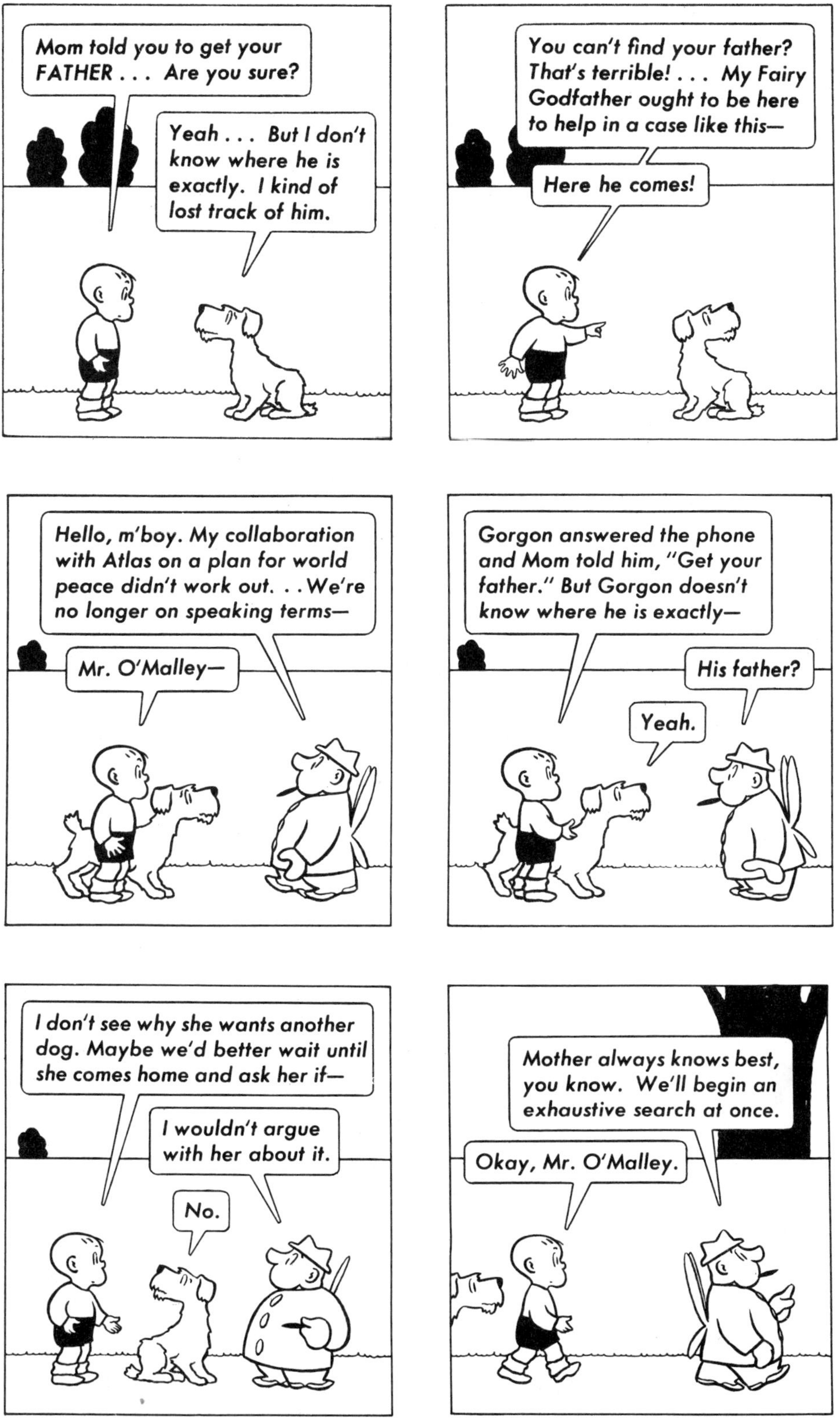
Mom told you to get your FATHER . . . Are you sure?
Yeah . . . But I don't know where he is exactly. I kind of lost track of him.
You can't find your father? That's terrible! . . . My Fairy Godfather ought to be here to help in a case like this—
Here he comes!
Hello, m'boy. My collaboration with Atlas on a plan for world peace didn't work out. . . We're no longer on speaking terms—
Mr. O'Malley—
Gorgon answered the phone and Mom told him, "Get your father." But Gorgon doesn't know where he is exactly—
His father?
Yeah.
I don't see why she wants another dog. Maybe we'd better wait until she comes home and ask her if—
I wouldn't argue with her about it.
No.
Mother always knows best, you know. We'll begin an exhaustive search at once.
Okay, Mr. O'Malley.

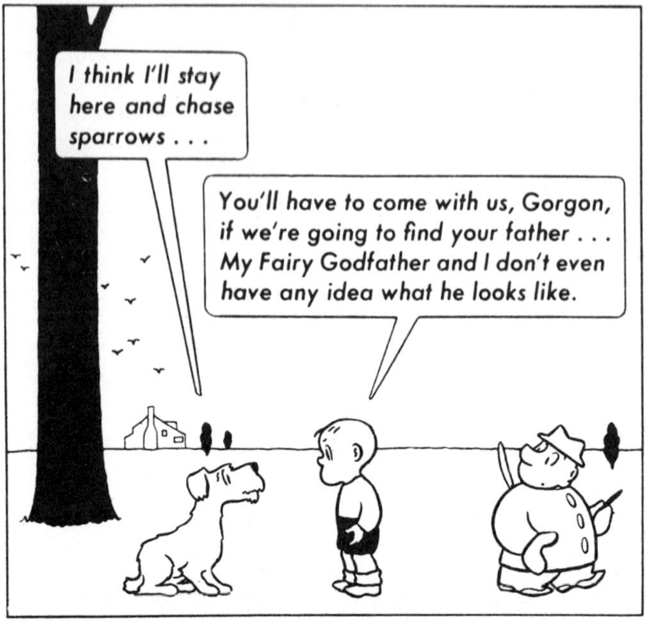
I think I'll stay here and chase sparrows . . .
You'll have to come with us, Gorgon, if we're going to find your father . . . My Fairy Godfather and I don't even have any idea what he looks like.

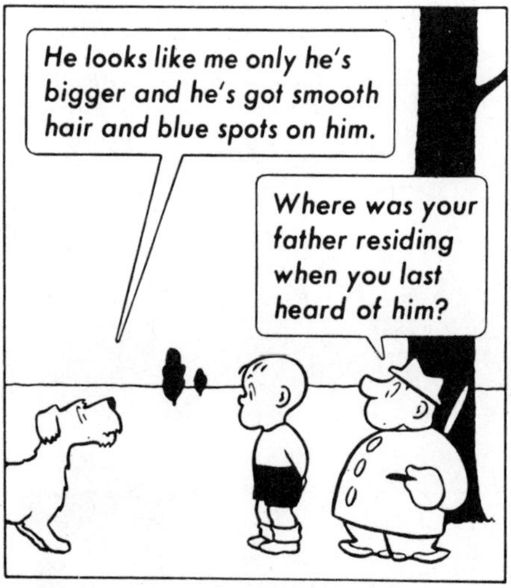
He looks like me only he's bigger and he's got smooth hair and blue spots on him.
Where was your father residing when you last heard of him?

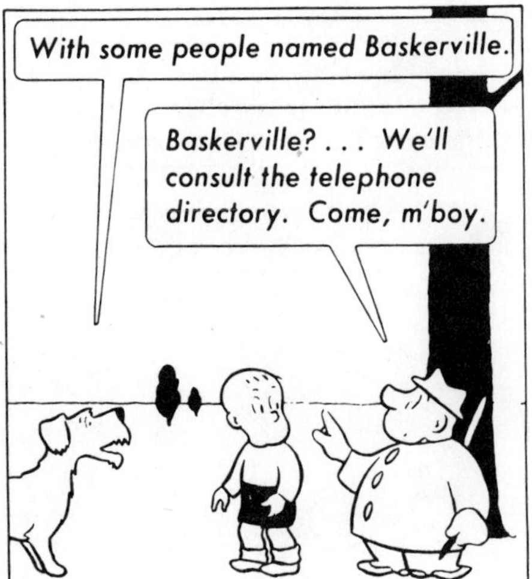
With some people named Baskerville.
Baskerville? . . . We'll consult the telephone directory. Come, m'boy.

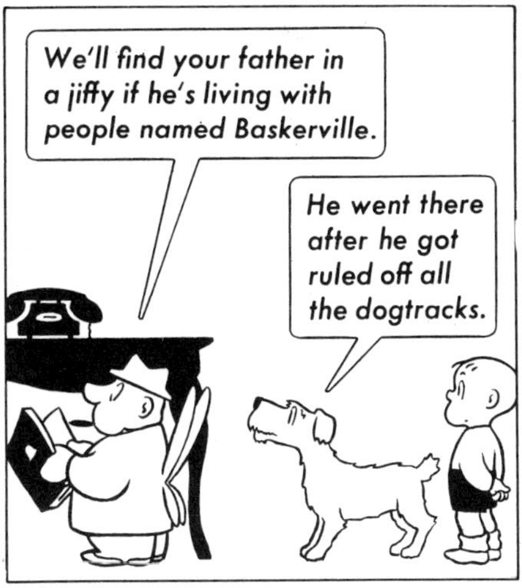
We'll find your father in a jiffy if he's living with people named Baskerville.
He went there after he got ruled off all the dogtracks.

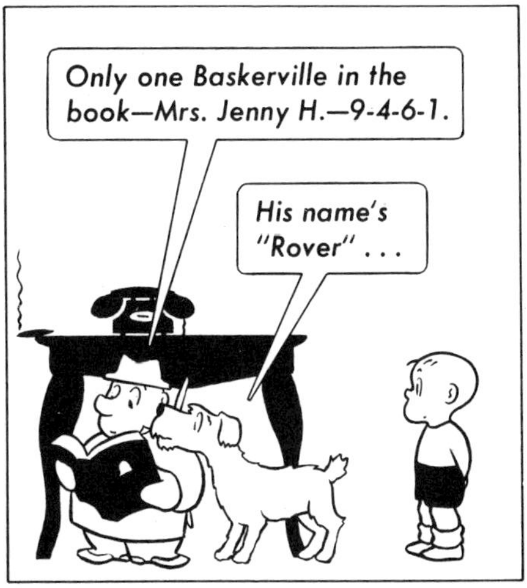
Only one Baskerville in the book—Mrs. Jenny H.—9-4-6-1.
His name's "Rover" . . .

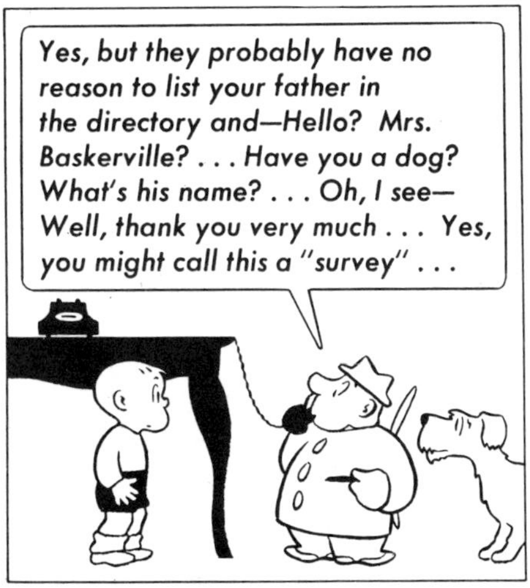
Yes, but they probably have no reason to list your father in the directory and—Hello? Mrs. Baskerville? . . . Have you a dog? What's his name? . . . Oh, I see— Well, thank you very much . . . Yes, you might call this a "survey" . . .

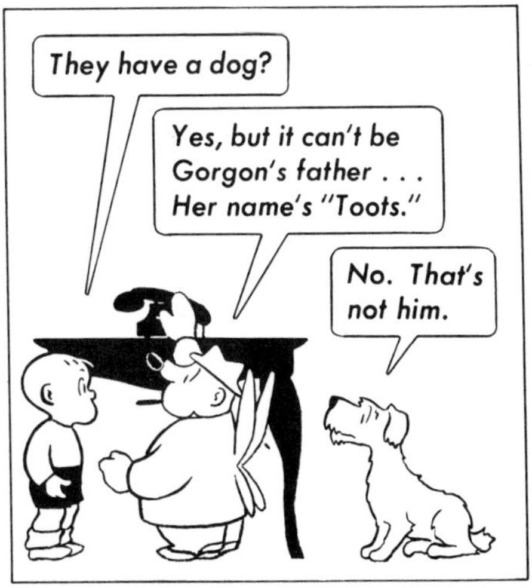
They have a dog?
Yes, but it can't be Gorgon's father . . . Her name's "Toots."
No. That's not him.

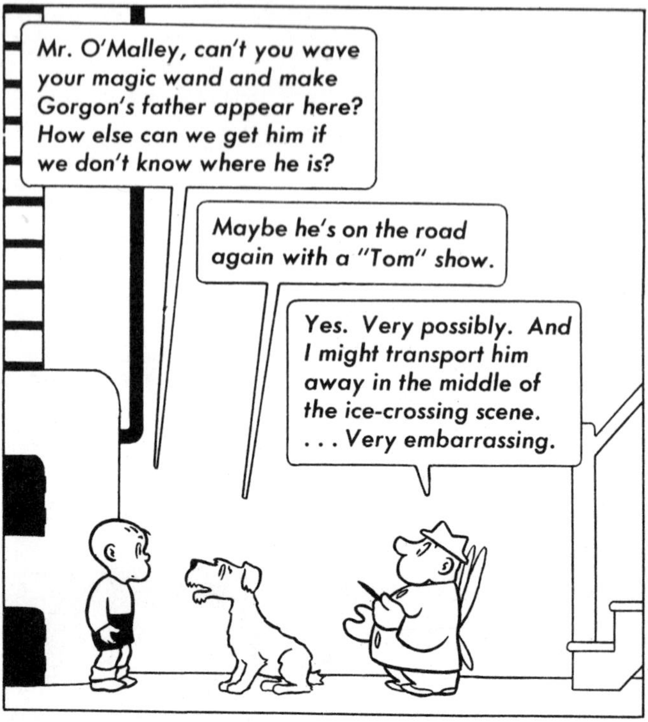
Mr. O'Malley, can't you wave your magic wand and make Gorgon's father appear here? How else can we get him if we don't know where he is?
Maybe he's on the road again with a "Tom" show.
Yes. Very possibly. And I might transport him away in the middle of the ice-crossing scene. . . . Very embarrassing.

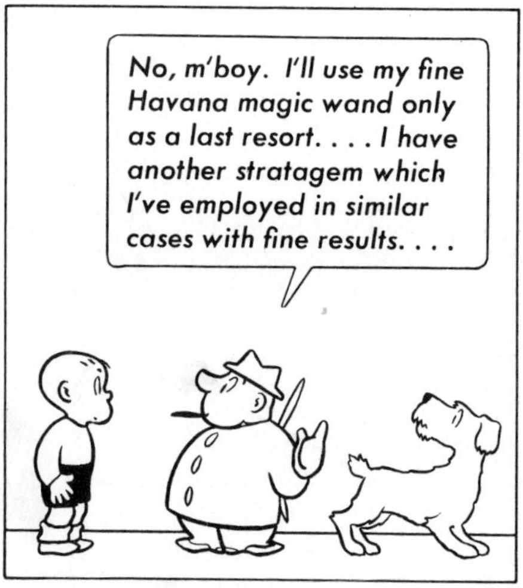
No, m'boy. I'll use my fine Havana magic wand only as a last resort. . . . I have another stratagem which I've employed in similar cases with fine results. . . .

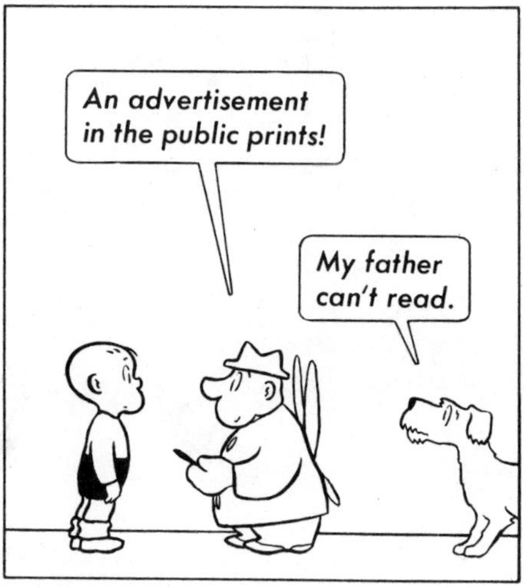
An advertisement in the public prints!
My father can't read.

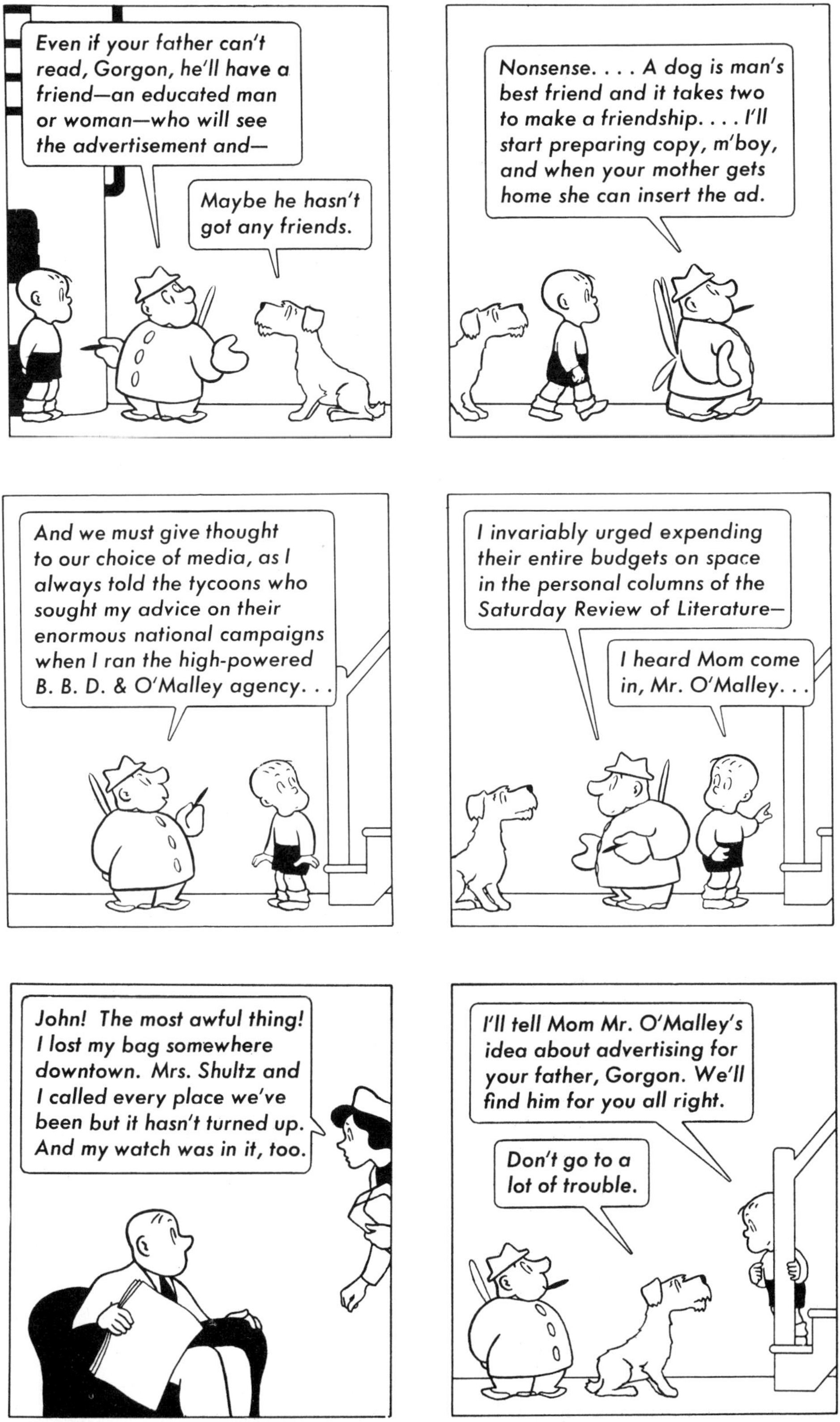
Even if your father can't read, Gorgon, he'll have a friend—an educated man or woman—who will see the advertisement and—
Maybe he hasn't got any friends.
Nonsense. . . . A dog is man's best friend and it takes two to make a friendship. . . . I'll start preparing copy, m'boy, and when your mother gets home she can insert the ad.
And we must give thought to our choice of media, as I always told the tycoons who sought my advice on their enormous national campaigns when I ran the high-powered B. B. D. & O'Malley agency. . .
I invariably urged expending their entire budgets on space in the personal columns of the Saturday Review of Literature—
I heard Mom come in, Mr. O'Malley. . .
John! The most awful thing! I lost my bag somewhere downtown. Mrs. Shultz and I called every place we've been but it hasn't turned up. And my watch was in it, too.
I'll tell Mom Mr. O'Malley's idea about advertising for your father, Gorgon. We'll find him for you all right.
Don't go to a lot of trouble.

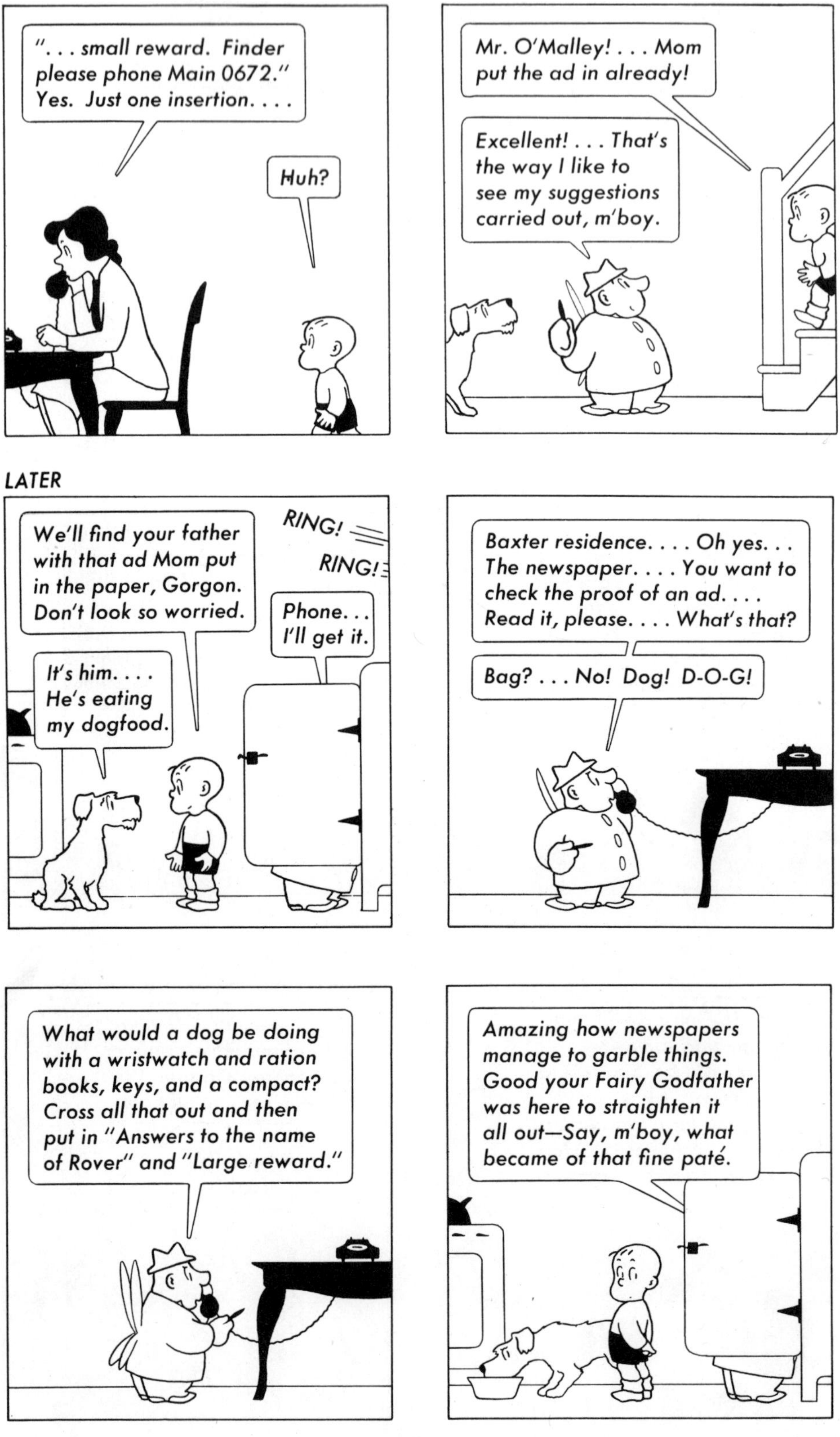
". . . small reward. Finder please phone Main 0672." Yes. Just one insertion. . . .
Huh?
Mr. O'Malley! . . . Mom put the ad in already!
Excellent! . . . That's the way I like to see my suggestions carried out, m'boy.
LATER
We'll find your father with that ad Mom put in the paper, Gorgon. Don't look so worried.
RING!
RING!
Phone. . . I'll get it.
It's him. . . . He's eating my dogfood.
Baxter residence. . . . Oh yes. . . The newspaper. . . . You want to check the proof of an ad. . . . Read it, please. . . . What's that?
Bag? . . . No! Dog! D-O-G!
What would a dog be doing with a wristwatch and ration books, keys, and a compact? Cross all that out and then put in "Answers to the name of Rover" and "Large reward."
Amazing how newspapers manage to garble things. Good your Fairy Godfather was here to straighten it all out—Say, m'boy, what became of that fine paté.

THE FOLLOWING DAY

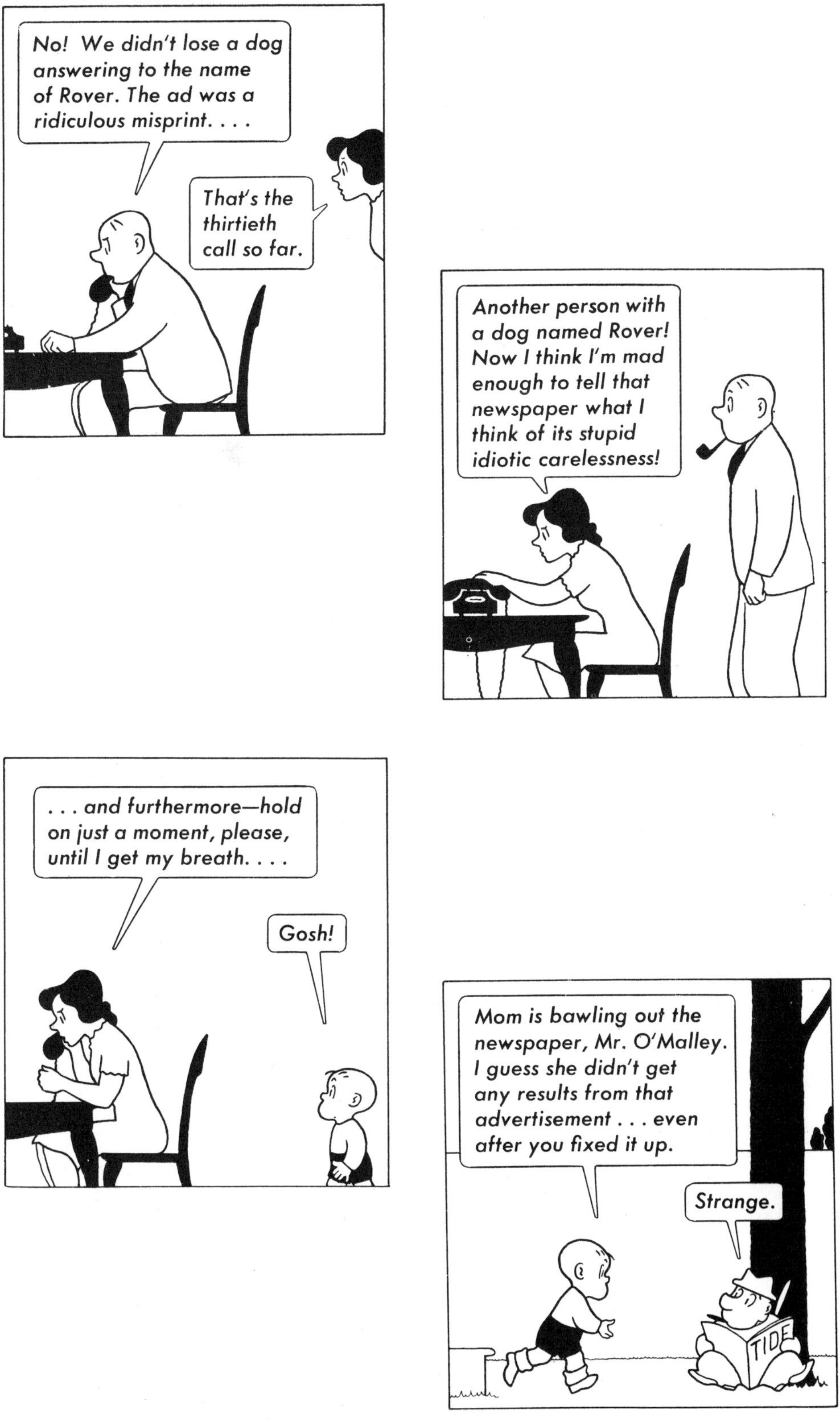
No! We didn't lose a dog answering to the name of Rover. The ad was a ridiculous misprint. . . .
That's the thirtieth call so far.
Another person with a dog named Rover! Now I think I'm mad enough to tell that newspaper what I think of its stupid idiotic carelessness!
. . . and furthermore—hold on just a moment, please, until I get my breath. . . .
Gosh!
Mom is bawling out the newspaper, Mr. O'Malley. I guess she didn't get any results from that advertisement . . . even after you fixed it up.
Strange.
TIDE

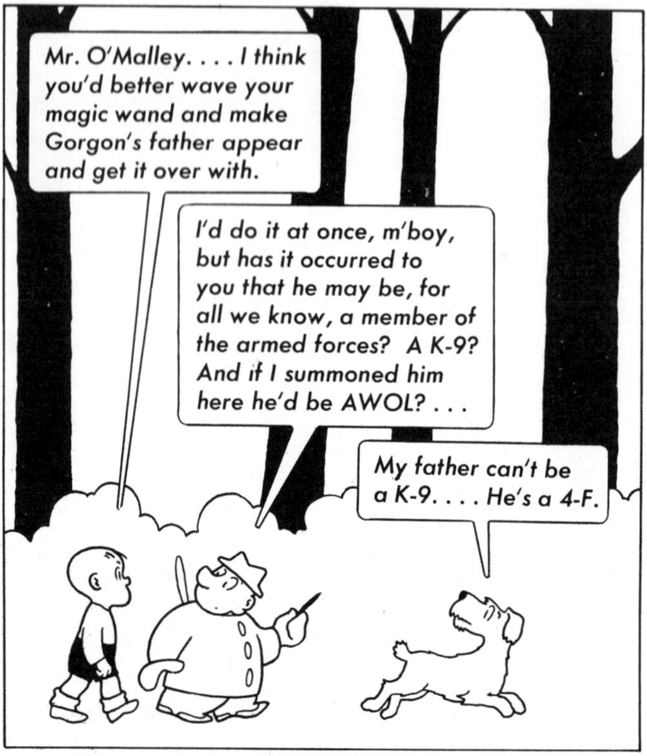
Mr. O'Malley. . . . I think you'd better wave your magic wand and make Gorgon's father appear and get it over with.
I'd do it at once, m'boy, but has it occurred to you that he may be, for all we know, a member of the armed forces? A K-9? And if I summoned him here he'd be AWOL? . . .
My father can't be a K-9. . . . He's a 4-F.

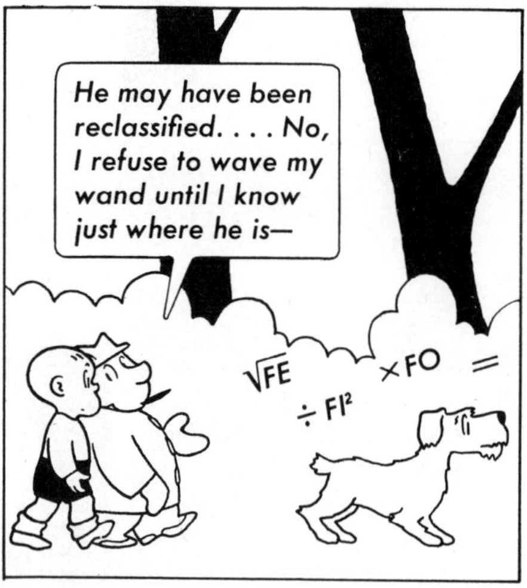
He may have been reclassified. . . . No, I refuse to wave my wand until I know just where he is—
√FE ÷ FI² × FO =

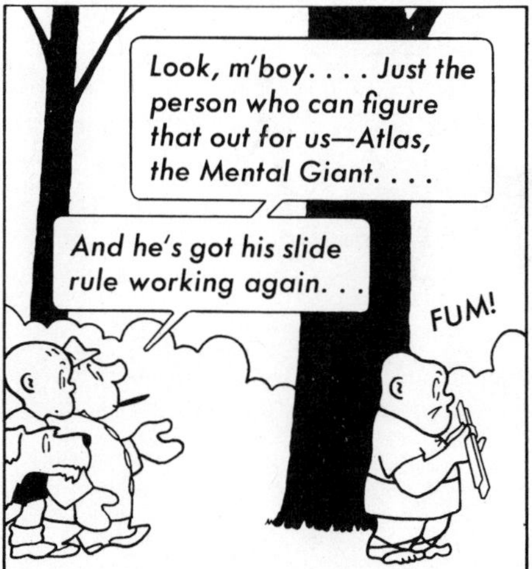
Look, m'boy. . . . Just the person who can figure that out for us—Atlas, the Mental Giant. . . .
And he's got his slide rule working again. . .
FUM!

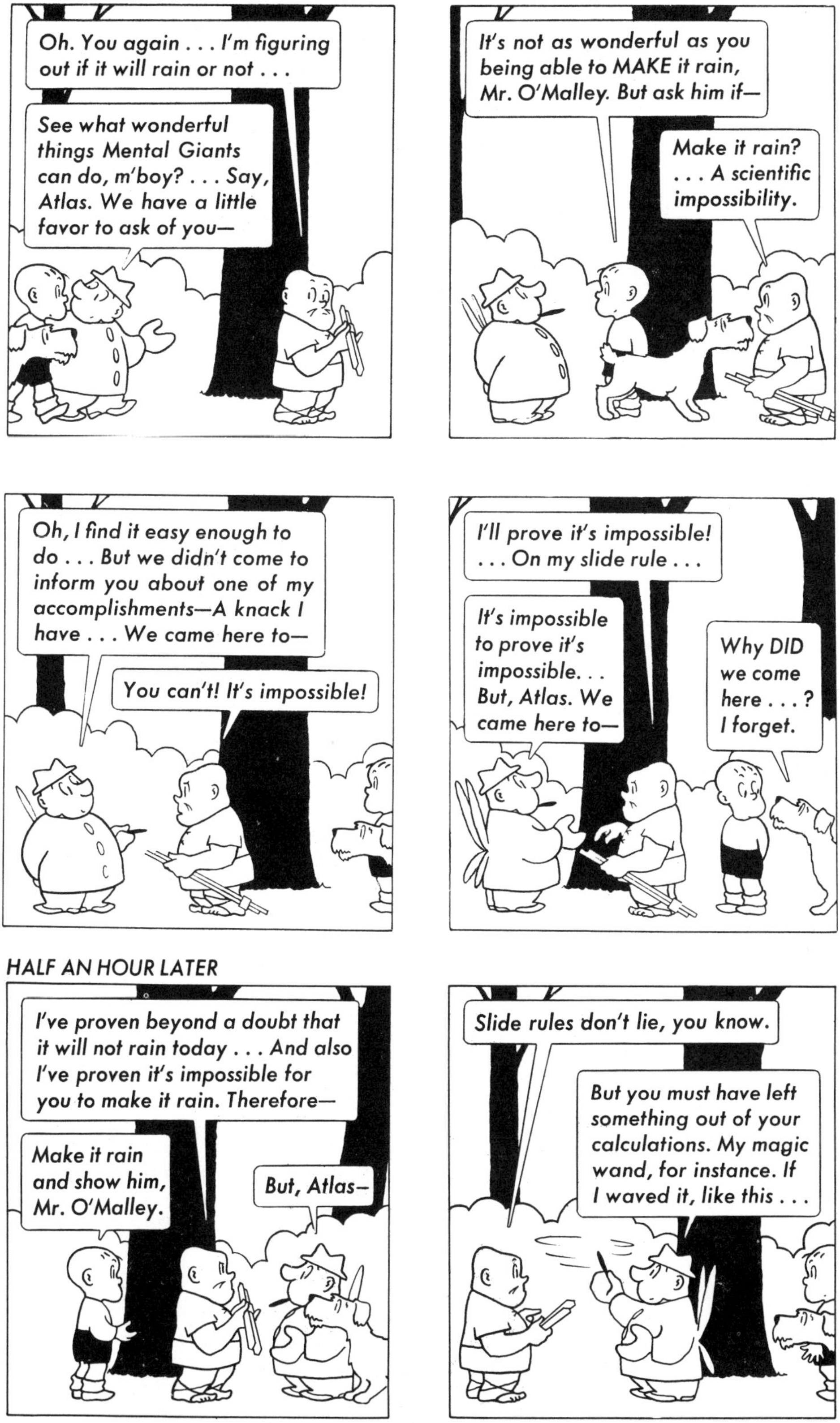
Oh. You again . . . I'm figuring out if it will rain or not . . .
See what wonderful things Mental Giants can do, m'boy? . . . Say, Atlas. We have a little favor to ask of you—
It's not as wonderful as you being able to MAKE it rain, Mr. O'Malley. But ask him if—
Make it rain? . . . A scientific impossibility.
Oh, I find it easy enough to do . . . But we didn't come to inform you about one of my accomplishments—A knack I have . . . We came here to—
You can't! It's impossible!
I'll prove it's impossible! . . . On my slide rule . . .
It's impossible to prove it's impossible. . . But, Atlas. We came here to—
Why DID we come here . . . ? I forget.
HALF AN HOUR LATER
I've proven beyond a doubt that it will not rain today . . . And also I've proven it's impossible for you to make it rain. Therefore—
Make it rain and show him, Mr. O'Malley.
But, Atlas—
Slide rules don't lie, you know.
But you must have left something out of your calculations. My magic wand, for instance. If I waved it, like this . . .

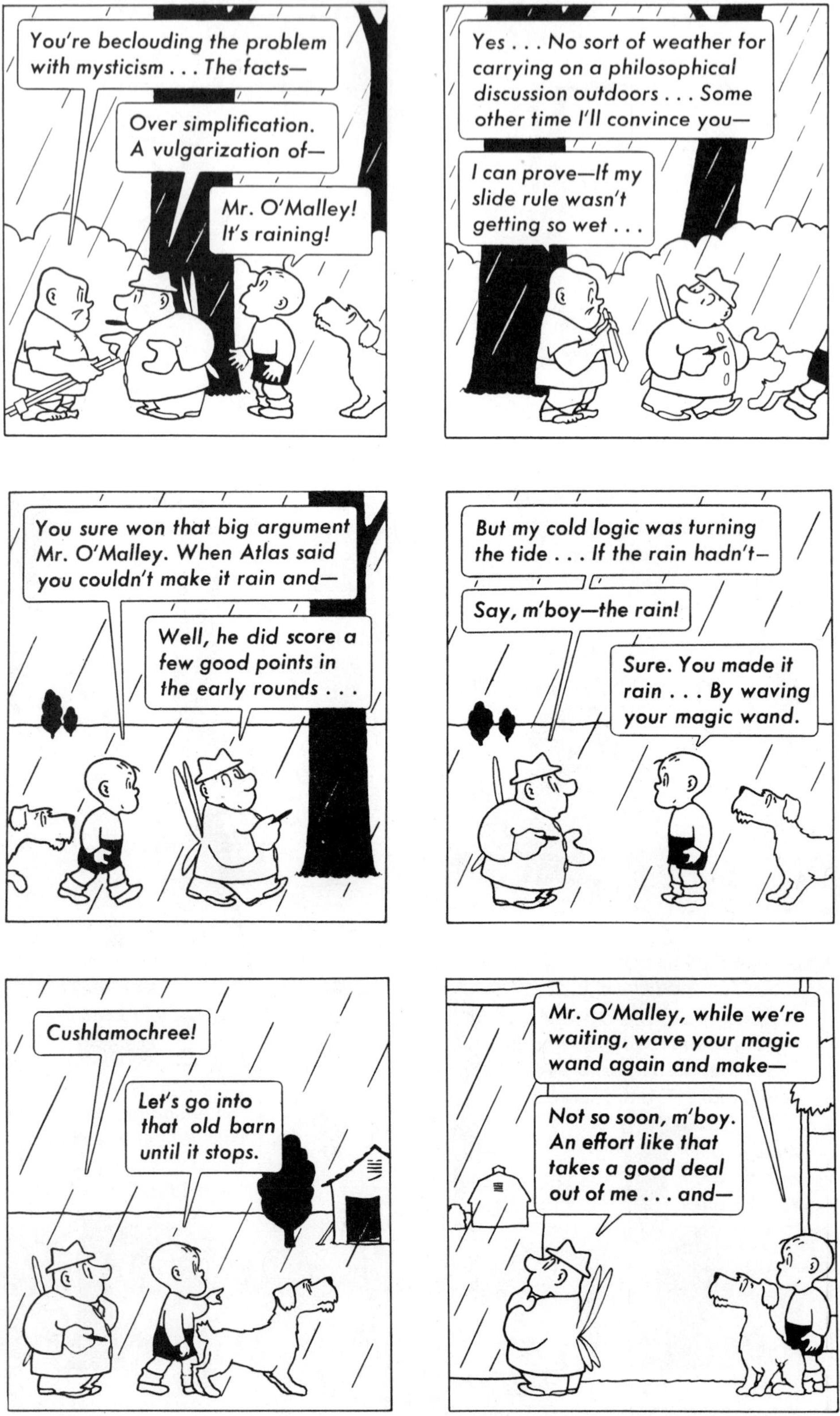
You're beclouding the problem with mysticism . . . The facts—
Over simplification. A vulgarization of—
Mr. O'Malley! It's raining!
Yes . . . No sort of weather for carrying on a philosophical discussion outdoors . . . Some other time I'll convince you—
I can prove—If my slide rule wasn't getting so wet . . .
You sure won that big argument Mr. O'Malley. When Atlas said you couldn't make it rain and—
Well, he did score a few good points in the early rounds . . .
But my cold logic was turning the tide . . . If the rain hadn't—
Say, m'boy—the rain!
Sure. You made it rain . . . By waving your magic wand.
Cushlamochree!
Let's go into that old barn until it stops.
Mr. O'Malley, while we're waiting, wave your magic wand again and make—
Not so soon, m'boy. An effort like that takes a good deal out of me . . . and—

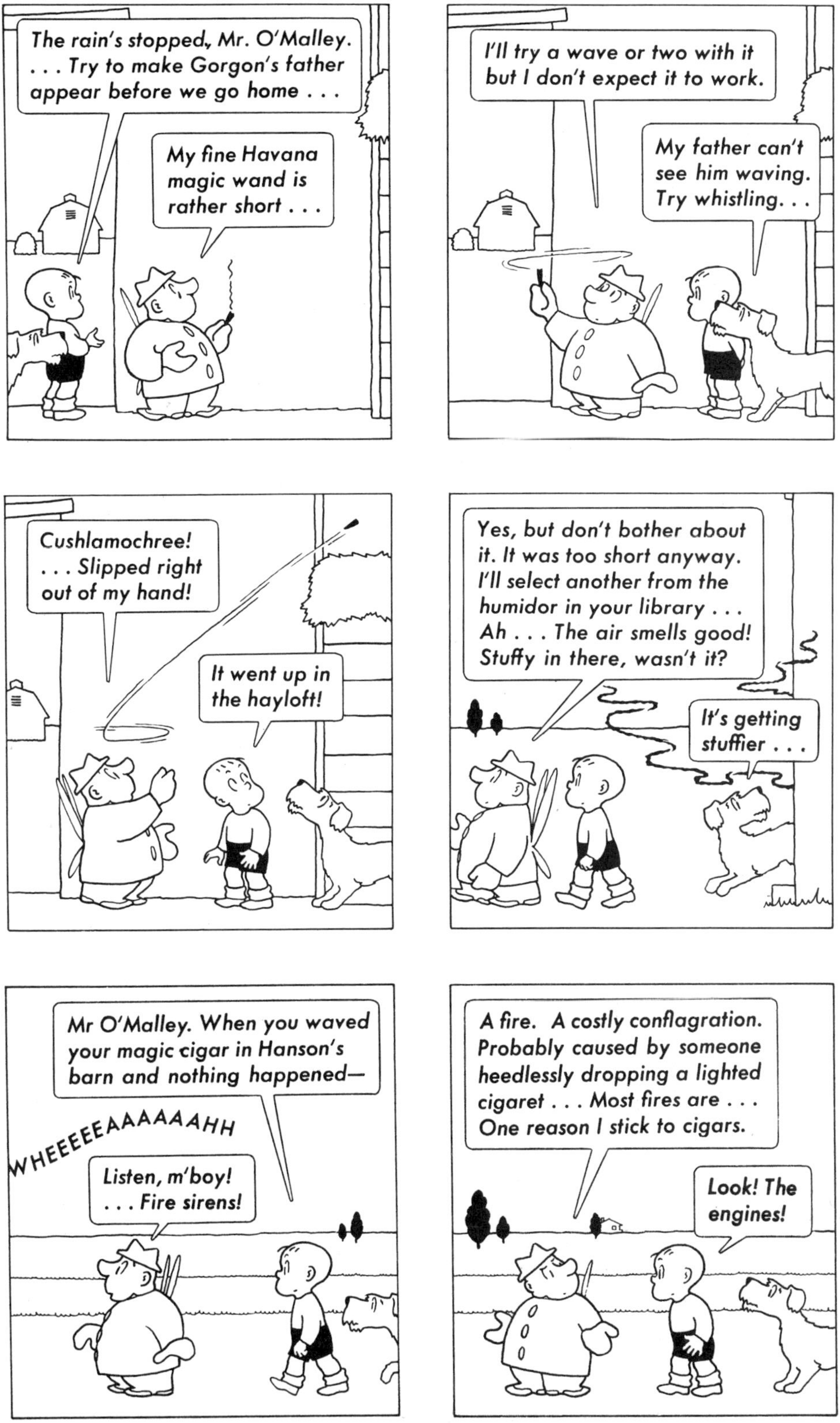
The rain's stopped, Mr. O'Malley. . . . Try to make Gorgon's father appear before we go home . . .
My fine Havana magic wand is rather short . . .
I'll try a wave or two with it but I don't expect it to work.
My father can't see him waving. Try whistling. . .
Cushlamochree! . . . Slipped right out of my hand!
It went up in the hayloft!
Yes, but don't bother about it. It was too short anyway. I'll select another from the humidor in your library . . . Ah . . . The air smells good! Stuffy in there, wasn't it?
It's getting stuffier . . .
Mr O'Malley. When you waved your magic cigar in Hanson's barn and nothing happened—
WHEEEEEAAAAAAHH
Listen, m'boy! . . . Fire sirens!
A fire. A costly conflagration. Probably caused by someone heedlessly dropping a lighted cigaret . . . Most fires are . . . One reason I stick to cigars.
Look! The engines!

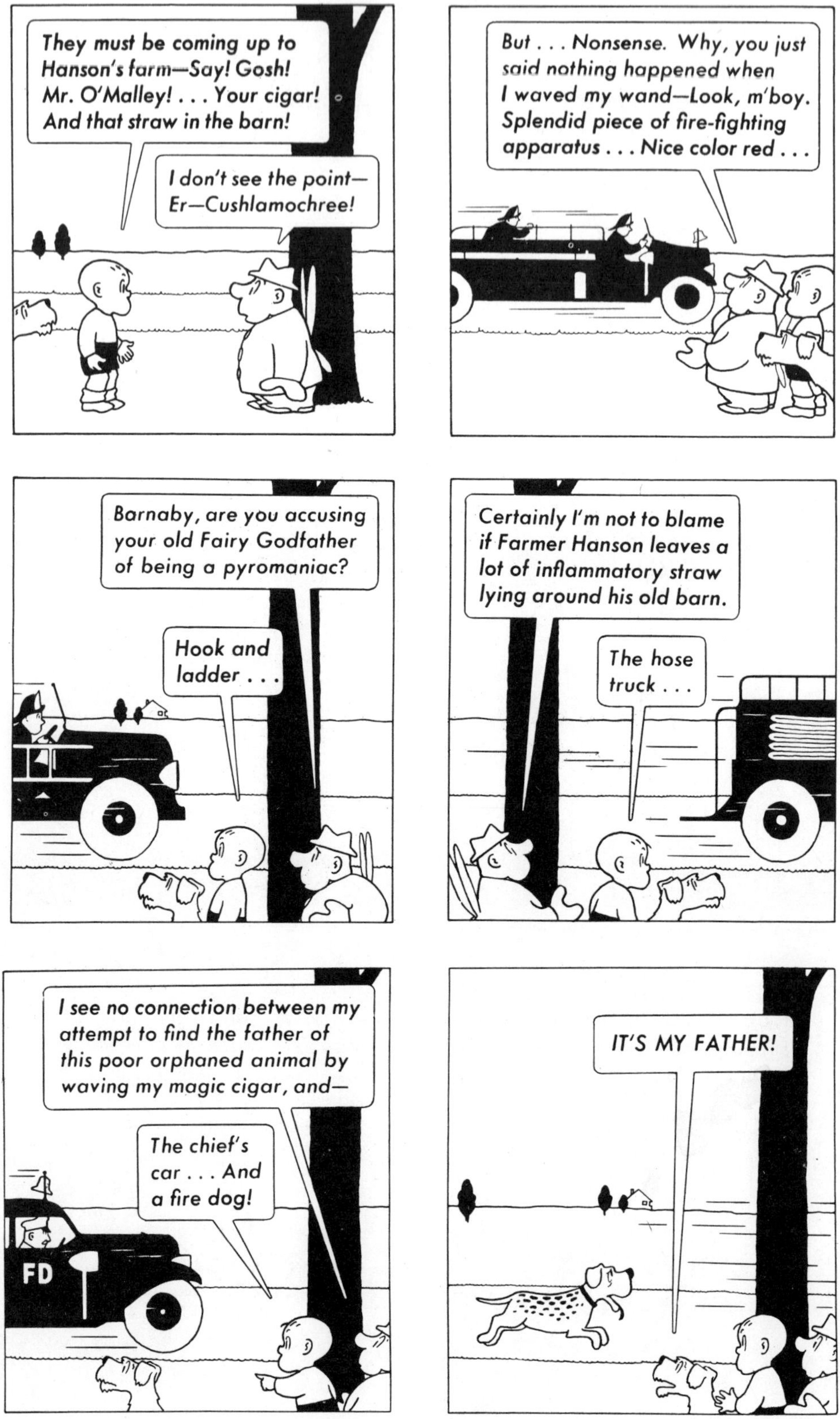
They must be coming up to Hanson's farm—Say! Gosh! Mr. O'Malley! . . . Your cigar! And that straw in the barn!
I don't see the point—Er—Cushlamochree!
But . . . Nonsense. Why, you just said nothing happened when I waved my wand—Look, m'boy. Splendid piece of fire-fighting apparatus . . . Nice color red . . .
Barnaby, are you accusing your old Fairy Godfather of being a pyromaniac?
Hook and ladder . . .
Certainly I'm not to blame if Farmer Hanson leaves a lot of inflammatory straw lying around his old barn.
The hose truck . . .
I see no connection between my attempt to find the father of this poor orphaned animal by waving my magic cigar, and—
The chief's car . . . And a fire dog!
FD
IT'S MY FATHER!

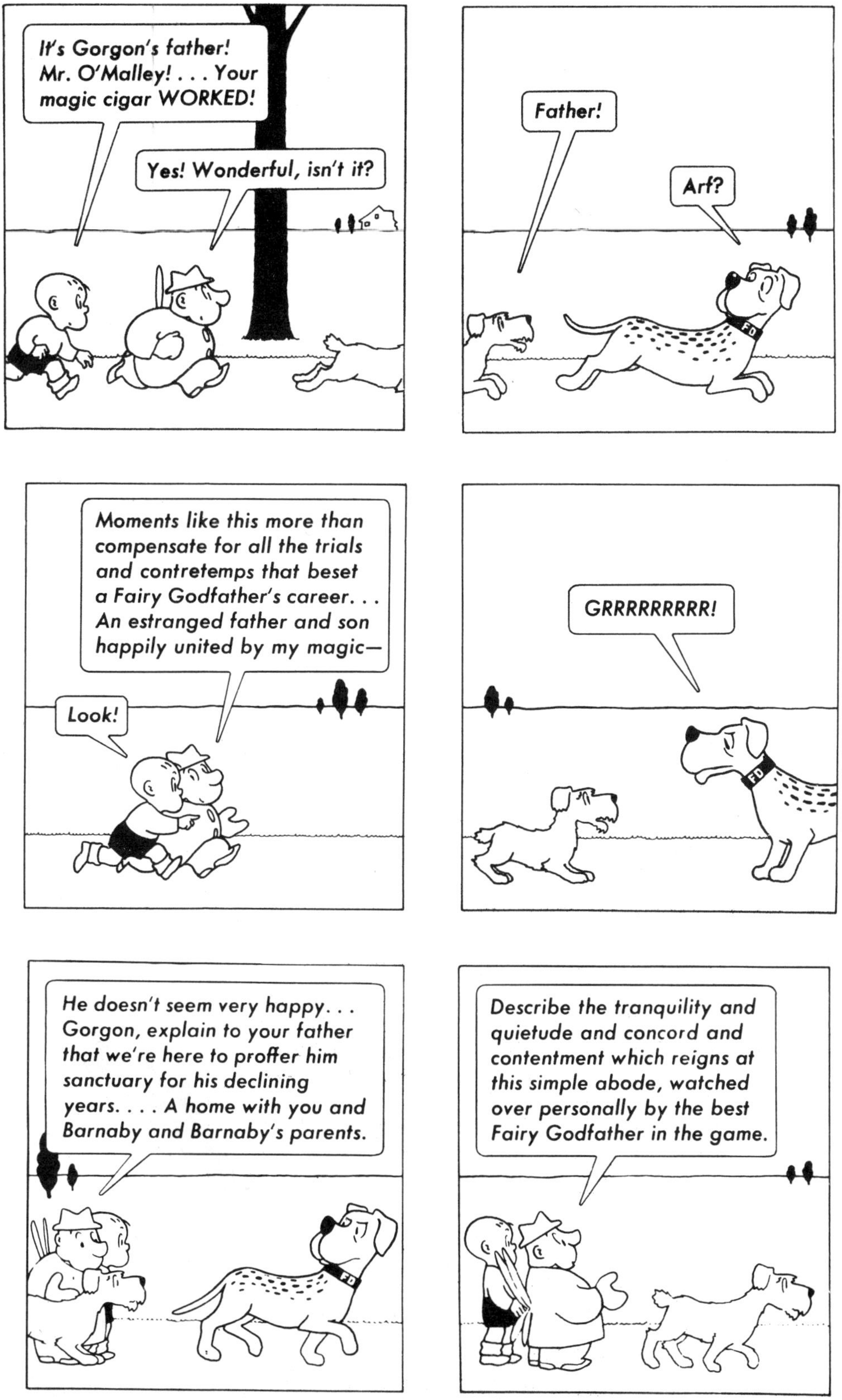
It's Gorgon's father! Mr. O'Malley! . . . Your magic cigar WORKED!
Yes! Wonderful, isn't it?
Father!
Arf?
Moments like this more than compensate for all the trials and contretemps that beset a Fairy Godfather's career. . . An estranged father and son happily united by my magic—
Look!
GRRRRRRRRR!
He doesn't seem very happy. . . Gorgon, explain to your father that we're here to proffer him sanctuary for his declining years. . . . A home with you and Barnaby and Barnaby's parents.
Describe the tranquility and quietude and concord and contentment which reigns at this simple abode, watched over personally by the best Fairy Godfather in the game.

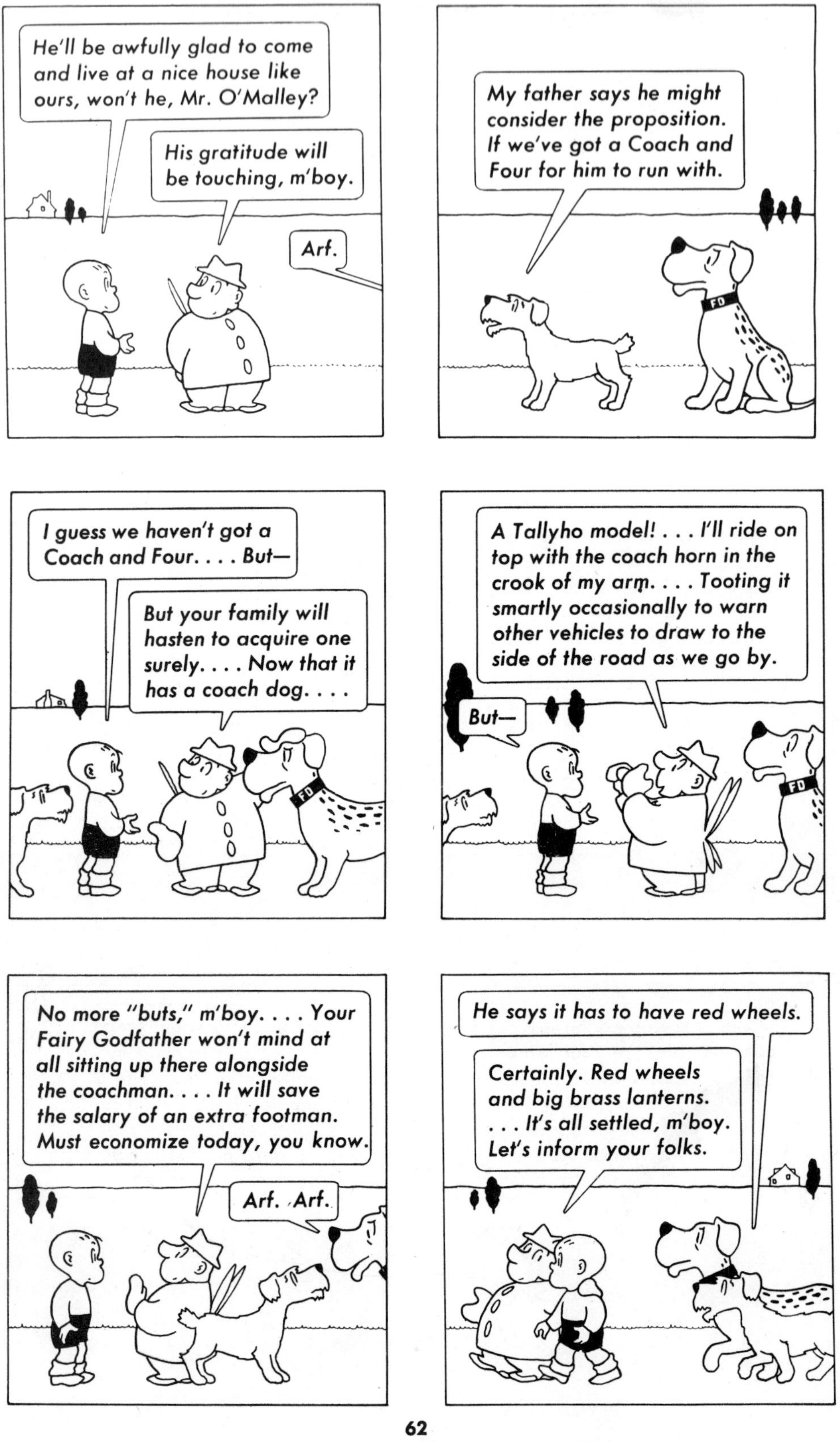
He'll be awfully glad to come and live at a nice house like ours, won't he, Mr. O'Malley?
His gratitude will be touching, m'boy.
Arf.
My father says he might consider the proposition. If we've got a Coach and Four for him to run with.
I guess we haven't got a Coach and Four. . . . But—
But your family will hasten to acquire one surely. . . . Now that it has a coach dog. . . .
FD
A Tallyho model! . . . I'll ride on top with the coach horn in the crook of my arm. . . . Tooting it smartly occasionally to warn other vehicles to draw to the side of the road as we go by.
But—
No more "buts," m'boy. . . . Your Fairy Godfather won't mind at all sitting up there alongside the coachman. . . . It will save the salary of an extra footman. Must economize today, you know.
Arf. Arf.
He says it has to have red wheels.
Certainly. Red wheels and big brass lanterns. . . . It's all settled, m'boy. Let's inform your folks.

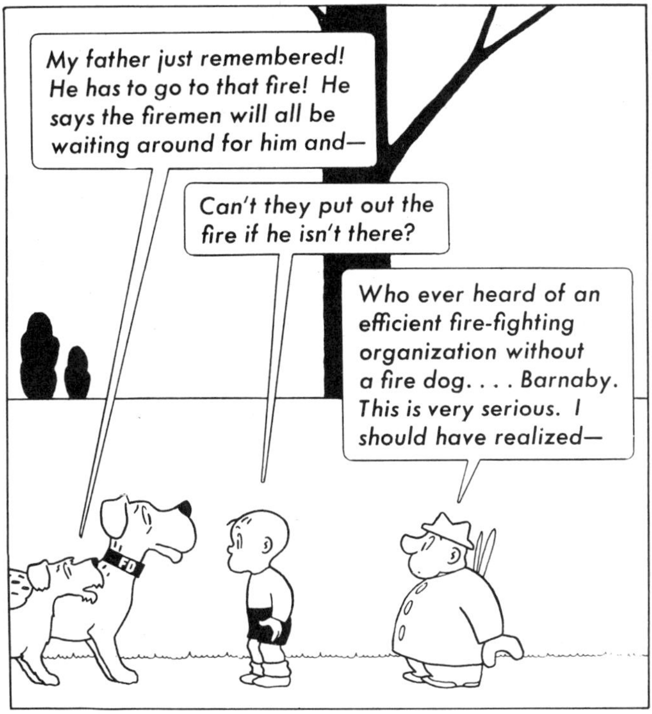
My father just remembered! He has to go to that fire! He says the firemen will all be waiting around for him and—
Can't they put out the fire if he isn't there?
Who ever heard of an efficient fire-fighting organization without a fire dog. . . . Barnaby. This is very serious. I should have realized—
FD

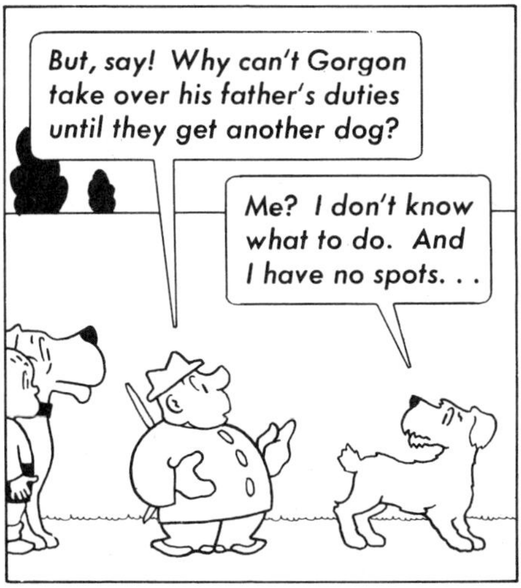
But, say! Why can't Gorgon take over his father's duties until they get another dog?
Me? I don't know what to do. And I have no spots. . .

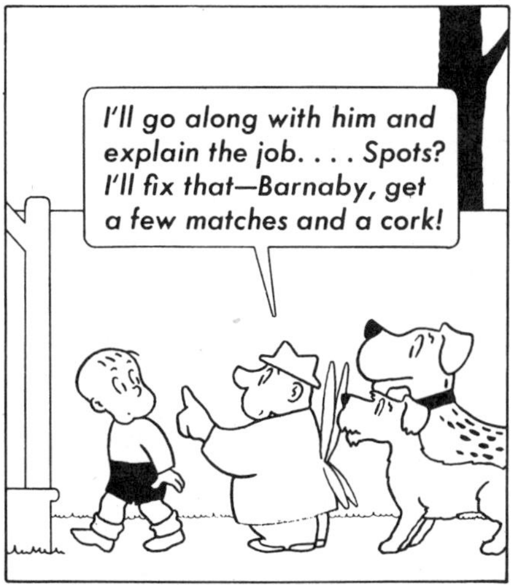
I'll go along with him and explain the job. . . . Spots? I'll fix that—Barnaby, get a few matches and a cork!

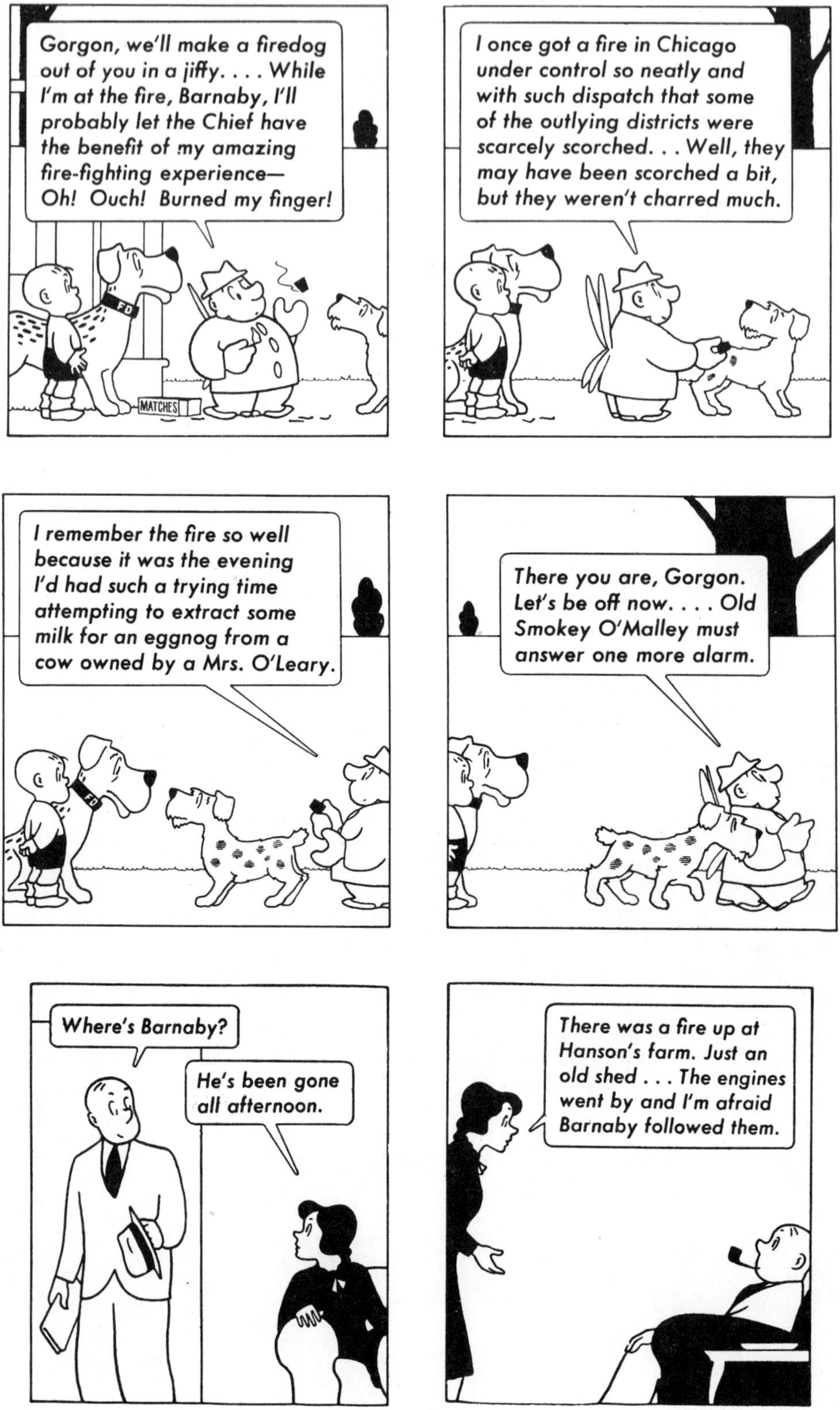
Gorgon, we'll make a firedog out of you in a jiffy. . . . While I'm at the fire, Barnaby, I'll probably let the Chief have the benefit of my amazing fire-fighting experience— Oh! Ouch! Burned my finger!
FD
MATCHES
I once got a fire in Chicago under control so neatly and with such dispatch that some of the outlying districts were scarcely scorched. . . Well, they may have been scorched a bit, but they weren't charred much.
I remember the fire so well because it was the evening I'd had such a trying time attempting to extract some milk for an eggnog from a cow owned by a Mrs. O'Leary.
FD
There you are, Gorgon. Let's be off now. . . . Old Smokey O'Malley must answer one more alarm.
Where's Barnaby?
He's been gone all afternoon.
There was a fire up at Hanson's farm. Just an old shed . . . The engines went by and I'm afraid Barnaby followed them.

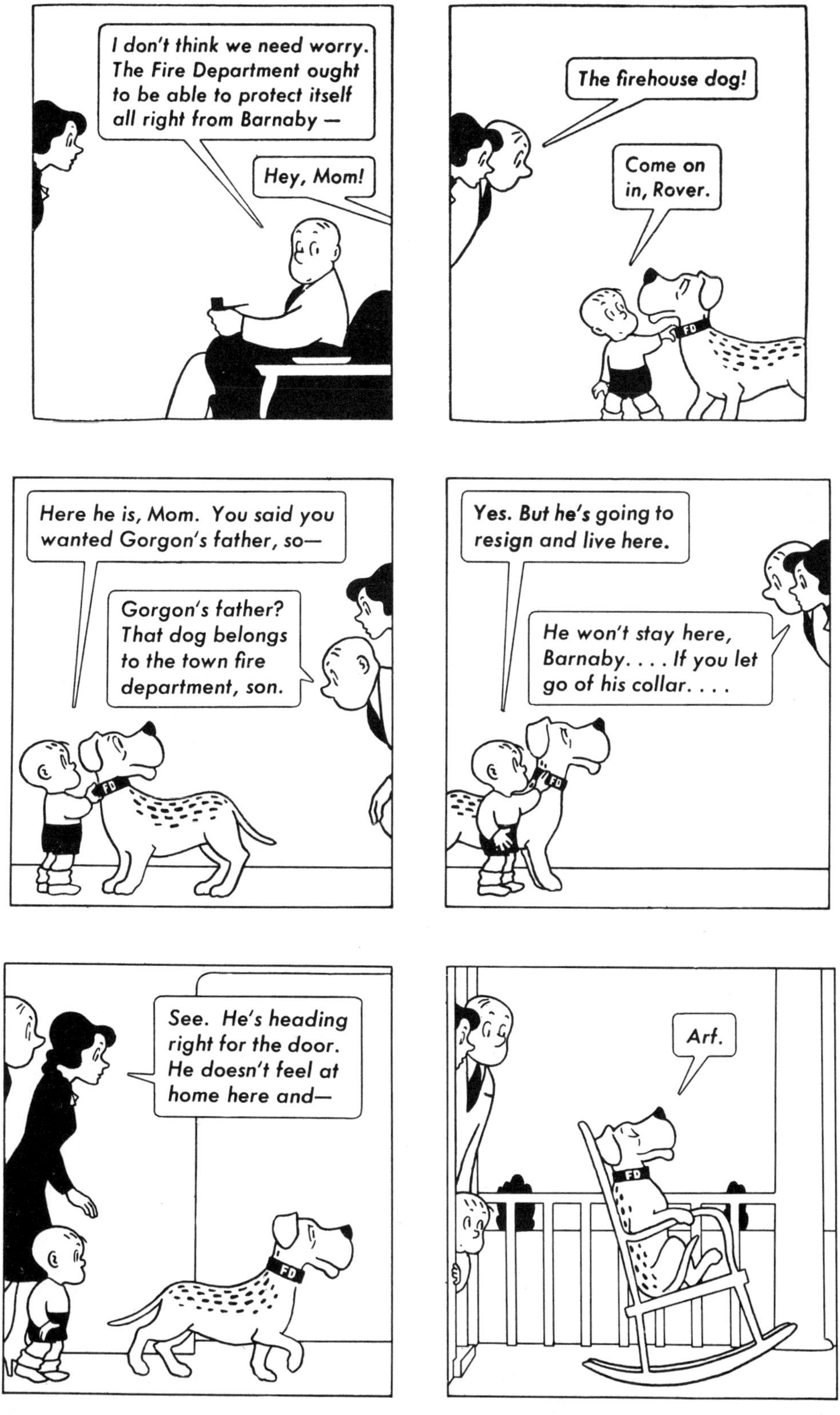
I don't think we need worry. The Fire Department ought to be able to protect itself all right from Barnaby —
Hey, Mom!
The firehouse dog!
Come on in, Rover.
Here he is, Mom. You said you wanted Gorgon's father, so—
Gorgon's father? That dog belongs to the town fire department, son.
FD
Yes. But he's going to resign and live here.
He won't stay here, Barnaby. . . . If you let go of his collar. . . .
FD
See. He's heading right for the door. He doesn't feel at home here and—
FD
Arf.
FD

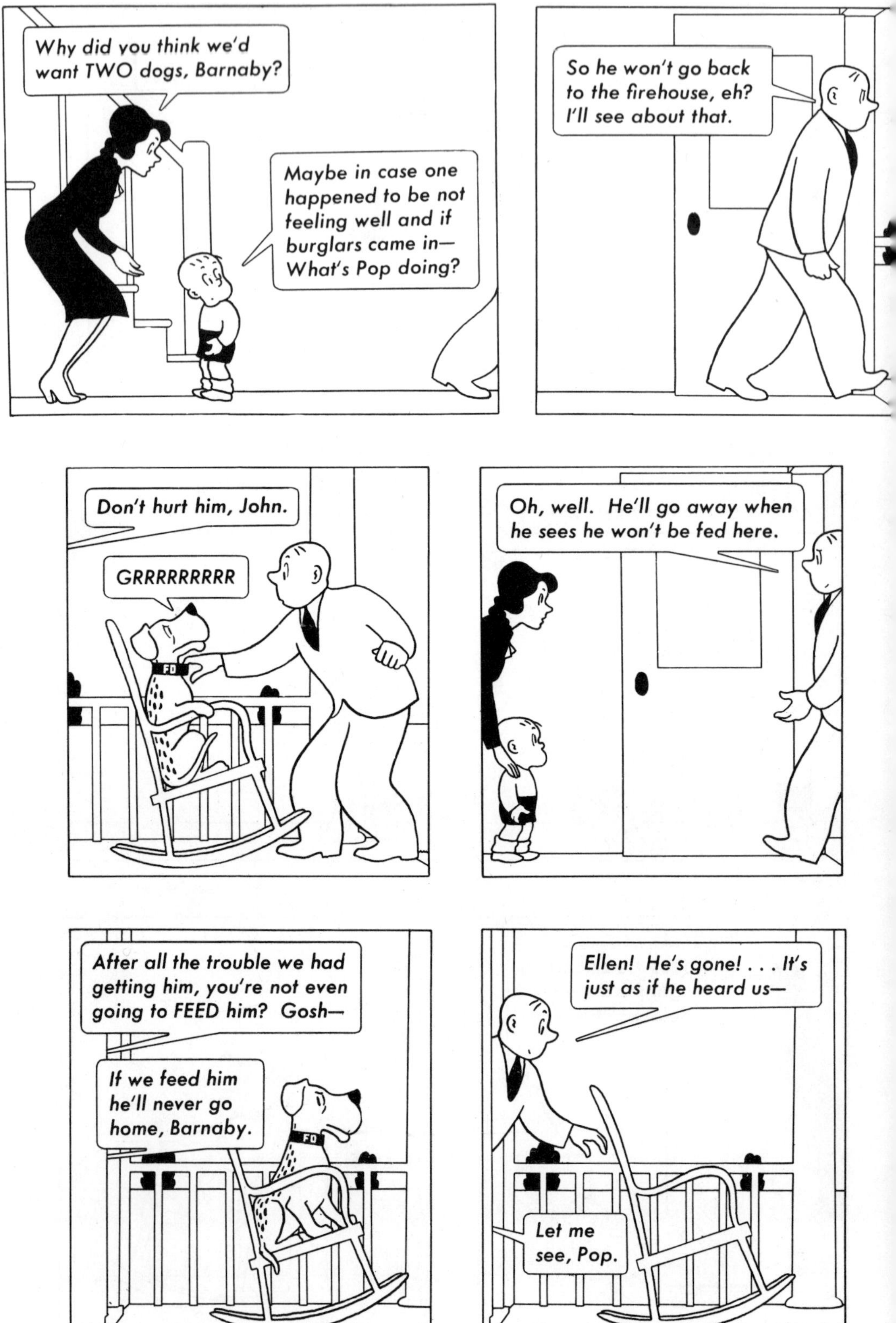
Why did you think we'd want TWO dogs, Barnaby?
Maybe in case one happened to be not feeling well and if burglars came in— What's Pop doing?
So he won't go back to the firehouse, eh? I'll see about that.
Don't hurt him, John.
GRRRRRRRRR
FD
Oh, well. He'll go away when he sees he won't be fed here.
After all the trouble we had getting him, you're not even going to FEED him? Gosh—
If we feed him he'll never go home, Barnaby.
FD
Ellen! He's gone! . . . It's just as if he heard us—
Let me see, Pop.

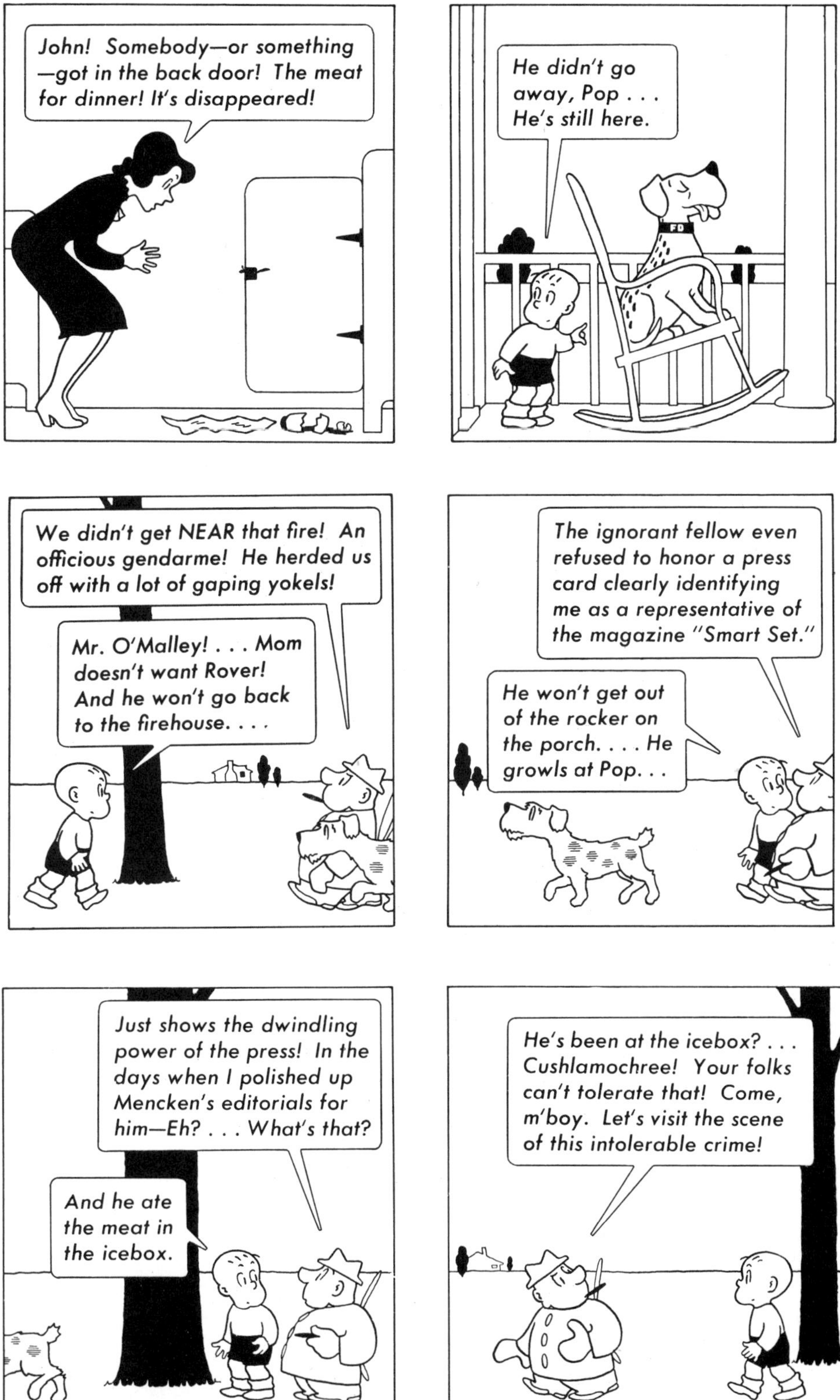
John! Somebody—or something —got in the back door! The meat for dinner! It's disappeared!
He didn't go away, Pop . . . He's still here.
FD
We didn't get NEAR that fire! An officious gendarme! He herded us off with a lot of gaping yokels!
Mr. O'Malley! . . . Mom doesn't want Rover! And he won't go back to the firehouse. . . .
The ignorant fellow even refused to honor a press card clearly identifying me as a representative of the magazine "Smart Set."
He won't get out of the rocker on the porch. . . . He growls at Pop. . .
Just shows the dwindling power of the press! In the days when I polished up Mencken's editorials for him—Eh? . . . What's that?
And he ate the meat in the icebox.
He's been at the icebox? . . . Cushlamochree! Your folks can't tolerate that! Come, m'boy. Let's visit the scene of this intolerable crime!

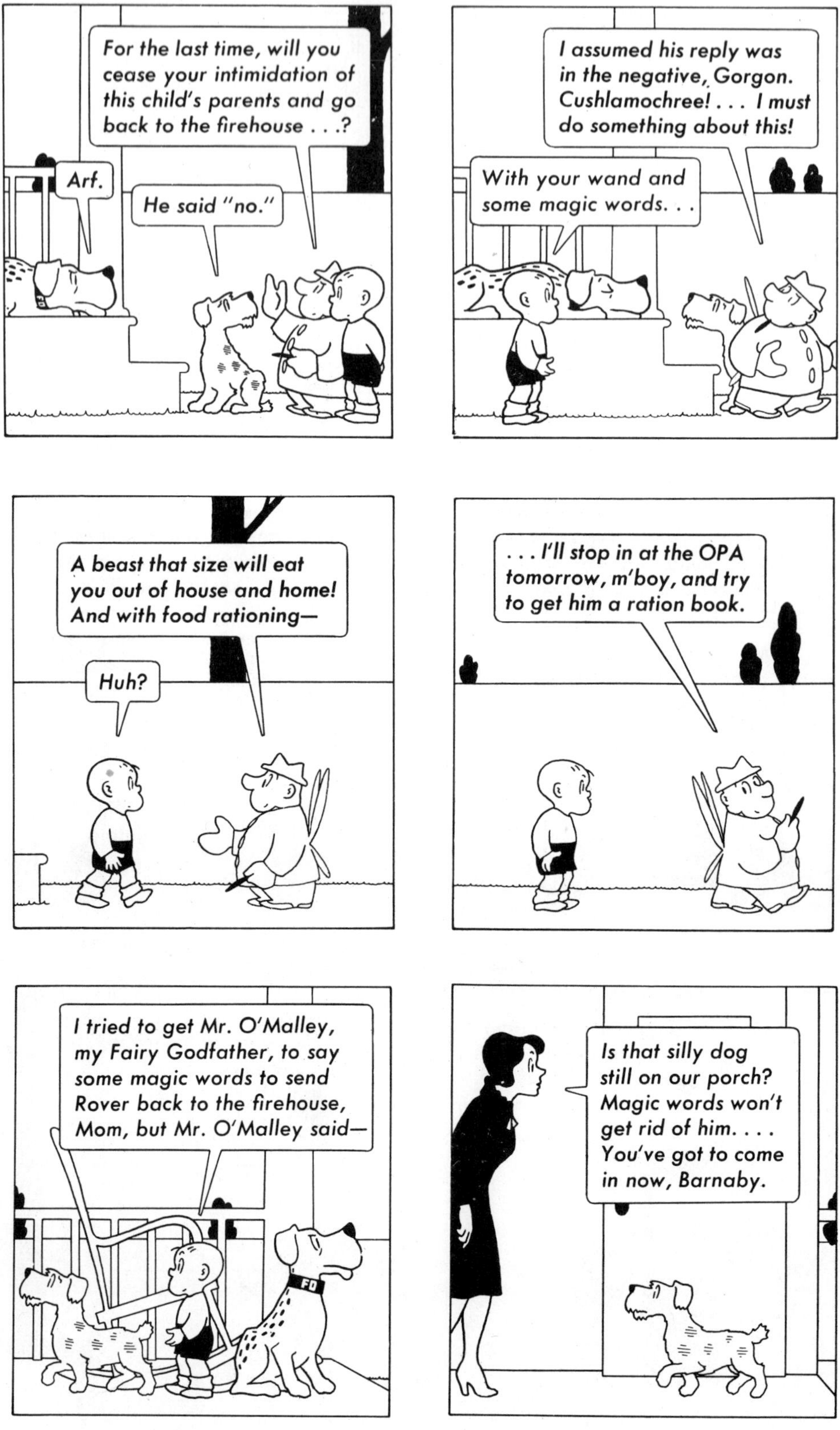
For the last time, will you cease your intimidation of this child's parents and go back to the firehouse . . .?
Arf.
He said "no."
I assumed his reply was in the negative, Gorgon. Cushlamochree! . . . I must do something about this!
With your wand and some magic words. . .
A beast that size will eat you out of house and home! And with food rationing—
Huh?
. . . I'll stop in at the OPA tomorrow, m'boy, and try to get him a ration book.
I tried to get Mr. O'Malley, my Fairy Godfather, to say some magic words to send Rover back to the firehouse, Mom, but Mr. O'Malley said—
FD
FD
Is that silly dog still on our porch? Magic words won't get rid of him. . . . You've got to come in now, Barnaby.

Time for your bath.
Bath?
FD
Hey, Mom! He's gone!

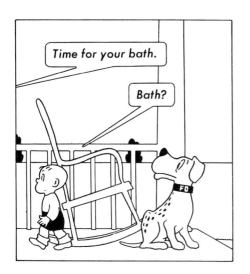

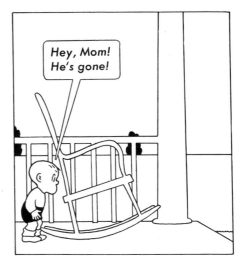

EPISODE FIVE

Man of the Hour

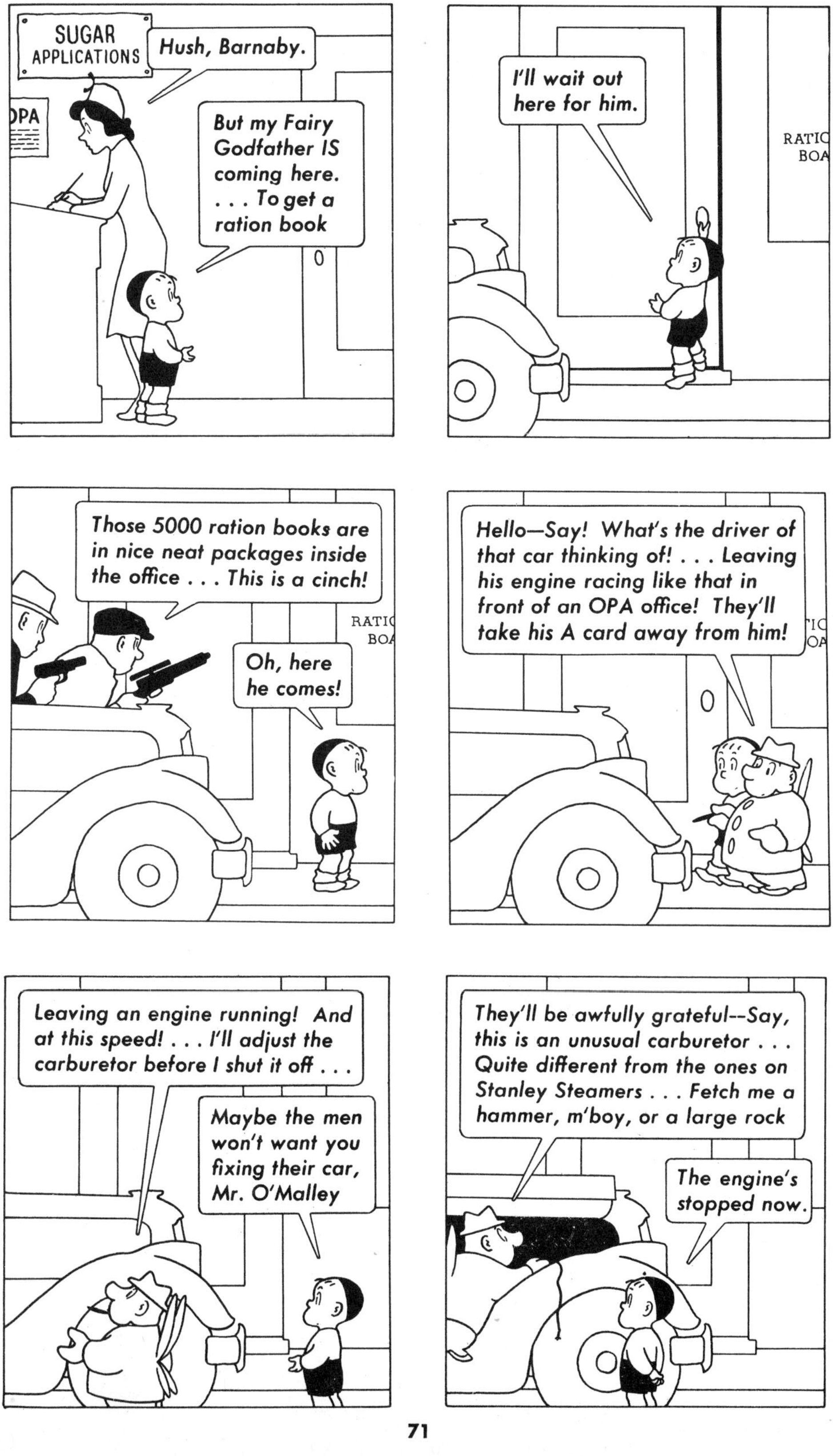
SUGAR APPLICATIONS
OPA
Hush, Barnaby.
But my Fairy Godfather IS coming here. . . . To get a ration book
I'll wait out here for him.
Those 5000 ration books are in nice neat packages inside the office . . . This is a cinch!
Oh, here he comes!
Hello—Say! What's the driver of that car thinking of! . . . Leaving his engine racing like that in front of an OPA office! They'll take his A card away from him!
Leaving an engine running! And at this speed! . . . I'll adjust the carburetor before I shut it off . . .
Maybe the men won't want you fixing their car, Mr. O'Malley
They'll be awfully grateful--Say, this is an unusual carburetor . . . Quite different from the ones on Stanley Steamers . . . Fetch me a hammer, m'boy, or a large rock
The engine's stopped now.

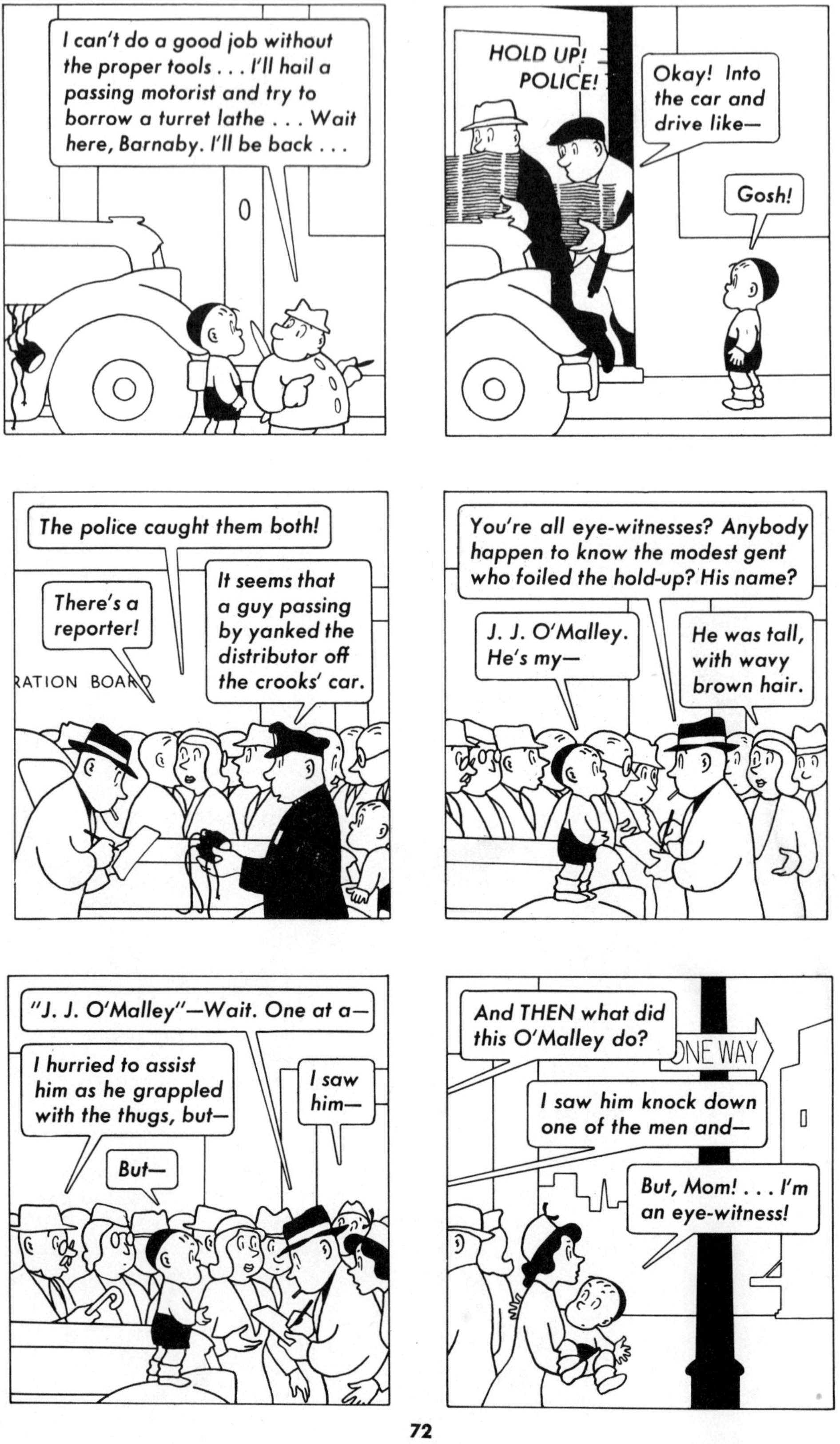
I can't do a good job without the proper tools . . . I'll hail a passing motorist and try to borrow a turret lathe . . . Wait here, Barnaby. I'll be back . . .
HOLD UP! POLICE!
Okay! Into the car and drive like—
Gosh!
The police caught them both!
There's a reporter!
It seems that a guy passing by yanked the distributor off the crooks' car.
RATION BOARD
You're all eye-witnesses? Anybody happen to know the modest gent who foiled the hold-up? His name?
J. J. O'Malley. He's my—
He was tall, with wavy brown hair.
"J. J. O'Malley"—Wait. One at a—
I hurried to assist him as he grappled with the thugs, but—
I saw him—
But—
And THEN what did this O'Malley do?
ONE WAY
I saw him knock down one of the men and—
But, Mom! . . . I'm an eye-witness!

THE NEXT EVENING

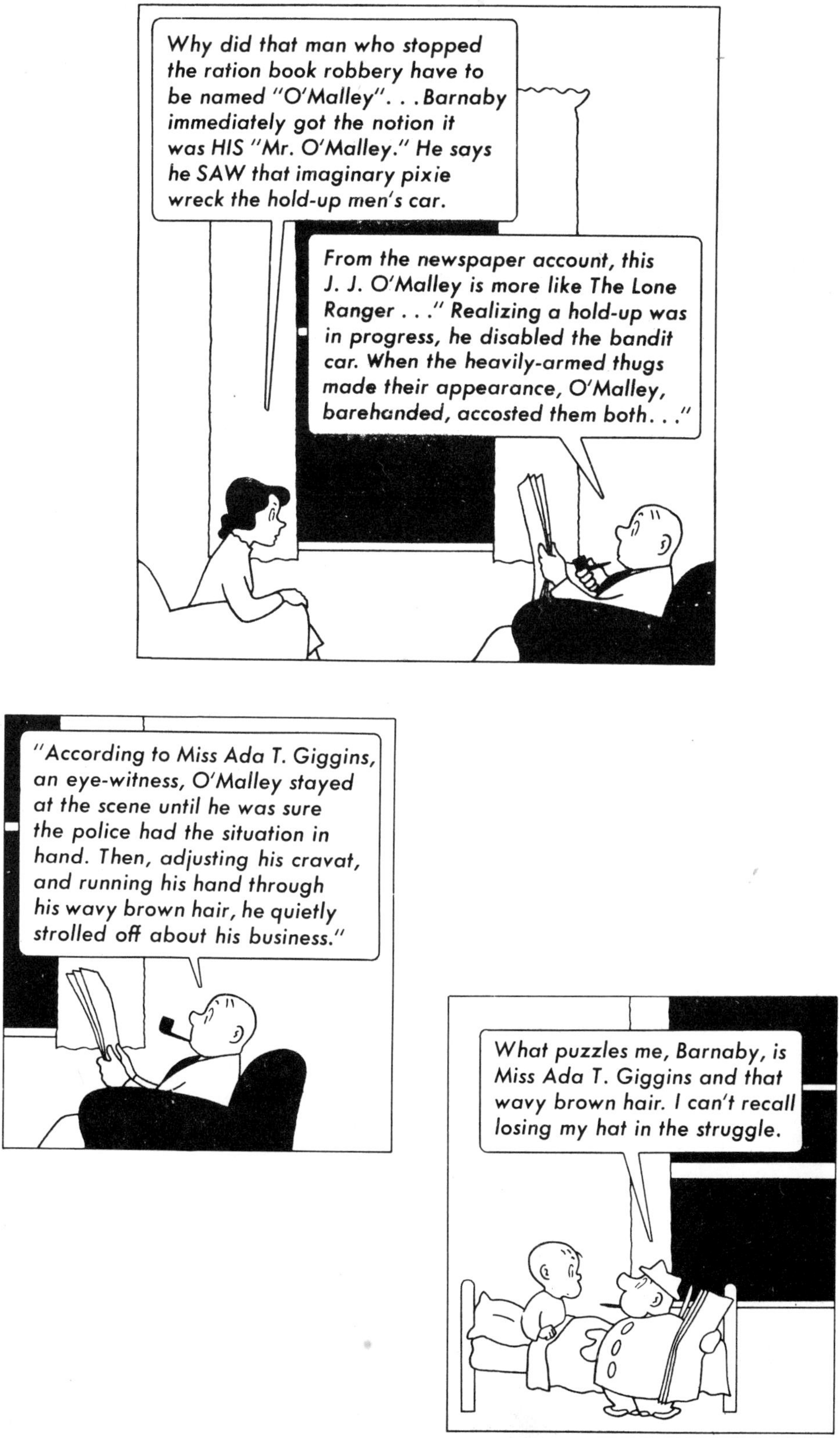

Why did that man who stopped the ration book robbery have to be named "O'Malley". . . Barnaby immediately got the notion it was HIS "Mr. O'Malley." He says he SAW that imaginary pixie wreck the hold-up men's car.
From the newspaper account, this J. J. O'Malley is more like The Lone Ranger . . ." Realizing a hold-up was in progress, he disabled the bandit car. When the heavily-armed thugs made their appearance, O'Malley, barehanded, accosted them both. . ."
"According to Miss Ada T. Giggins, an eye-witness, O'Malley stayed at the scene until he was sure the police had the situation in hand. Then, adjusting his cravat, and running his hand through his wavy brown hair, he quietly strolled off about his business."
What puzzles me, Barnaby, is Miss Ada T. Giggins and that wavy brown hair. I can't recall losing my hat in the struggle.

THE FOLLOWING DAY

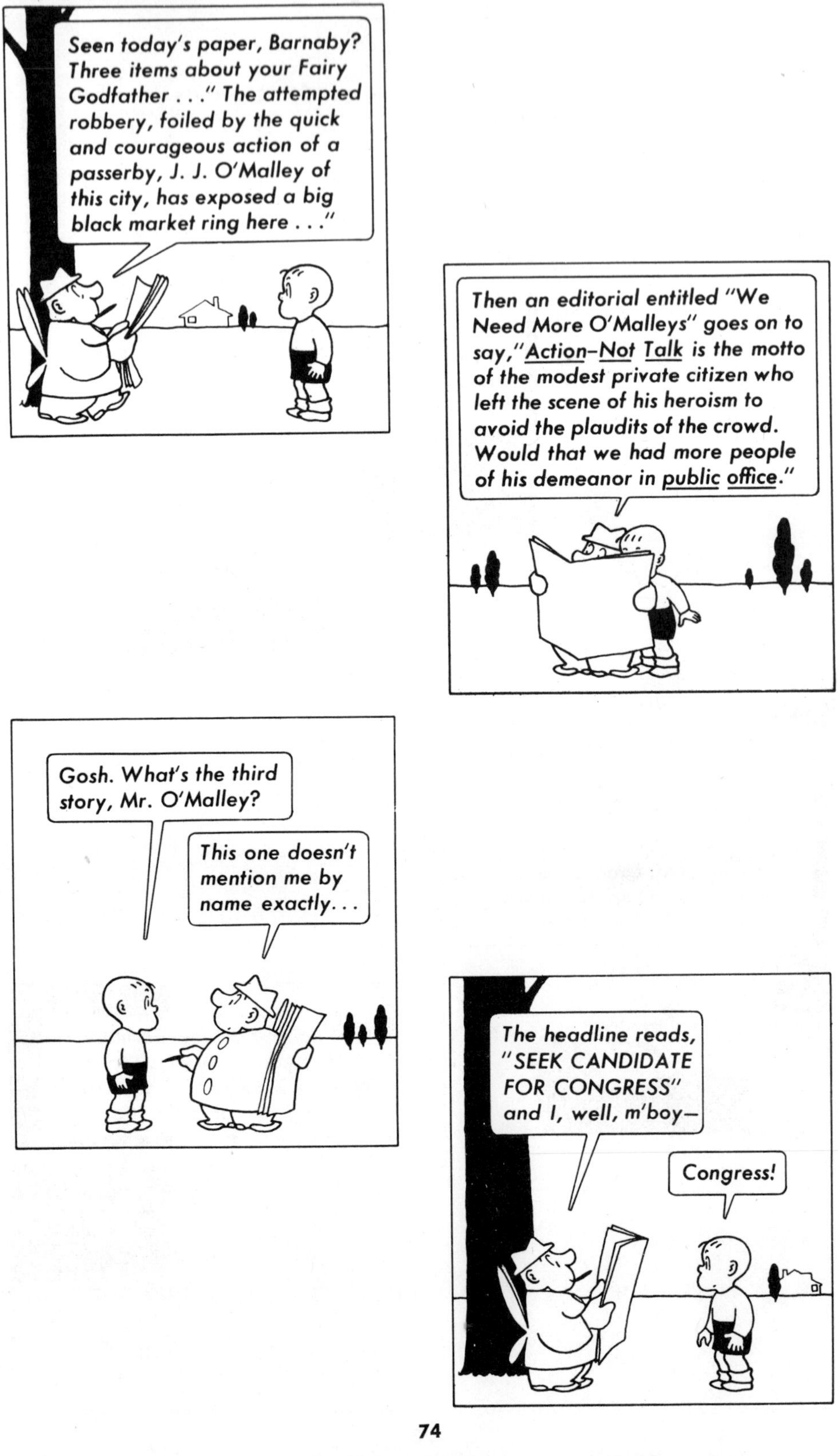
Seen today's paper, Barnaby? Three items about your Fairy Godfather . . ." The attempted robbery, foiled by the quick and courageous action of a passerby, J. J. O'Malley of this city, has exposed a big black market ring here . . ."
Then an editorial entitled "We Need More O'Malleys" goes on to say, "Action–Not Talk is the motto of the modest private citizen who left the scene of his heroism to avoid the plaudits of the crowd. Would that we had more people of his demeanor in public office."
Gosh. What's the third story, Mr. O'Malley?
This one doesn't mention me by name exactly. . .
The headline reads, "SEEK CANDIDATE FOR CONGRESS" and I, well, m'boy—
Congress!

THE NEXT NIGHT

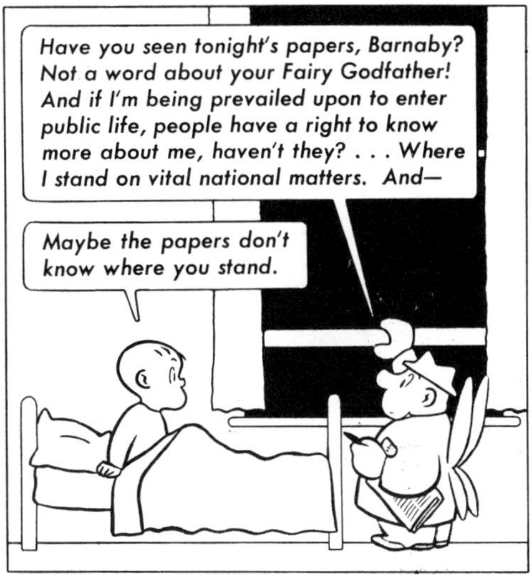
Have you seen tonight's papers, Barnaby? Not a word about your Fairy Godfather! And if I'm being prevailed upon to enter public life, people have a right to know more about me, haven't they? . . . Where I stand on vital national matters. And—
Maybe the papers don't know where you stand.

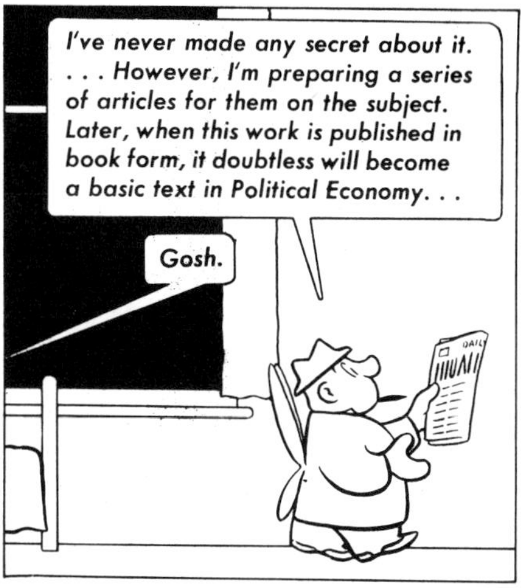
I've never made any secret about it. . . . However, I'm preparing a series of articles for them on the subject. Later, when this work is published in book form, it doubtless will become a basic text in Political Economy. . .
Gosh.

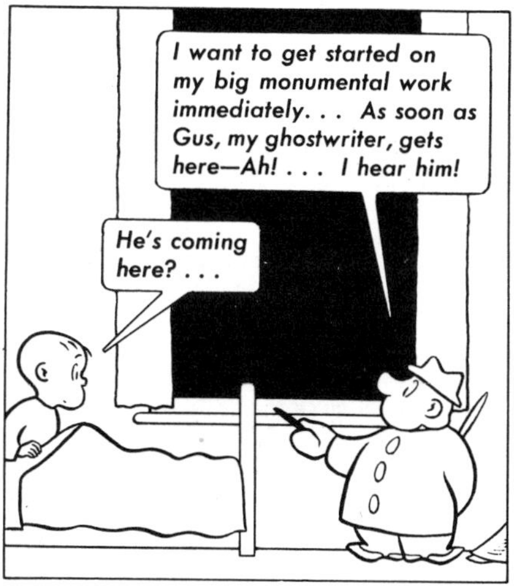
I want to get started on my big monumental work immediately. . . As soon as Gus, my ghostwriter, gets here—Ah! . . . I hear him!
He's coming here? . . .

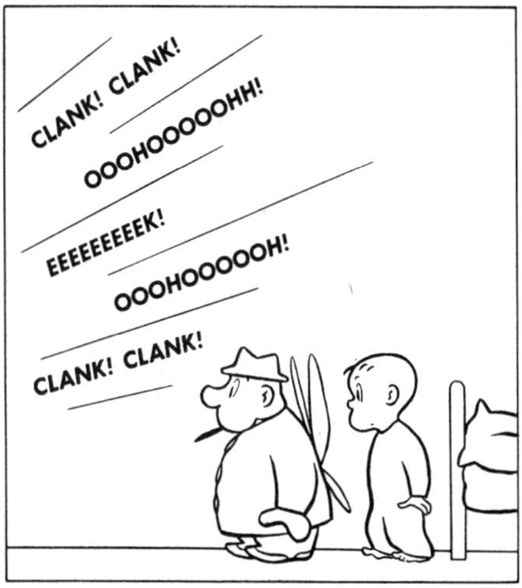
CLANK! CLANK!
OOOHOOOOOHH!
EEEEEEEEK!
OOOHOOOOOH!
CLANK! CLANK!

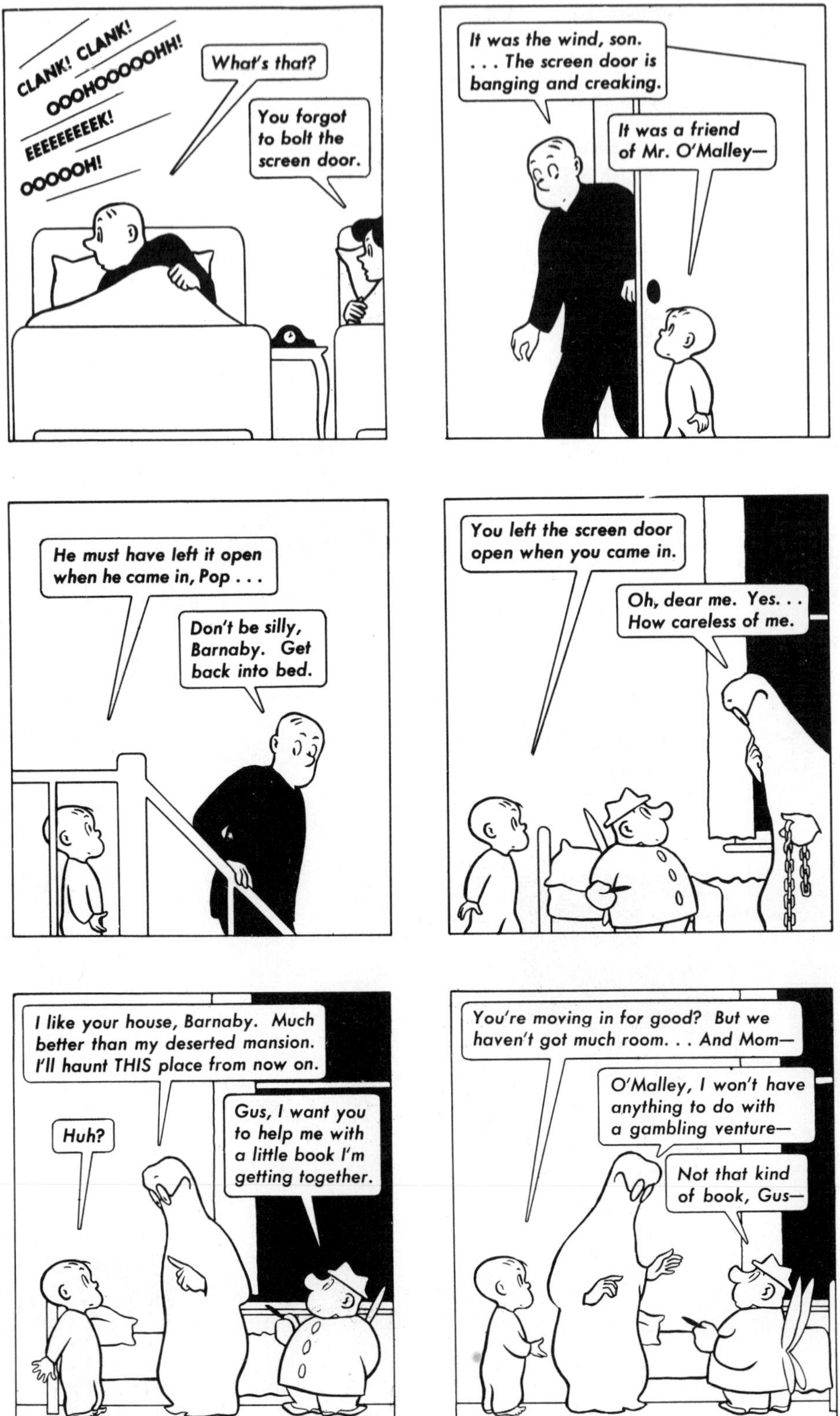
CLANK! CLANK!
OOOHOOOOOHH!
EEEEEEEEEK!
OOOOOH!
What's that?
You forgot to bolt the screen door.
It was the wind, son. . . . The screen door is banging and creaking.
It was a friend of Mr. O'Malley—
He must have left it open when he came in, Pop . . .
Don't be silly, Barnaby. Get back into bed.
You left the screen door open when you came in.
Oh, dear me. Yes. . . How careless of me.
I like your house, Barnaby. Much better than my deserted mansion. I'll haunt THIS place from now on.
Huh?
Gus, I want you to help me with a little book I'm getting together.
You're moving in for good? But we haven't got much room. . . And Mom—
O'Malley, I won't have anything to do with a gambling venture—
Not that kind of book, Gus—

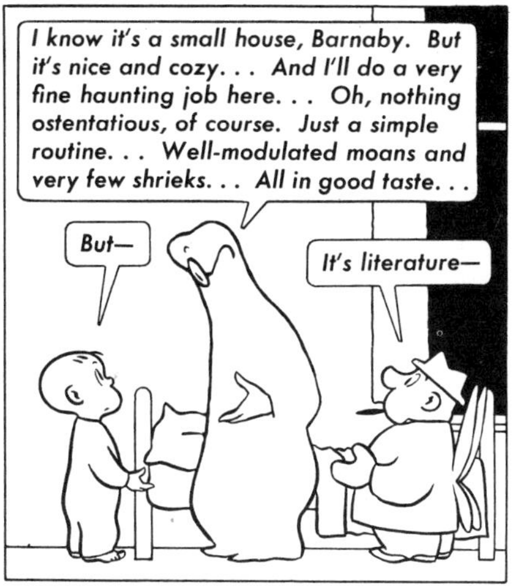
I know it's a small house, Barnaby. But it's nice and cozy. . . And I'll do a very fine haunting job here. . . Oh, nothing ostentatious, of course. Just a simple routine. . . Well-modulated moans and very few shrieks. . . All in good taste. . .
But—
It's literature—

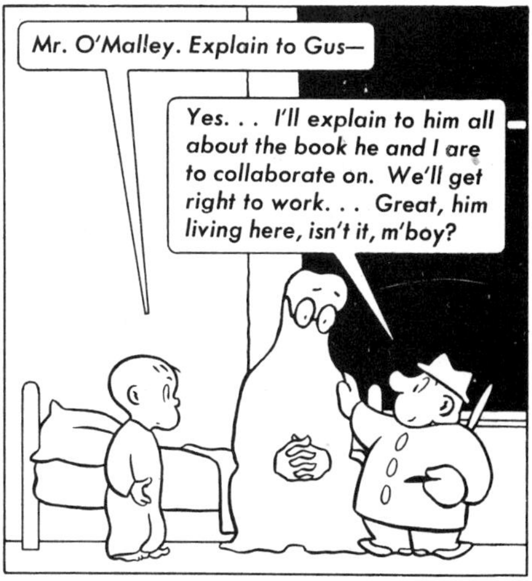
Mr. O'Malley. Explain to Gus—
Yes. . . I'll explain to him all about the book he and I are to collaborate on. We'll get right to work. . . Great, him living here, isn't it, m'boy?

THE NEXT DAY

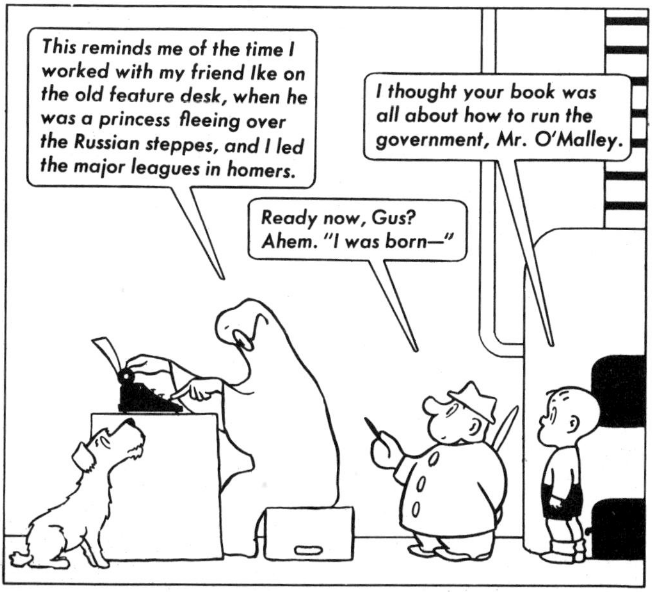
This reminds me of the time I worked with my friend Ike on the old feature desk, when he was a princess fleeing over the Russian steppes, and I led the major leagues in homers.
Ready now, Gus? Ahem. "I was born—"
I thought your book was all about how to run the government, Mr. O'Malley.

Hush, Barnaby. This is background material... The first chapter will be somewhat autobiographical... Even though the story of my life has been written time and again—

Gosh, I never knew that...

Oh, yes. Scores of times. By a man named Horatio Alger... Now, let's see, Gus... Where were we? Yes. "I was born—"

HOURS LATER

It's difficult, recalling the events of one's early life... I should have taken notes as I went along. ... You've got how I was born in a log cabin, Gus? And how I got out of my cradle one night to play a cadenza for my most recent concerto on the grand piano in our music room? ... And the time I was showing a kid on our block by the name of Paul Bunyan a few tricks with my hatchet and I chopped down that cherry tree? ... And then how I toddled right up to the pater and said, "Father, dear Father, come home with me now" ... And—

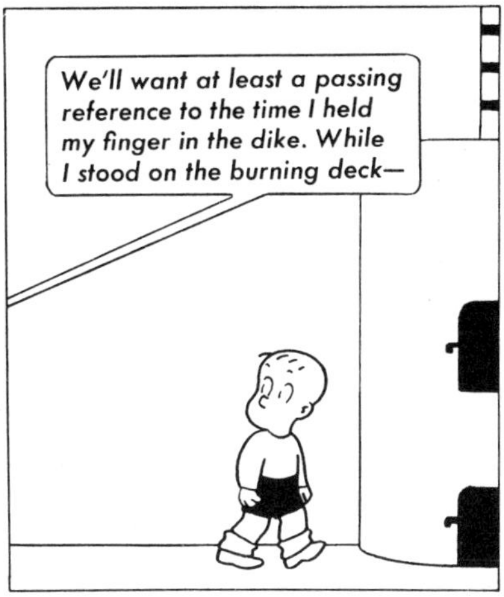
We'll want at least a passing reference to the time I held my finger in the dike. While I stood on the burning deck—

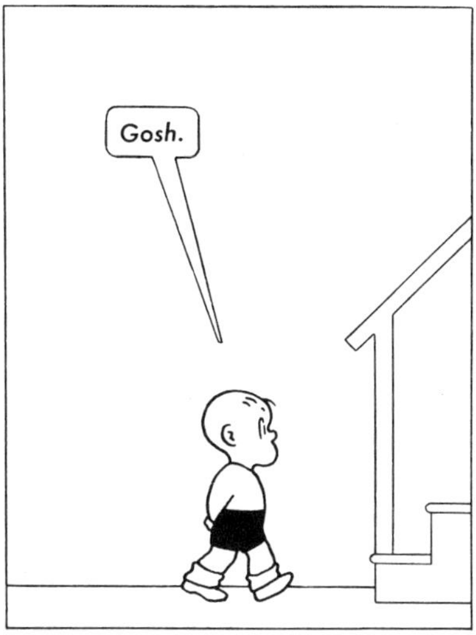
Gosh.

SEVERAL DAYS LATER

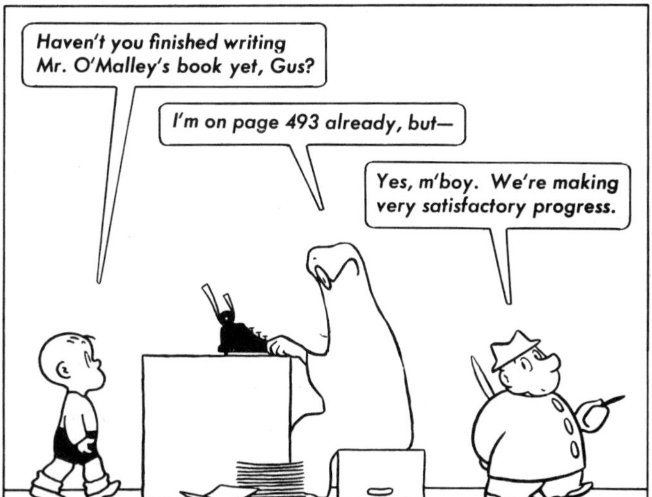
Haven't you finished writing Mr. O'Malley's book yet, Gus?
I'm on page 493 already, but—
Yes, m'boy. We're making very satisfactory progress.

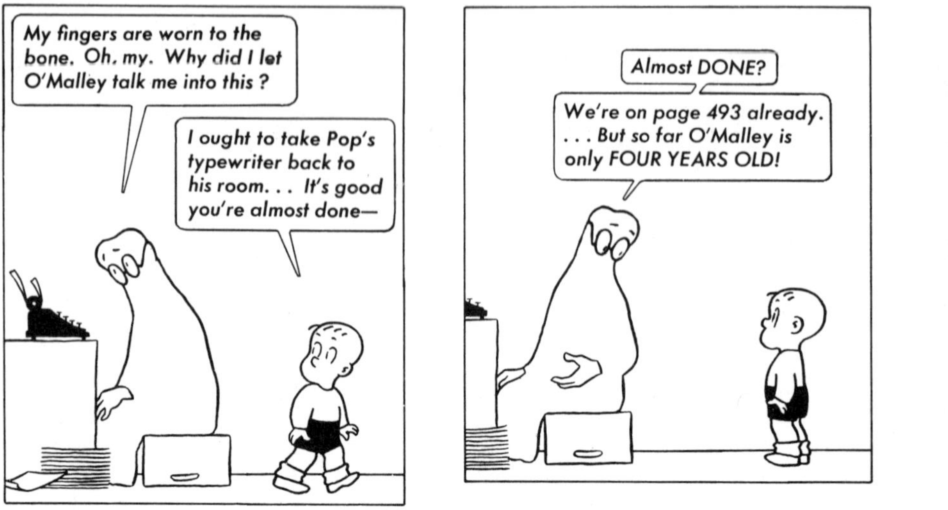
My fingers are worn to the bone. Oh, my. Why did I let O'Malley talk me into this ?
I ought to take Pop's typewriter back to his room. . . It's good you're almost done—
Almost DONE?
We're on page 493 already. . . . But so far O'Malley is only FOUR YEARS OLD!

THAT AFTERNOON

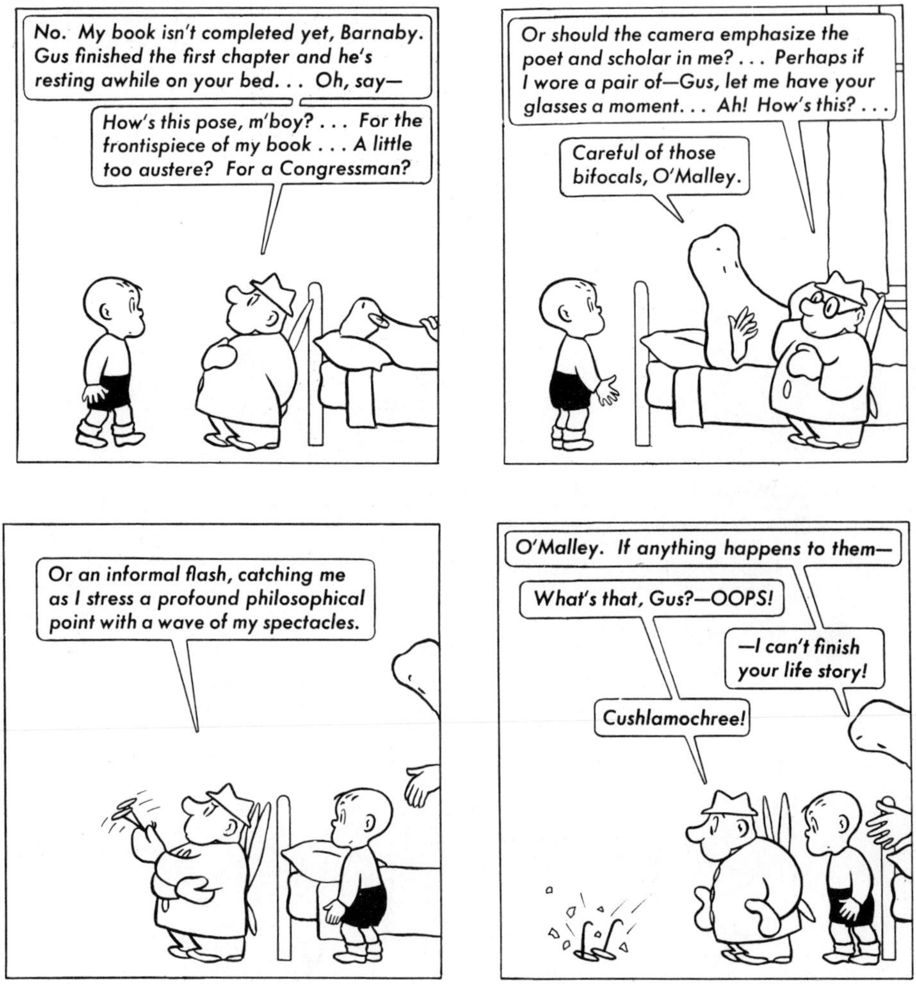
No. My book isn't completed yet, Barnaby. Gus finished the first chapter and he's resting awhile on your bed. . . Oh, say—
How's this pose, m'boy? . . . For the frontispiece of my book . . . A little too austere? For a Congressman?
Or should the camera emphasize the poet and scholar in me? . . . Perhaps if I wore a pair of—Gus, let me have your glasses a moment. . . Ah! How's this? . . .
Careful of those bifocals, O'Malley.
Or an informal flash, catching me as I stress a profound philosophical point with a wave of my spectacles.
O'Malley. If anything happens to them—
What's that, Gus?—OOPS!
—I can't finish your life story!
Cushlamochree!

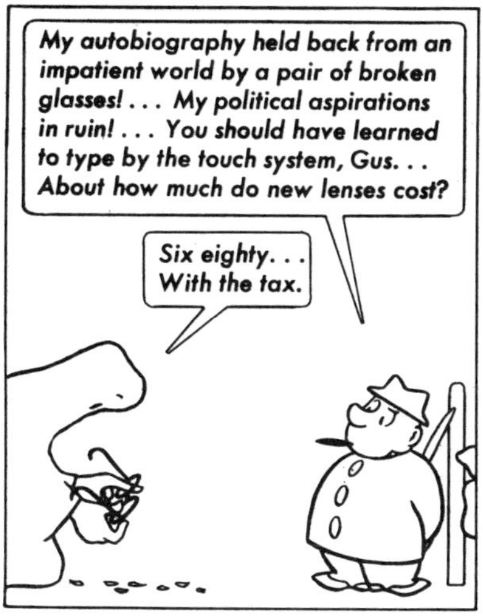
My autobiography held back from an impatient world by a pair of broken glasses! . . . My political aspirations in ruin! . . . You should have learned to type by the touch system, Gus. . . About how much do new lenses cost?
Six eighty. . . With the tax.

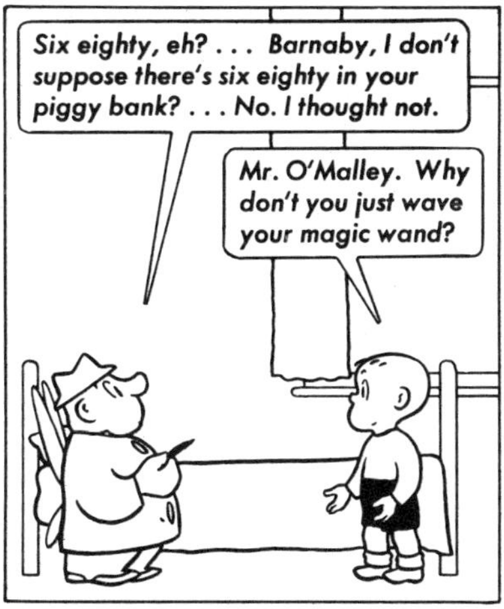
Six eighty, eh? . . . Barnaby, I don't suppose there's six eighty in your piggy bank? . . . No. I thought not.
Mr. O'Malley. Why don't you just wave your magic wand?

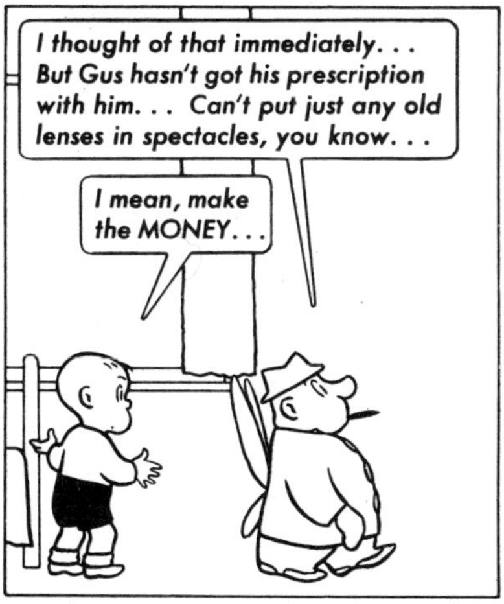
I thought of that immediately. . . But Gus hasn't got his prescription with him. . . Can't put just any old lenses in spectacles, you know. . .
I mean, make the MONEY. . .

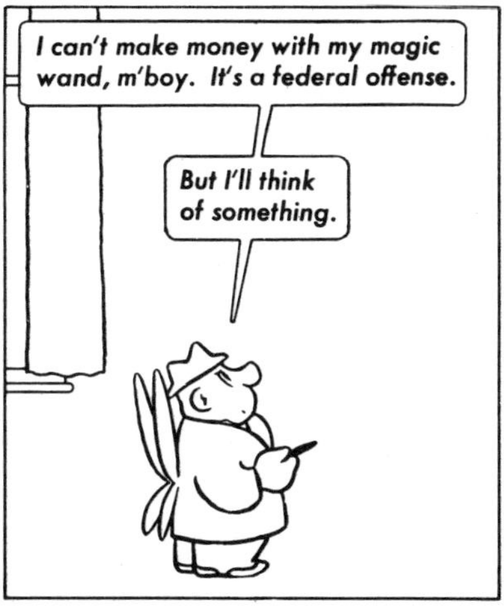
I can't make money with my magic wand, m'boy. It's a federal offense.
But I'll think of something.

EPISODE SIX

The Testimonial Dinner

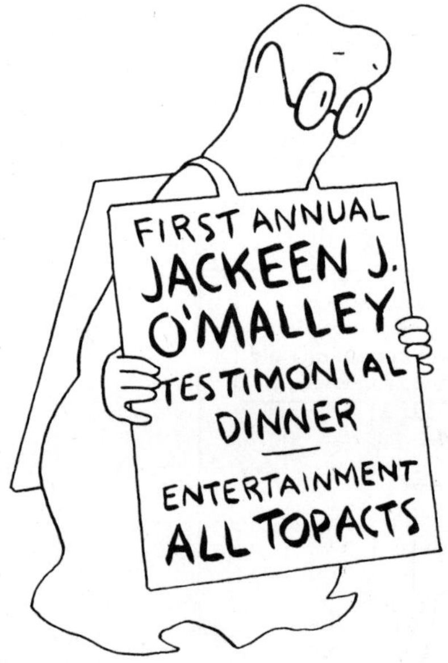
FIRST ANNUAL
JACKEEN J. O'MALLEY
TESTIMONIAL DINNER
ENTERTAINMENT
ALL TOP ACTS

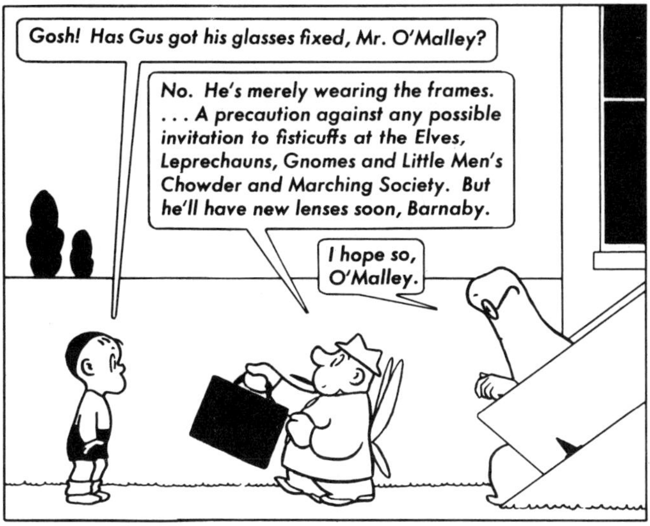
Gosh! Has Gus got his glasses fixed, Mr. O'Malley?
No. He's merely wearing the frames. . . . A precaution against any possible invitation to fisticuffs at the Elves, Leprechauns, Gnomes and Little Men's Chowder and Marching Society. But he'll have new lenses soon, Barnaby.
I hope so, O'Malley.

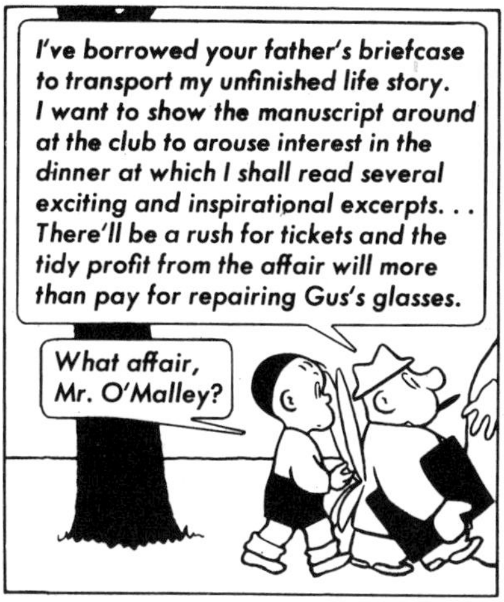
I've borrowed your father's briefcase to transport my unfinished life story. I want to show the manuscript around at the club to arouse interest in the dinner at which I shall read several exciting and inspirational excerpts. . . There'll be a rush for tickets and the tidy profit from the affair will more than pay for repairing Gus's glasses.
What affair, Mr. O'Malley?

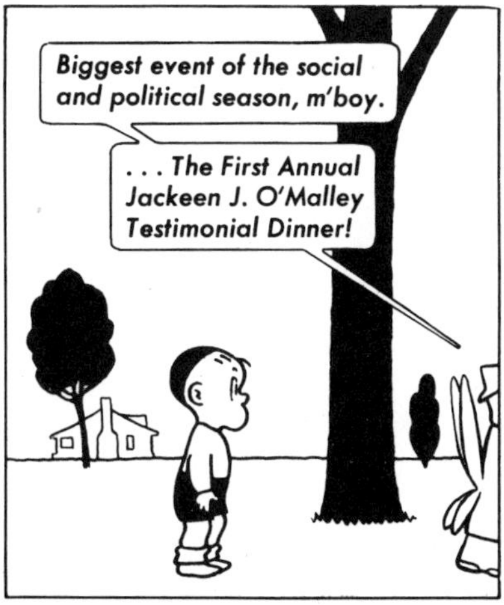
Biggest event of the social and political season, m'boy.
. . . The First Annual Jackeen J. O'Malley Testimonial Dinner!

LATER

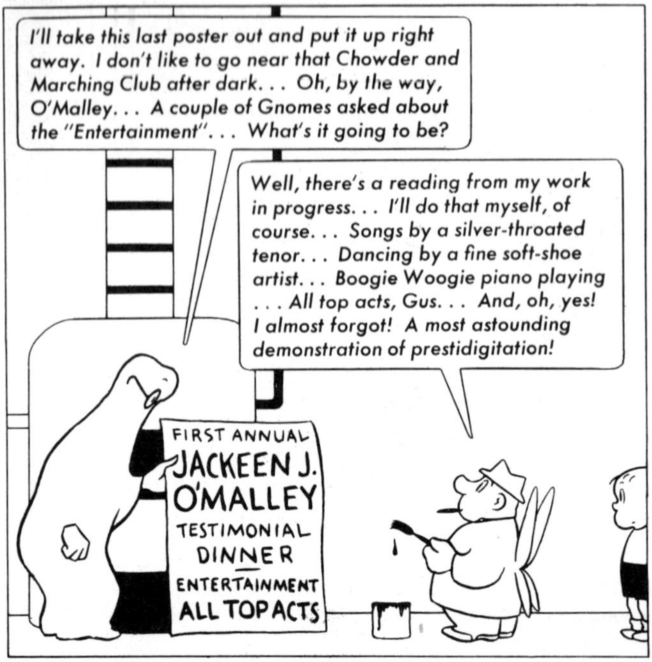
I'll take this last poster out and put it up right away. I don't like to go near that Chowder and Marching Club after dark. . . Oh, by the way, O'Malley. . . A couple of Gnomes asked about the "Entertainment". . . What's it going to be?
Well, there's a reading from my work in progress. . . I'll do that myself, of course. . . Songs by a silver-throated tenor. . . Dancing by a fine soft-shoe artist. . . Boogie Woogie piano playing . . . All top acts, Gus. . . And, oh, yes! I almost forgot! A most astounding demonstration of prestidigitation!
FIRST ANNUAL
JACKEEN J. O'MALLEY
TESTIMONIAL
DINNER
ENTERTAINMENT
ALL TOP ACTS

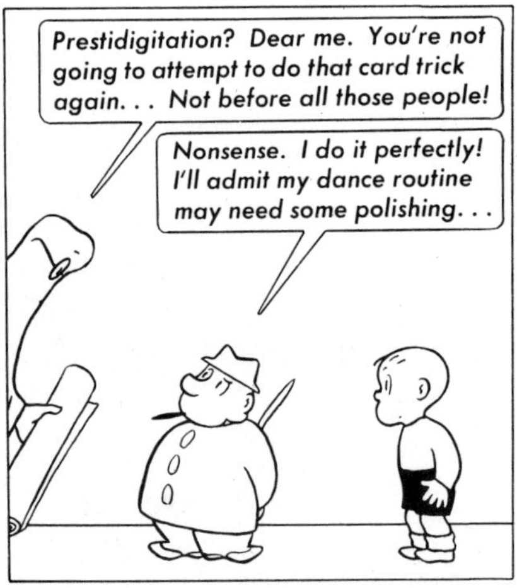
Prestidigitation? Dear me. You're not going to attempt to do that card trick again. . . Not before all those people!
Nonsense. I do it perfectly! I'll admit my dance routine may need some polishing. . .

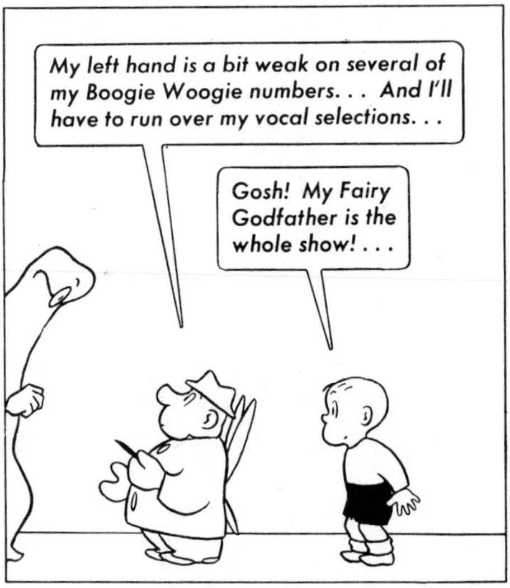
My left hand is a bit weak on several of my Boogie Woogie numbers. . . And I'll have to run over my vocal selections. . .
Gosh! My Fairy Godfather is the whole show! . . .

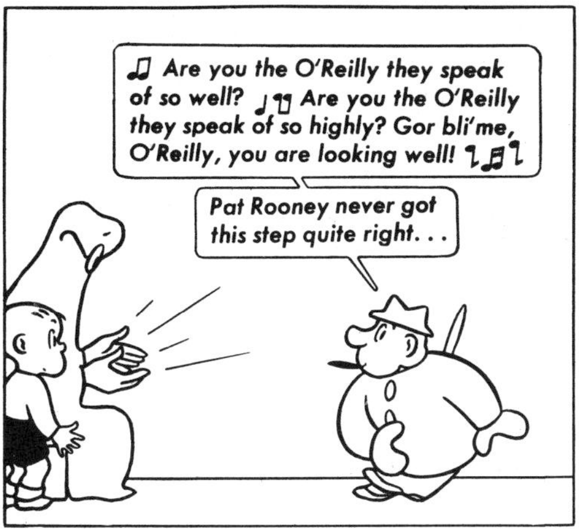
♫ Are you the O'Reilly they speak of so well? ♩♫ Are you the O'Reilly they speak of so highly? Gor bli'me, O'Reilly, you are looking well! ♪♬♪
Pat Rooney never got this step quite right. . .

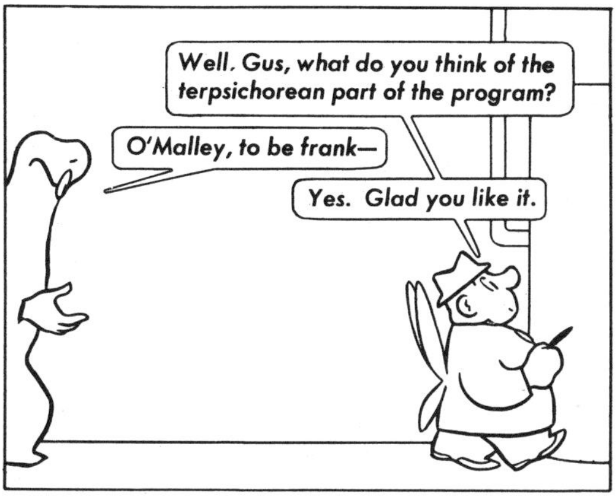
Well, Gus, what do you think of the terpsichorean part of the program?
O'Malley, to be frank—
Yes. Glad you like it.

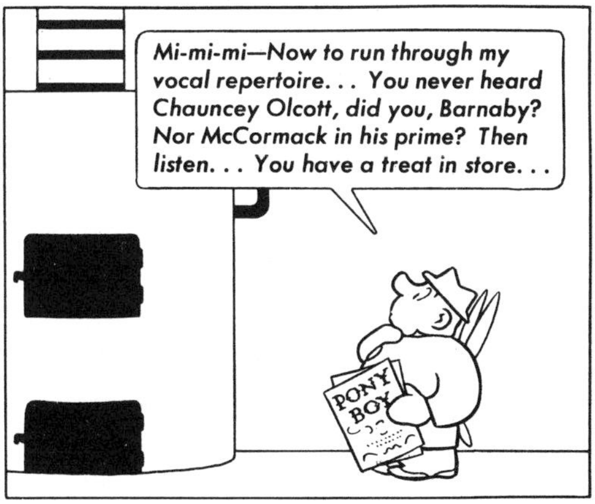
Mi-mi-mi—Now to run through my vocal repertoire. . . You never heard Chauncey Olcott, did you, Barnaby? Nor McCormack in his prime? Then listen. . . You have a treat in store. . .
PONY BOY

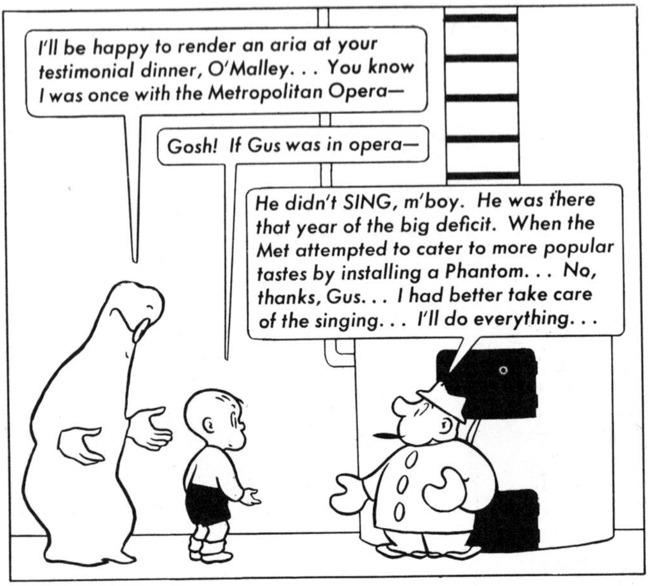
I'll be happy to render an aria at your testimonial dinner, O'Malley. . . You know I was once with the Metropolitan Opera—
Gosh! If Gus was in opera—
He didn't SING, m'boy. He was there that year of the big deficit. When the Met attempted to cater to more popular tastes by installing a Phantom. . . No, thanks, Gus. . . I had better take care of the singing. . . I'll do everything. . .

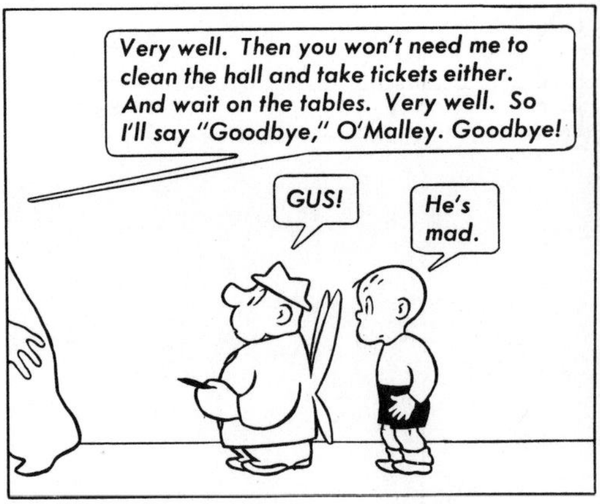
Very well. Then you won't need me to clean the hall and take tickets either. And wait on the tables. Very well. So I'll say "Goodbye," O'Malley. Goodbye!
GUS!
He's mad.

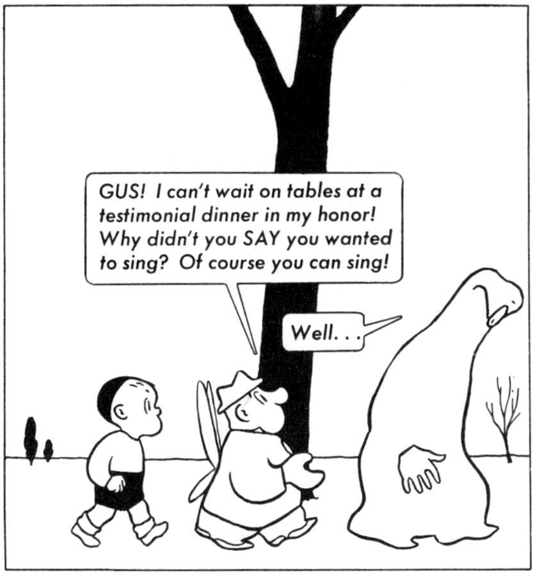
GUS! I can't wait on tables at a testimonial dinner in my honor! Why didn't you SAY you wanted to sing? Of course you can sing!
Well. . .

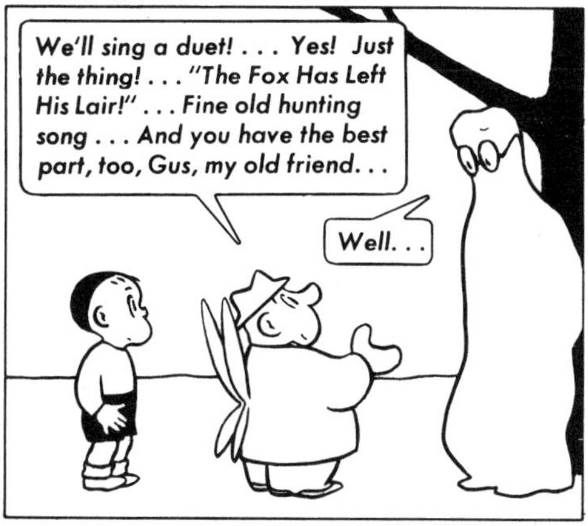
We'll sing a duet! . . . Yes! Just the thing! . . . "The Fox Has Left His Lair!" . . . Fine old hunting song . . . And you have the best part, too, Gus, my old friend. . .
Well. . .

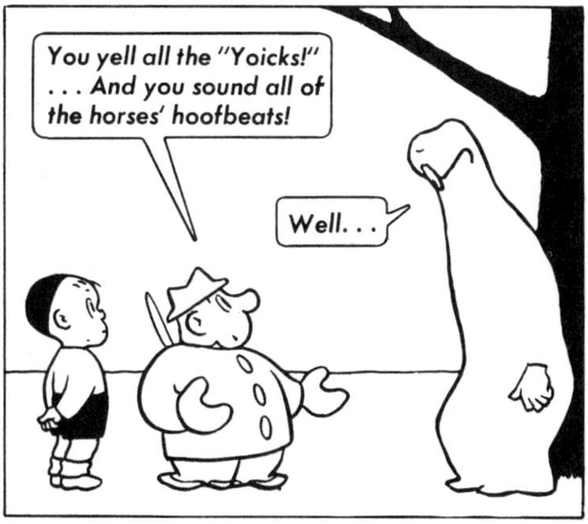
You yell all the "Yoicks!" . . . And you sound all of the horses' hoofbeats!
Well. . .

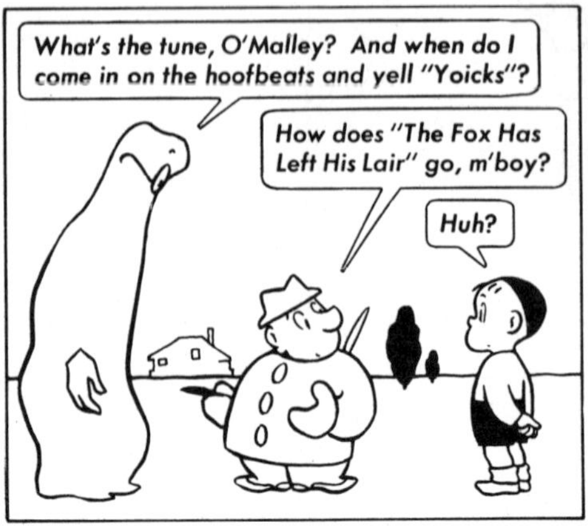
What's the tune, O'Malley? And when do I come in on the hoofbeats and yell "Yoicks"?
How does "The Fox Has Left His Lair" go, m'boy?
Huh?

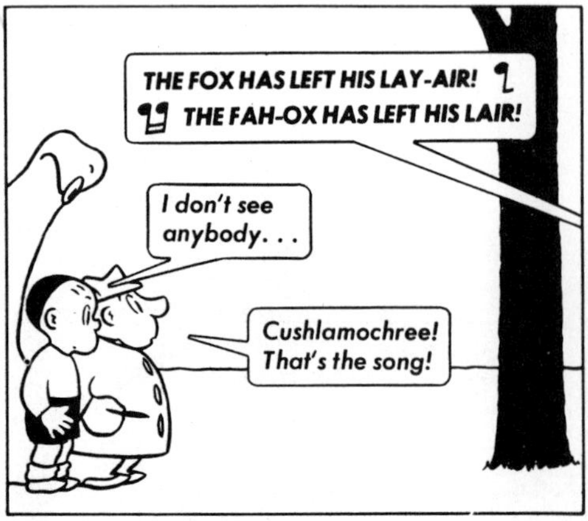
THE FOX HAS LEFT HIS LAY-AIR!
THE FAH-OX HAS LEFT HIS LAIR!
I don't see anybody. . .
Cushlamochree! That's the song!

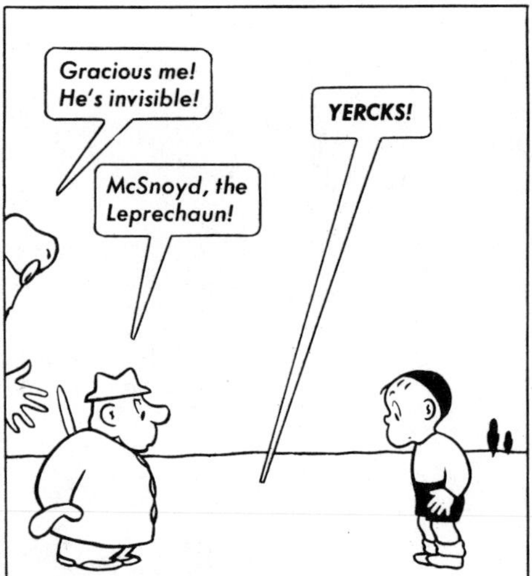
Gracious me! He's invisible!
McSnoyd, the Leprechaun!
YERCKS!

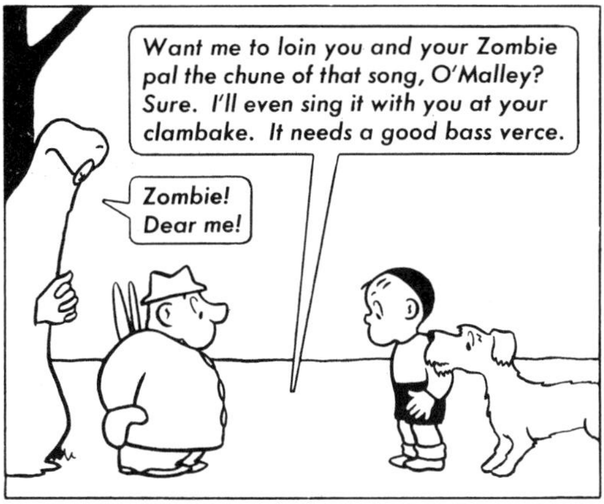
Want me to loin you and your Zombie pal the chune of that song, O'Malley? Sure. I'll even sing it with you at your clambake. It needs a good bass verce.
Zombie! Dear me!

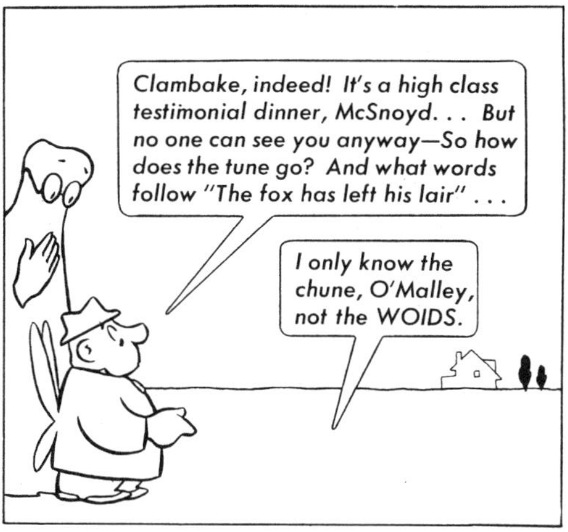
Clambake, indeed! It's a high class testimonial dinner, McSnoyd. . . But no one can see you anyway—So how does the tune go? And what words follow "The fox has left his lair" . . .
I only know the chune, O'Malley, not the WOIDS.

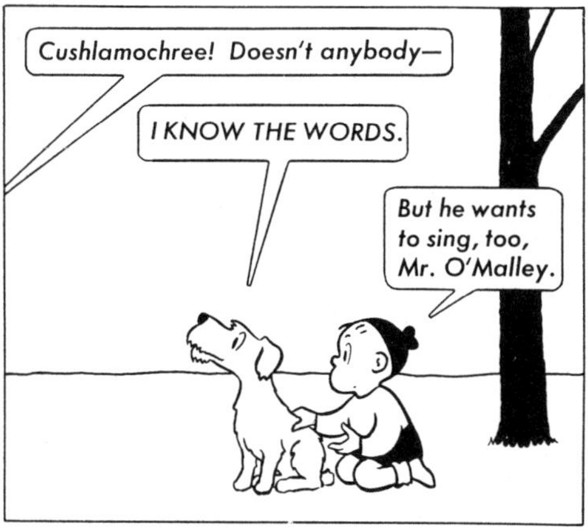
Cushlamochree! Doesn't anybody—
I KNOW THE WORDS.
But he wants to sing, too, Mr. O'Malley.

THE DAY AFTER

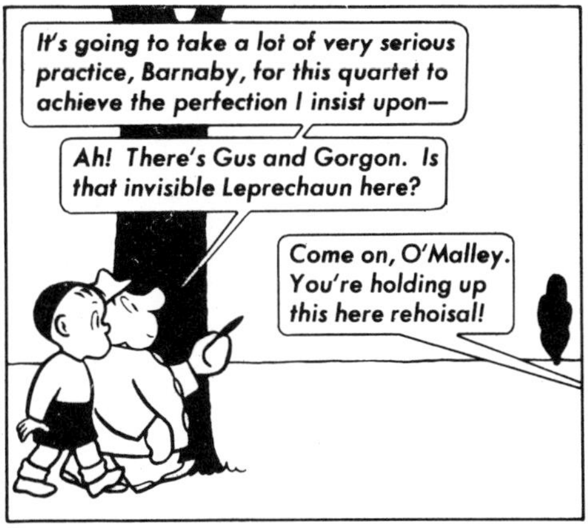
It's going to take a lot of very serious practice, Barnaby, for this quartet to achieve the perfection I insist upon—
Ah! There's Gus and Gorgon. Is that invisible Leprechaun here?
Come on, O'Malley. You're holding up this here rehoisal!

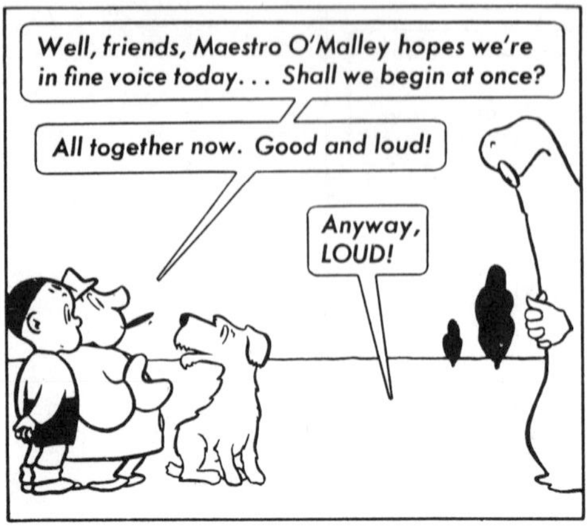
Well, friends, Maestro O'Malley hopes we're in fine voice today. . . Shall we begin at once?
All together now. Good and loud!
Anyway, LOUD!

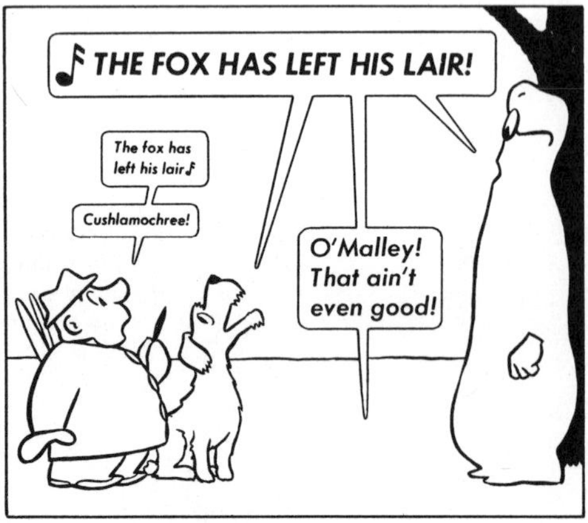
THE FOX HAS LEFT HIS LAIR!
The fox has left his lair
Cushlamochree!
O'Malley! That ain't even good!

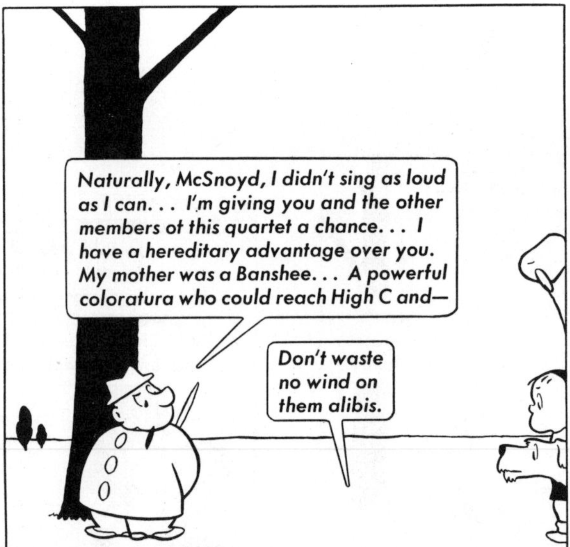
Naturally, McSnoyd, I didn't sing as loud as I can. . . I'm giving you and the other members of this quartet a chance. . . I have a hereditary advantage over you. My mother was a Banshee. . . A powerful coloratura who could reach High C and—
Don't waste no wind on them alibis.

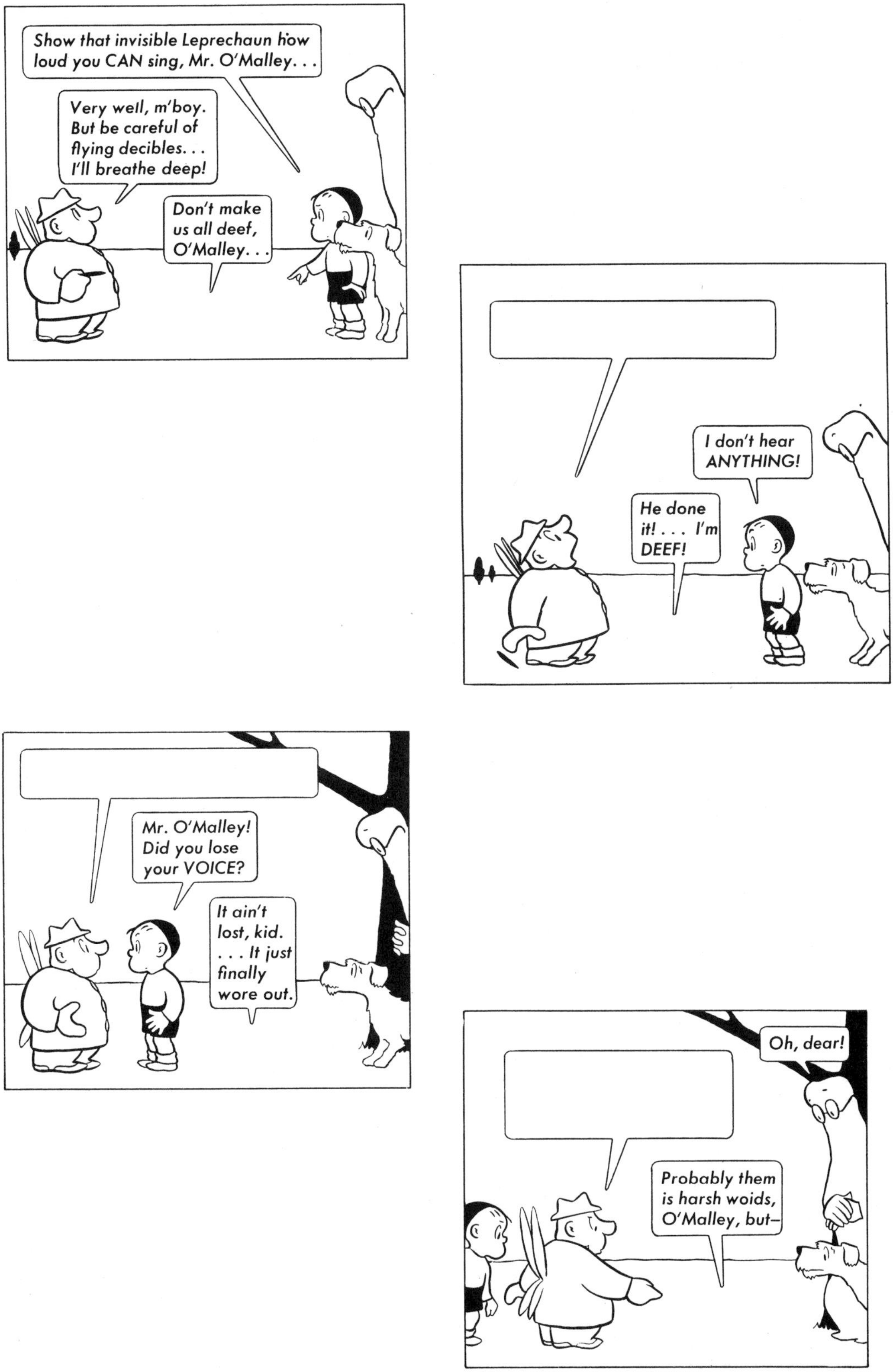
Show that invisible Leprechaun how loud you CAN sing, Mr. O'Malley. . .
Very well, m'boy. But be careful of flying decibles. . . I'll breathe deep!
Don't make us all deef, O'Malley. . .
I don't hear ANYTHING!
He done it! . . . I'm DEEF!
Mr. O'Malley! Did you lose your VOICE?
It ain't lost, kid. . . . It just finally wore out.
Oh, dear!
Probably them is harsh woids, O'Malley, but–

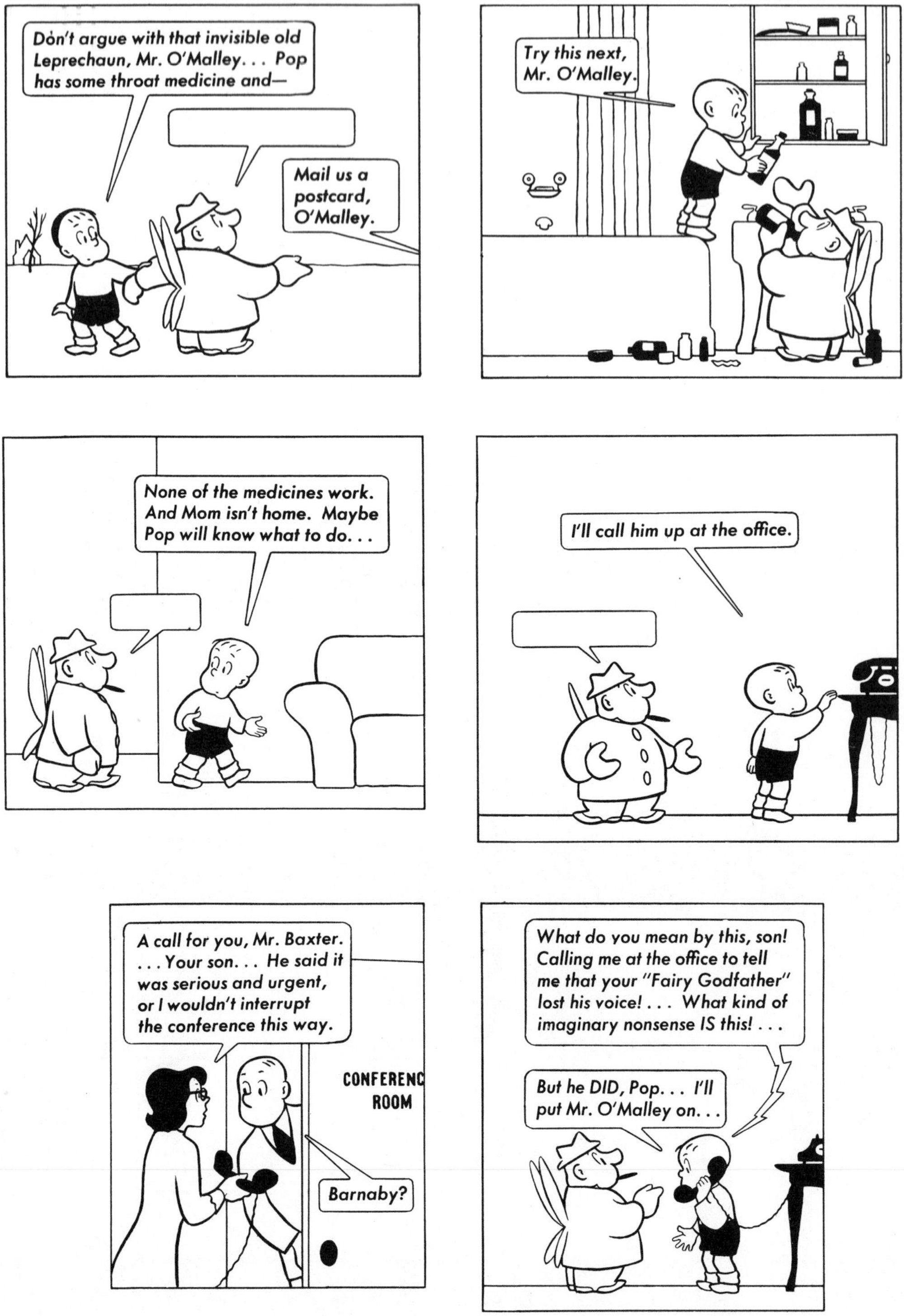
Don't argue with that invisible old Leprechaun, Mr. O'Malley. . . Pop has some throat medicine and—
Mail us a postcard, O'Malley.
Try this next, Mr. O'Malley.
None of the medicines work. And Mom isn't home. Maybe Pop will know what to do. . .
I'll call him up at the office.
A call for you, Mr. Baxter. . . . Your son. . . He said it was serious and urgent, or I wouldn't interrupt the conference this way.
CONFERENC
ROOM
Barnaby?
What do you mean by this, son! Calling me at the office to tell me that your "Fairy Godfather" lost his voice! . . . What kind of imaginary nonsense IS this! . . .
But he DID, Pop. . . I'll put Mr. O'Malley on. . .

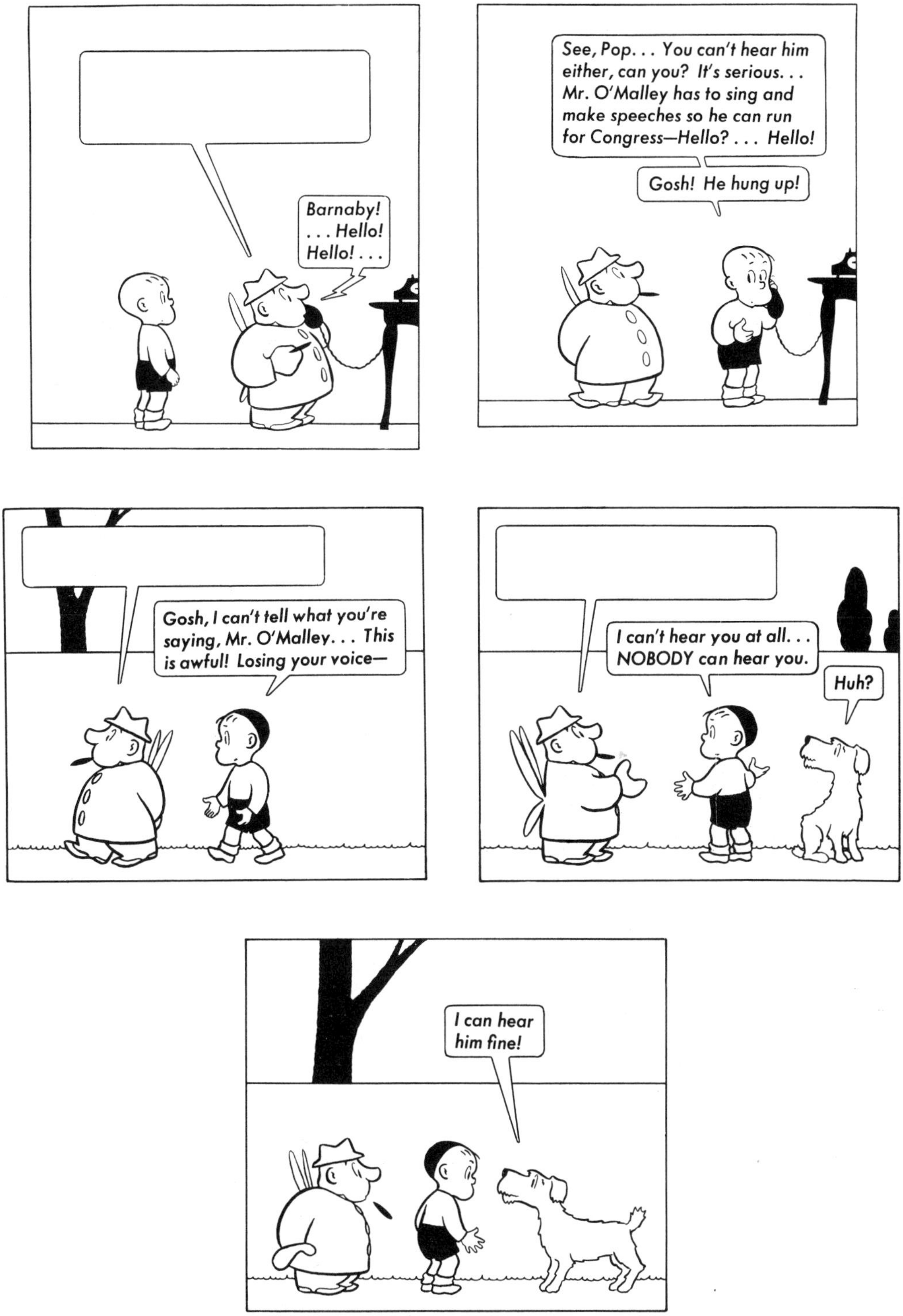
Barnaby! . . . Hello! Hello! . . .
See, Pop. . . You can't hear him either, can you? It's serious. . . Mr. O'Malley has to sing and make speeches so he can run for Congress—Hello? . . . Hello!
Gosh! He hung up!
Gosh, I can't tell what you're saying, Mr. O'Malley. . . This is awful! Losing your voice—
I can't hear you at all. . . NOBODY can hear you.
Huh?
I can hear him fine!

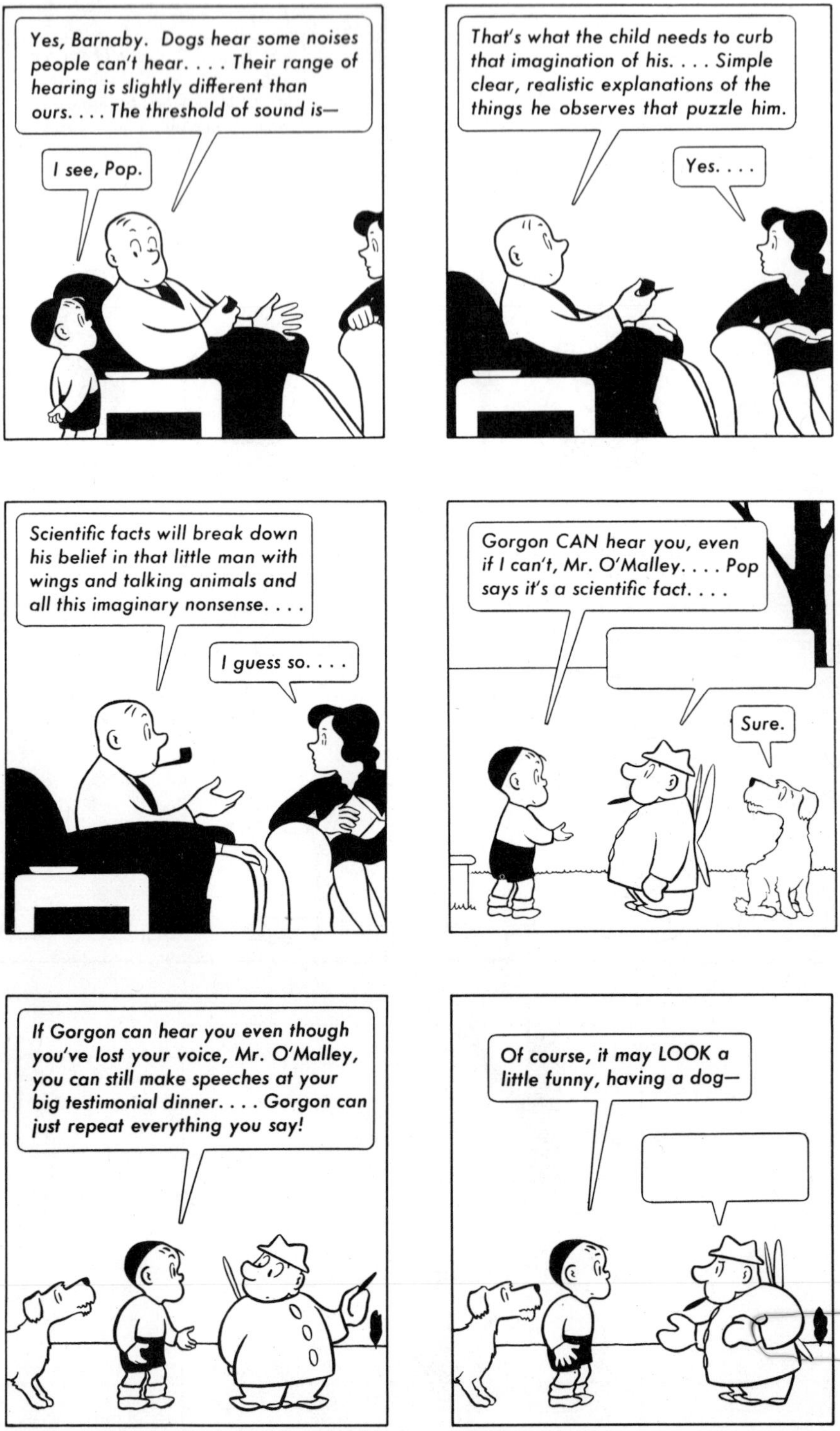
Yes, Barnaby. Dogs hear some noises people can't hear. . . . Their range of hearing is slightly different than ours. . . . The threshold of sound is—
I see, Pop.
That's what the child needs to curb that imagination of his. . . . Simple clear, realistic explanations of the things he observes that puzzle him.
Yes. . . .
Scientific facts will break down his belief in that little man with wings and talking animals and all this imaginary nonsense. . . .
I guess so. . . .
Gorgon CAN hear you, even if I can't, Mr. O'Malley. . . . Pop says it's a scientific fact. . . .
Sure.
If Gorgon can hear you even though you've lost your voice, Mr. O'Malley, you can still make speeches at your big testimonial dinner. . . . Gorgon can just repeat everything you say!
Of course, it may LOOK a little funny, having a dog—

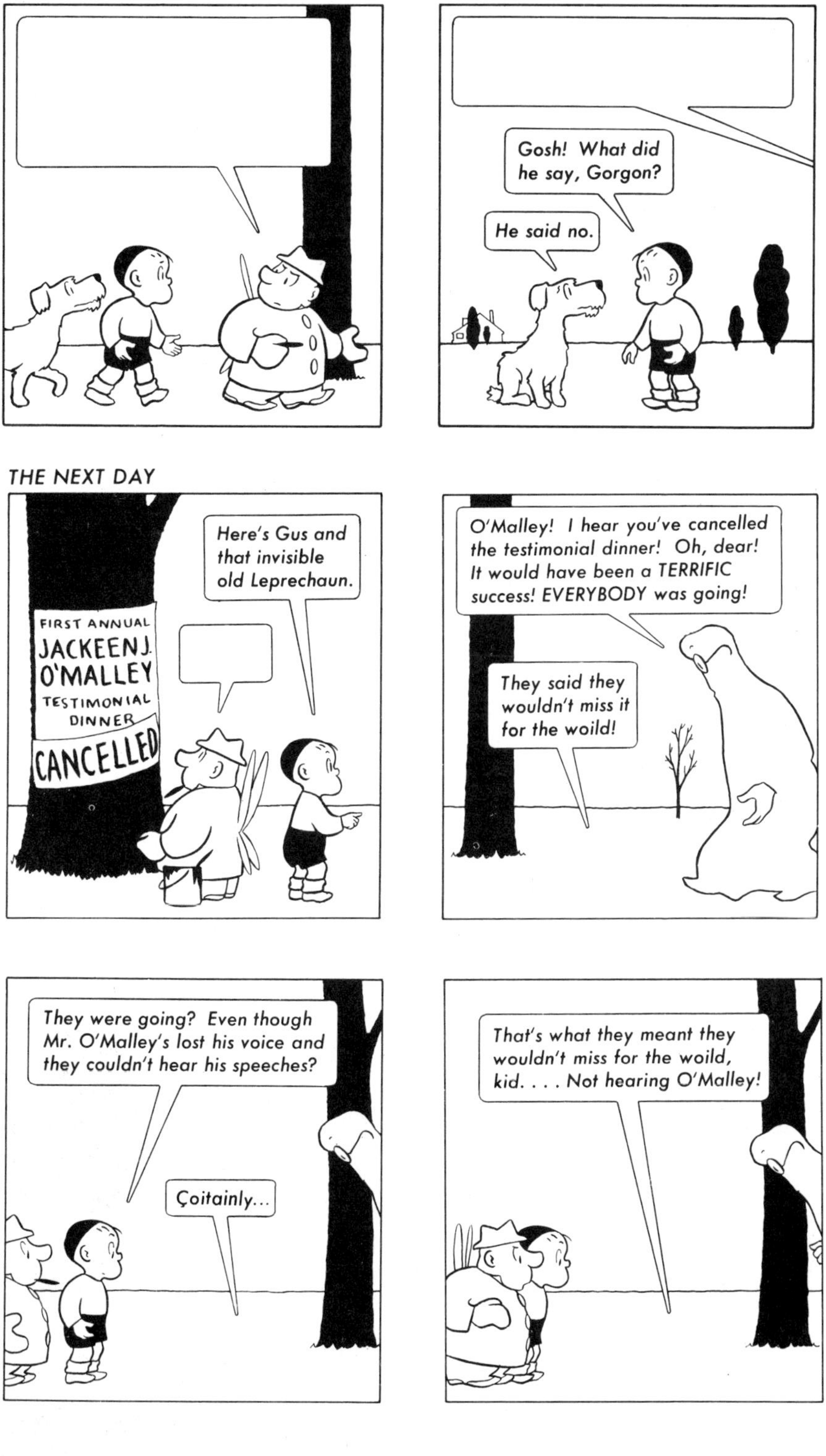
Gosh! What did he say, Gorgon?
He said no.
THE NEXT DAY
FIRST ANNUAL JACKEEN J. O'MALLEY TESTIMONIAL DINNER
CANCELLED
Here's Gus and that invisible old Leprechaun.
O'Malley! I hear you've cancelled the testimonial dinner! Oh, dear! It would have been a TERRIFIC success! EVERYBODY was going!
They said they wouldn't miss it for the woild!
They were going? Even though Mr. O'Malley's lost his voice and they couldn't hear his speeches?
Çoitainly...
That's what they meant they wouldn't miss for the woild, kid. . . . Not hearing O'Malley!

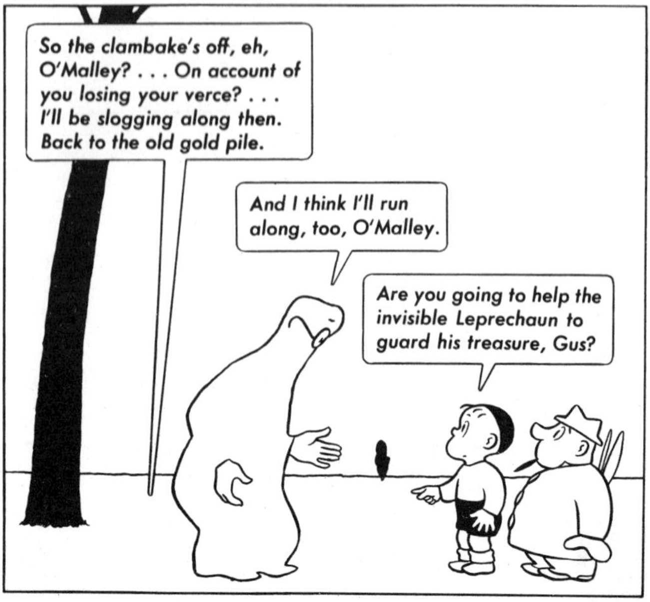
So the clambake's off, eh, O'Malley? . . . On account of you losing your verce? . . . I'll be slogging along then. Back to the old gold pile.
And I think I'll run along, too, O'Malley.
Are you going to help the invisible Leprechaun to guard his treasure, Gus?

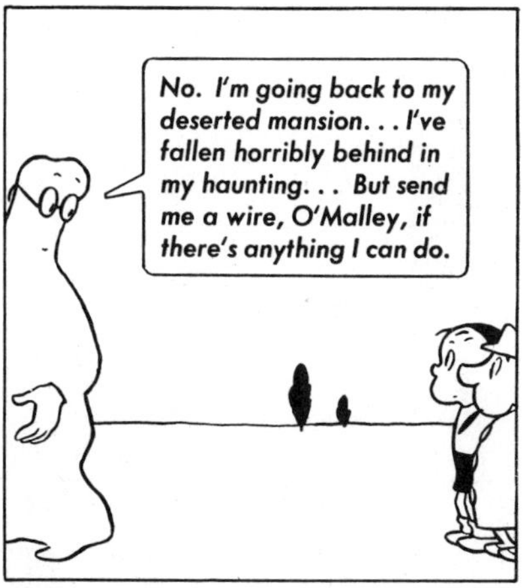
No. I'm going back to my deserted mansion. . . I've fallen horribly behind in my haunting. . . But send me a wire, O'Malley, if there's anything I can do.

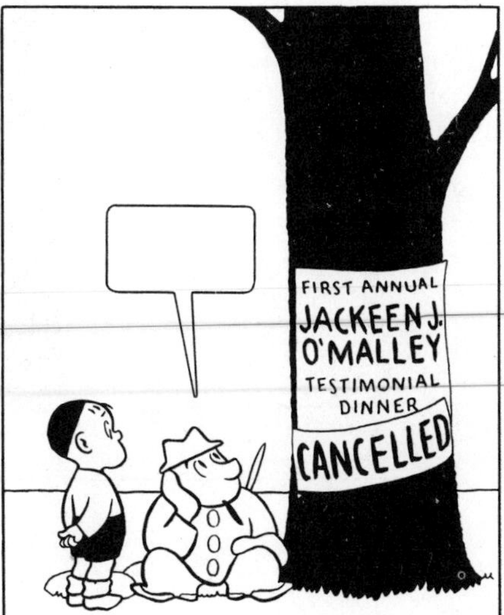
FIRST ANNUAL
JACKEEN J. O'MALLEY
TESTIMONIAL DINNER
CANCELLED

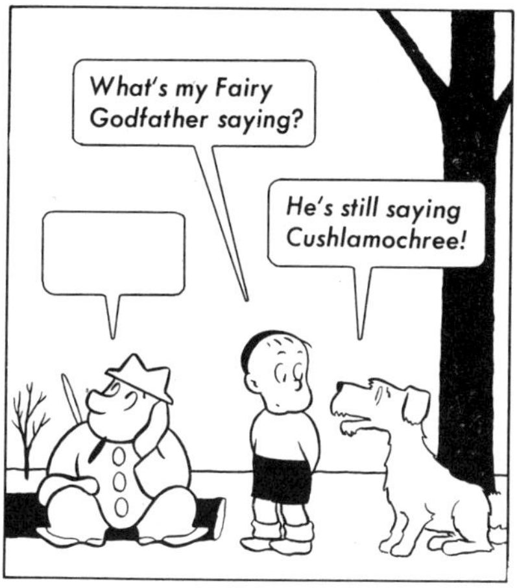
What's my Fairy Godfather saying?
He's still saying Cushlamochree!

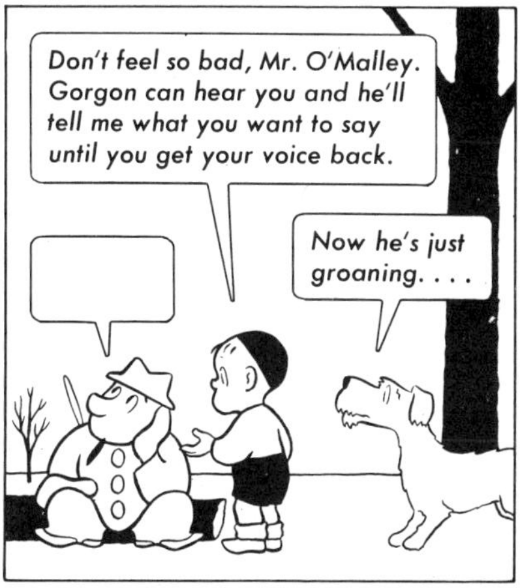
Don't feel so bad, Mr. O'Malley. Gorgon can hear you and he'll tell me what you want to say until you get your voice back.
Now he's just groaning. . . .

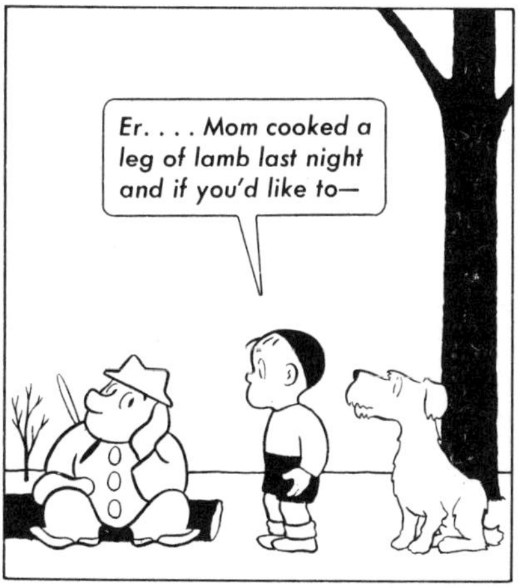
Er. . . . Mom cooked a leg of lamb last night and if you'd like to—

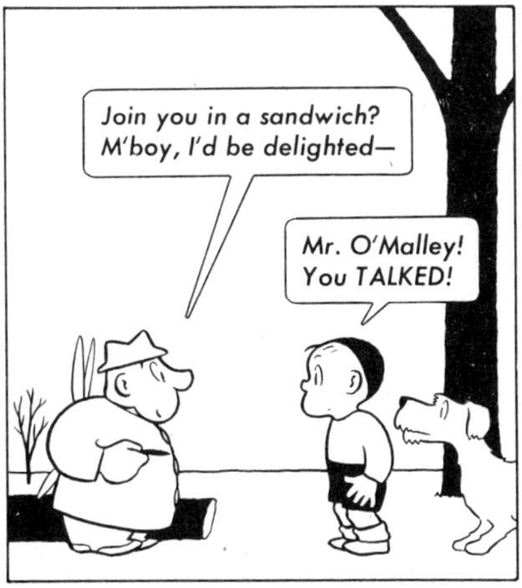
Join you in a sandwich? M'boy, I'd be delighted—
Mr. O'Malley! You TALKED!

EPISODE SEVEN
O'Malley for Congress!

I see Boss Snagg hasn't chosen a candidate for our district's congressional vacancy yet . . .

The opposition candidate, Beauregard W. Mintleaf, got his campaign off to a flying start, lambasting Snagg's political machine.

Does Boss Snagg pick people to go to Congress, Pop?

Mintleaf has got a lot of money behind him. . . If Boss Snagg is going to win this year he's got to dig up somebody different from his usual political hacks.

Who can he run?

Mr. O'Malley! Before you can go to Congress, you have to see Boss Snagg!

O'MALLEY FOR CONGRESS

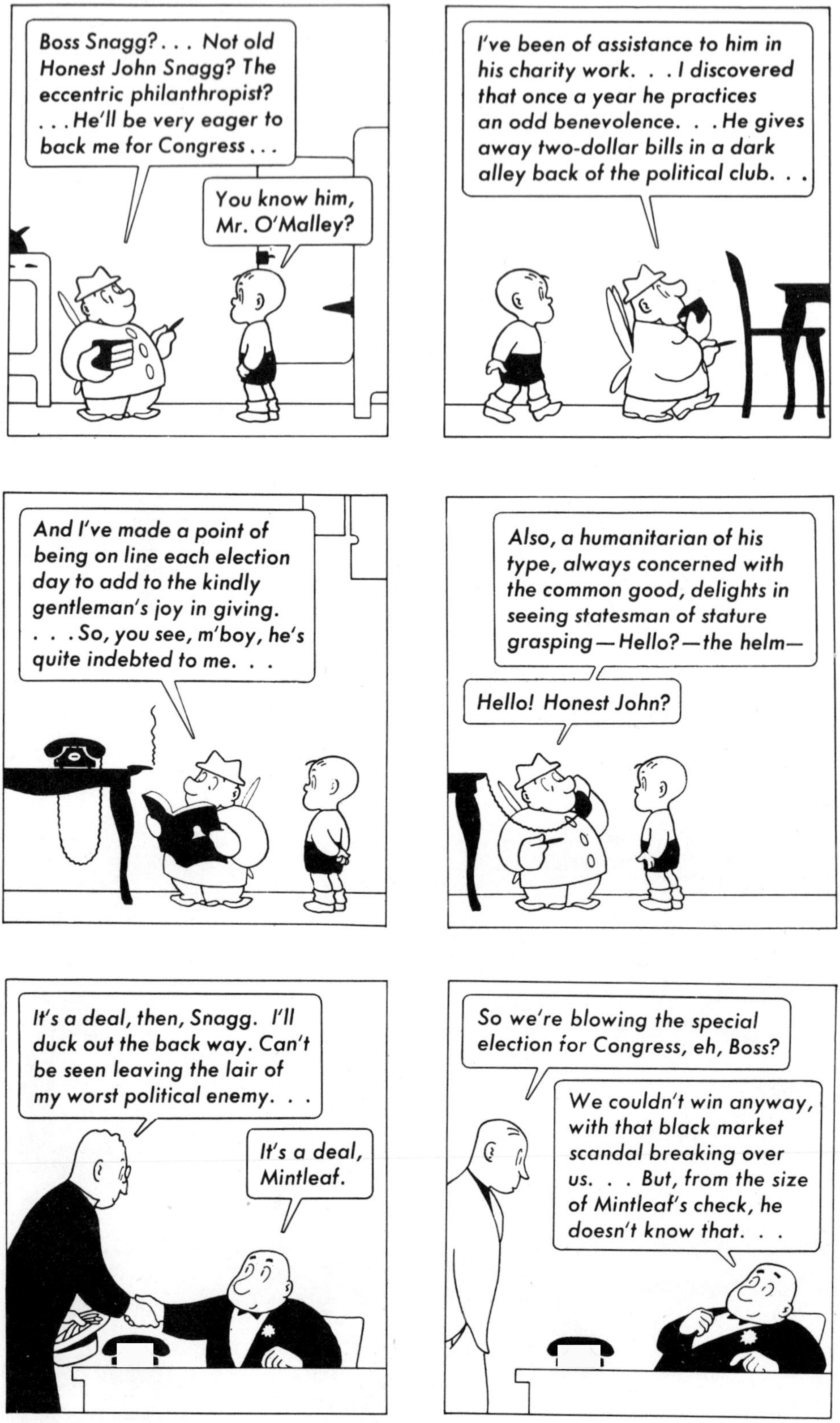
Boss Snagg? . . . Not old Honest John Snagg? The eccentric philanthropist? . . . He'll be very eager to back me for Congress . . .
You know him, Mr. O'Malley?
I've been of assistance to him in his charity work. . . I discovered that once a year he practices an odd benevolence. . . He gives away two-dollar bills in a dark alley back of the political club. . .
And I've made a point of being on line each election day to add to the kindly gentleman's joy in giving. . . . So, you see, m'boy, he's quite indebted to me. . .
Also, a humanitarian of his type, always concerned with the common good, delights in seeing statesman of stature grasping—Hello?—the helm—
Hello! Honest John?
It's a deal, then, Snagg. I'll duck out the back way. Can't be seen leaving the lair of my worst political enemy. . .
It's a deal, Mintleaf.
So we're blowing the special election for Congress, eh, Boss?
We couldn't win anyway, with that black market scandal breaking over us. . . But, from the size of Mintleaf's check, he doesn't know that. . .

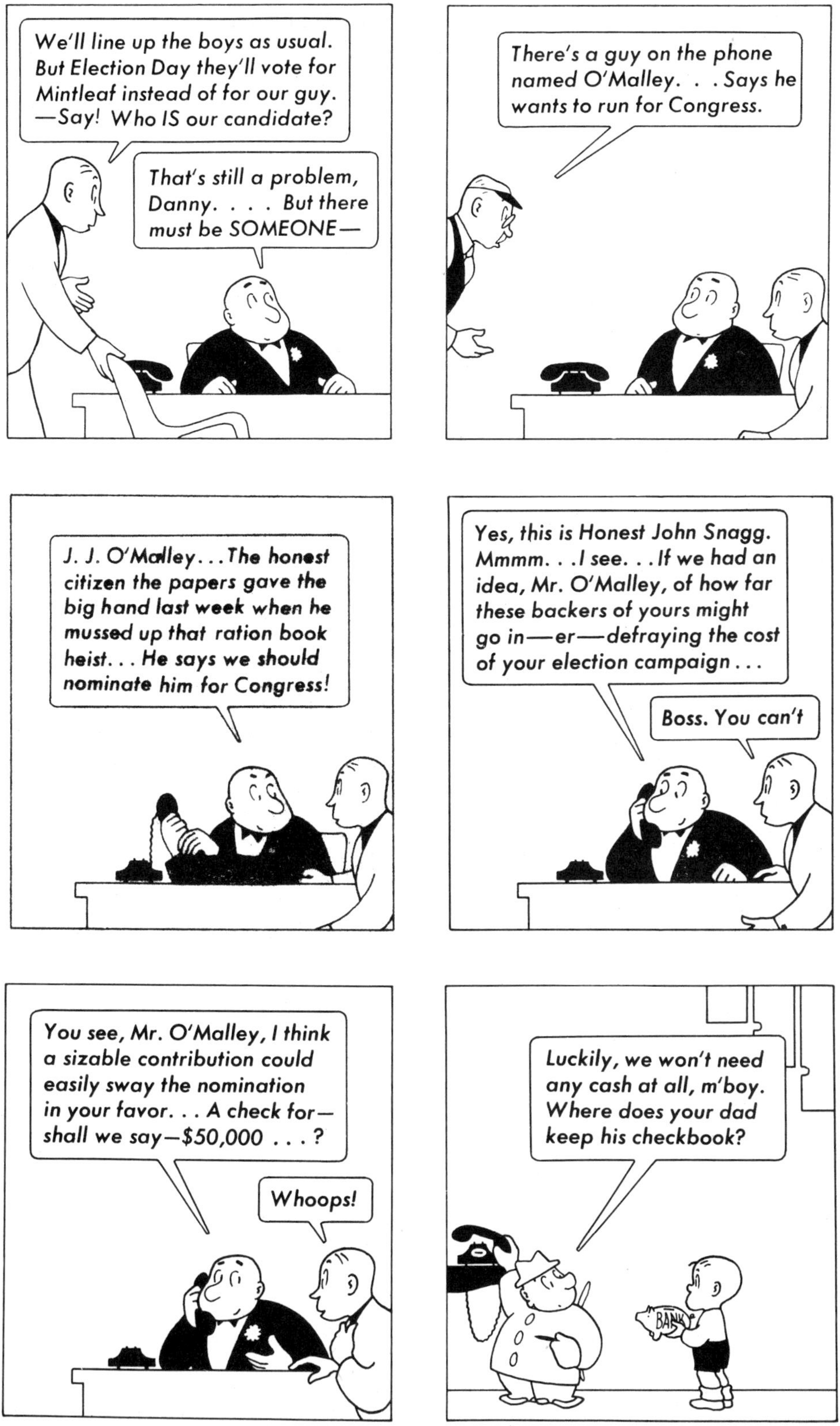
We'll line up the boys as usual. But Election Day they'll vote for Mintleaf instead of for our guy. —Say! Who IS our candidate?
That's still a problem, Danny. . . . But there must be SOMEONE—
There's a guy on the phone named O'Malley. . . Says he wants to run for Congress.
J. J. O'Malley. . . The honest citizen the papers gave the big hand last week when he mussed up that ration book heist. . . He says we should nominate him for Congress!
Yes, this is Honest John Snagg. Mmmm. . . I see. . . If we had an idea, Mr. O'Malley, of how far these backers of yours might go in—er—defraying the cost of your election campaign . . .
Boss. You can't
You see, Mr. O'Malley, I think a sizable contribution could easily sway the nomination in your favor. . . A check for—shall we say—$50,000 . . . ?
Whoops!
Luckily, we won't need any cash at all, m'boy. Where does your dad keep his checkbook?
BANK

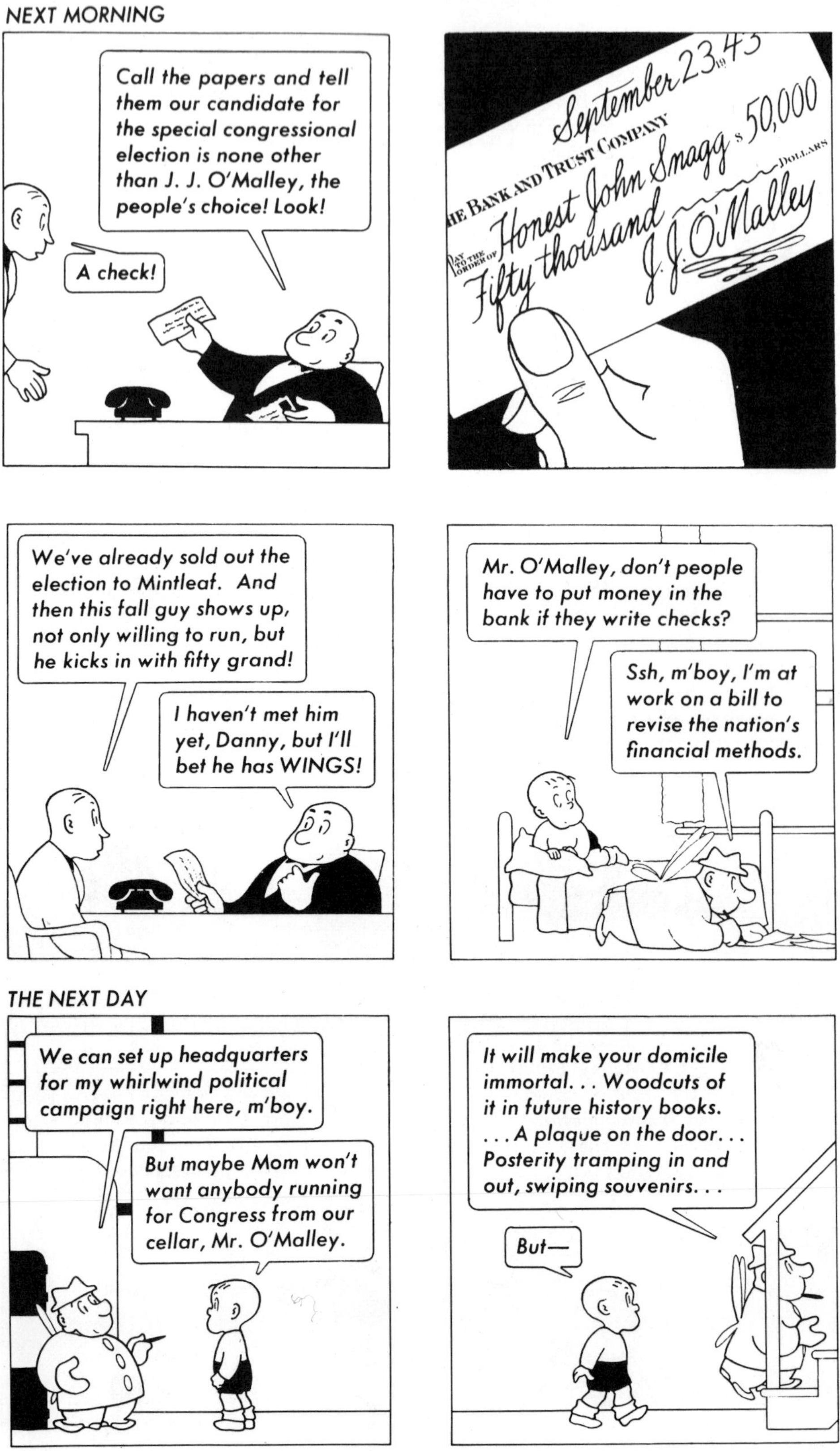
NEXT MORNING
Call the papers and tell them our candidate for the special congressional election is none other than J. J. O'Malley, the people's choice! Look!
A check!
September 23 1943
HE BANK AND TRUST COMPANY
Honest John Snagg $ 50,000
Fifty thousand
DOLLARS
J. J. O'Malley
We've already sold out the election to Mintleaf. And then this fall guy shows up, not only willing to run, but he kicks in with fifty grand!
I haven't met him yet, Danny, but I'll bet he has WINGS!
Mr. O'Malley, don't people have to put money in the bank if they write checks?
Ssh, m'boy, I'm at work on a bill to revise the nation's financial methods.
THE NEXT DAY
We can set up headquarters for my whirlwind political campaign right here, m'boy.
But maybe Mom won't want anybody running for Congress from our cellar, Mr. O'Malley.
It will make your domicile immortal. . . Woodcuts of it in future history books. . . . A plaque on the door. . . Posterity tramping in and out, swiping souvenirs. . .
But—

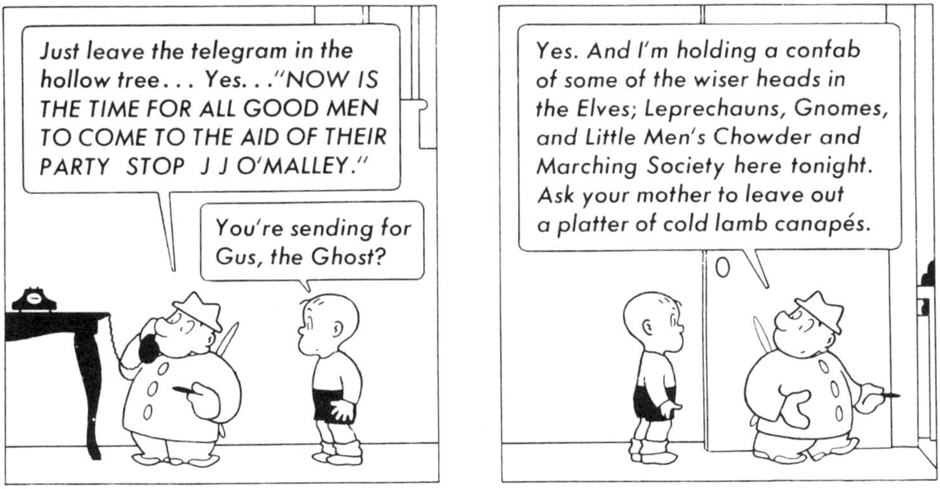
Just leave the telegram in the hollow tree... Yes..."NOW IS THE TIME FOR ALL GOOD MEN TO COME TO THE AID OF THEIR PARTY STOP J J O'MALLEY."
You're sending for Gus, the Ghost?
Yes. And I'm holding a confab of some of the wiser heads in the Elves; Leprechauns, Gnomes, and Little Men's Chowder and Marching Society here tonight. Ask your mother to leave out a platter of cold lamb canapés.

THAT EVENING

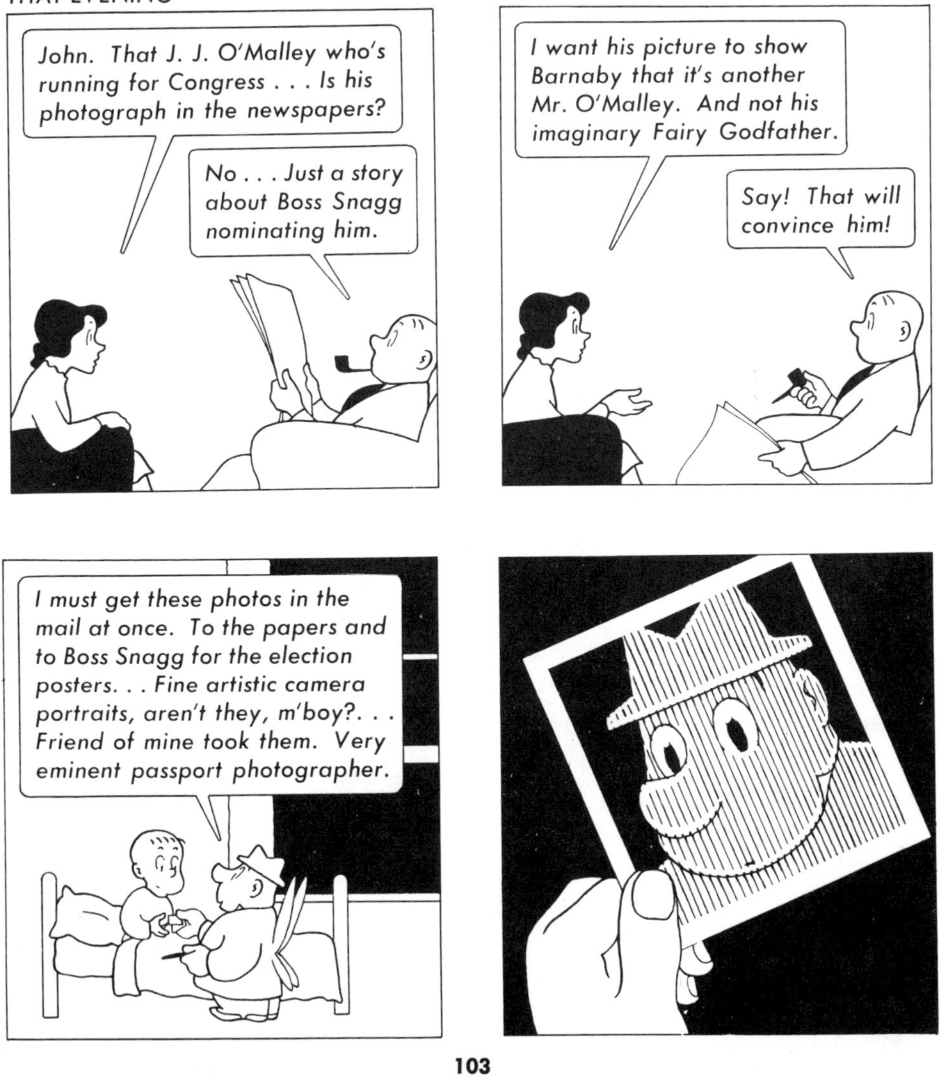
John. That J. J. O'Malley who's running for Congress . . . Is his photograph in the newspapers?
No . . . Just a story about Boss Snagg nominating him.
I want his picture to show Barnaby that it's another Mr. O'Malley. And not his imaginary Fairy Godfather.
Say! That will convince him!
I must get these photos in the mail at once. To the papers and to Boss Snagg for the election posters... Fine artistic camera portraits, aren't they, m'boy?... Friend of mine took them. Very eminent passport photographer.

THE FOLLOWING EVENING

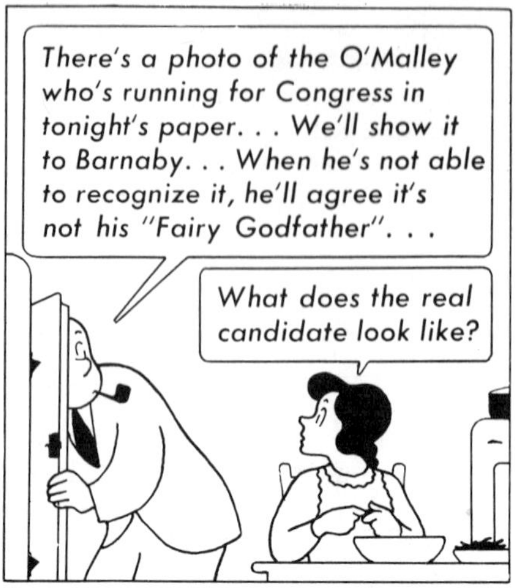
There's a photo of the O'Malley who's running for Congress in tonight's paper. . . We'll show it to Barnaby. . . When he's not able to recognize it, he'll agree it's not his "Fairy Godfather". . .
What does the real candidate look like?

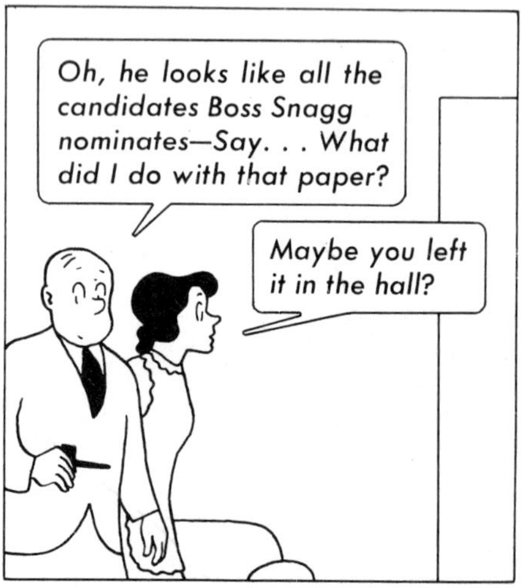
Oh, he looks like all the candidates Boss Snagg nominates—Say. . . What did I do with that paper?
Maybe you left it in the hall?

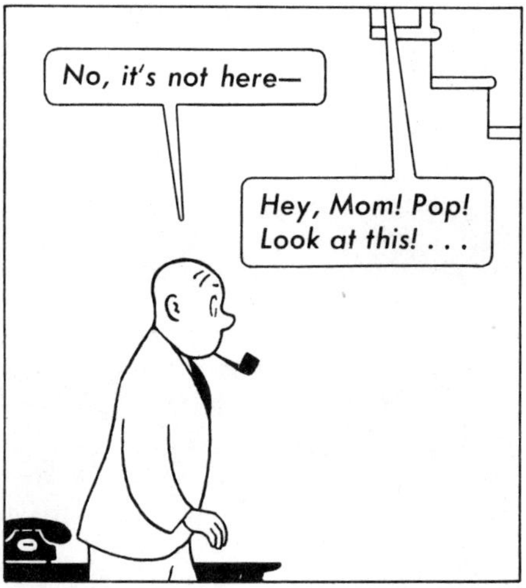
No, it's not here—
Hey, Mom! Pop! Look at this! . . .

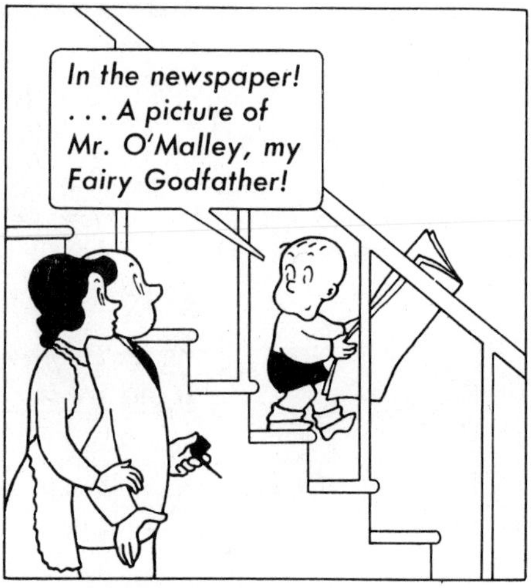
In the newspaper! . . . A picture of Mr. O'Malley, my Fairy Godfather!

A DAY LATER

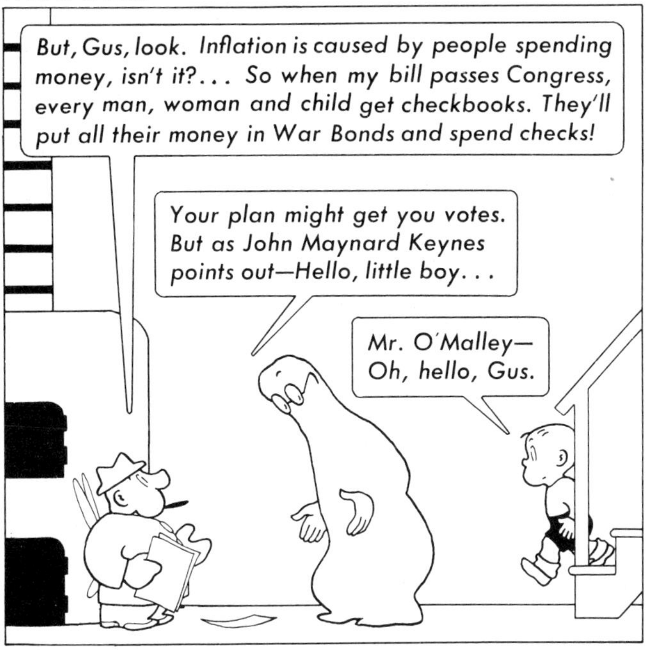

But, Gus, look. Inflation is caused by people spending money, isn't it?. . . So when my bill passes Congress, every man, woman and child get checkbooks. They'll put all their money in War Bonds and spend checks!
Your plan might get you votes. But as John Maynard Keynes points out—Hello, little boy. . .
Mr. O'Malley— Oh, hello, Gus.

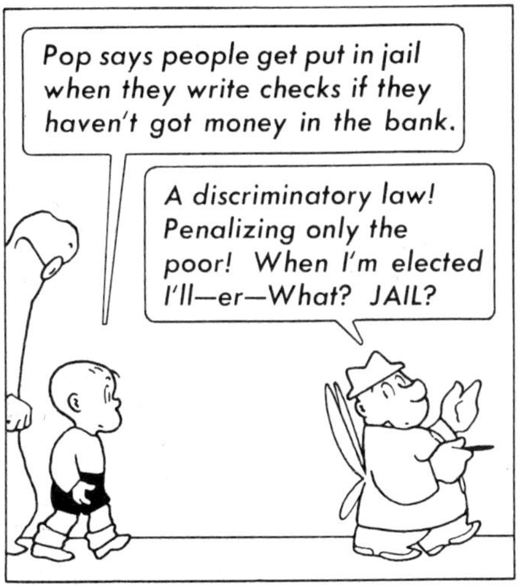

Pop says people get put in jail when they write checks if they haven't got money in the bank.
A discriminatory law! Penalizing only the poor! When I'm elected I'll—er—What? JAIL?

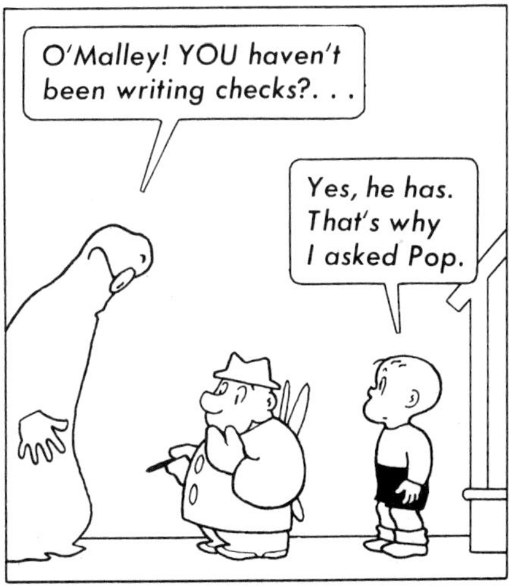

O'Malley! YOU haven't been writing checks?. . .
Yes, he has. That's why I asked Pop.

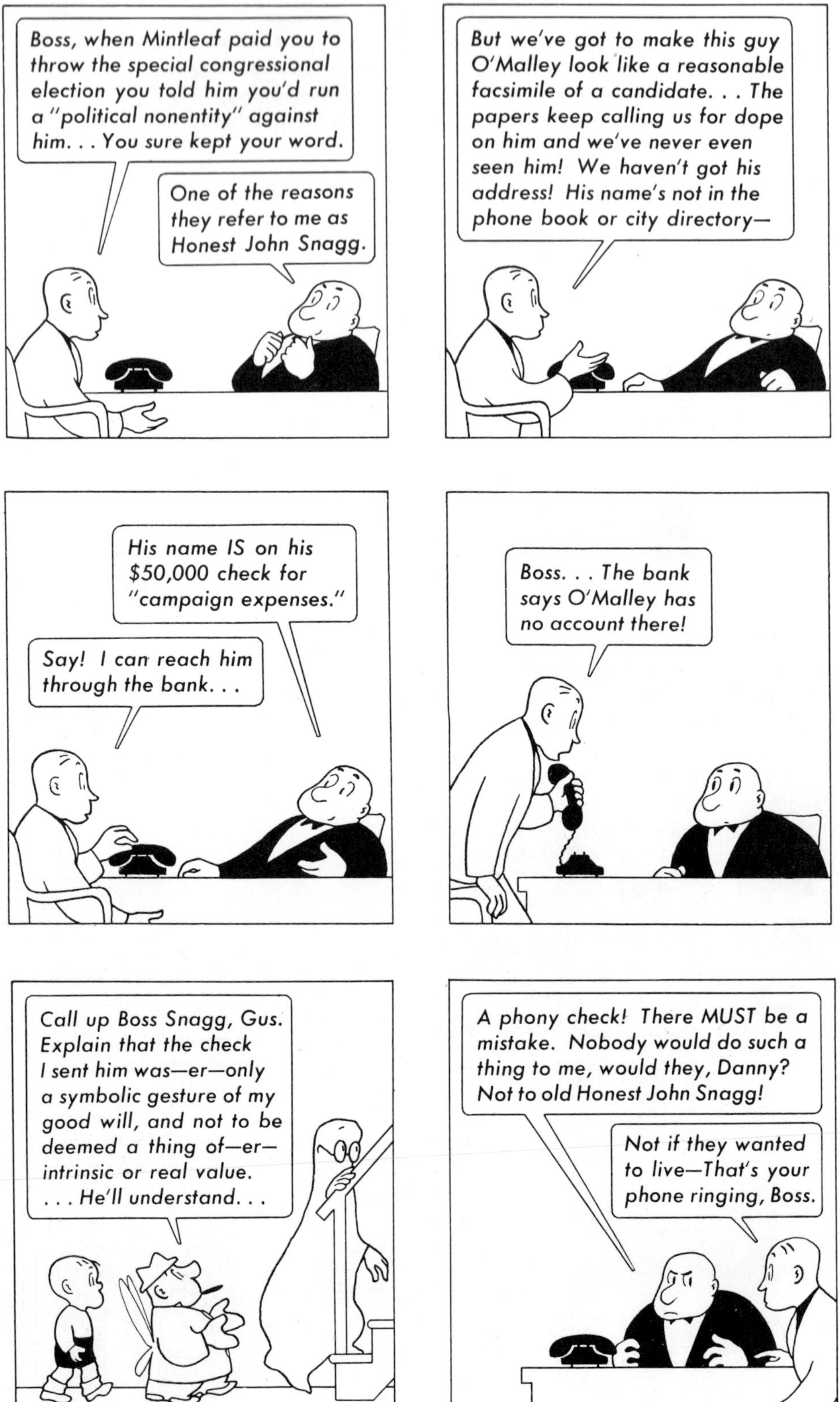
Boss, when Mintleaf paid you to throw the special congressional election you told him you'd run a "political nonentity" against him. . . You sure kept your word.
One of the reasons they refer to me as Honest John Snagg.
But we've got to make this guy O'Malley look like a reasonable facsimile of a candidate. . . The papers keep calling us for dope on him and we've never even seen him! We haven't got his address! His name's not in the phone book or city directory—
Say! I can reach him through the bank. . .
His name IS on his $50,000 check for "campaign expenses."
Boss. . . The bank says O'Malley has no account there!
Call up Boss Snagg, Gus. Explain that the check I sent him was—er—only a symbolic gesture of my good will, and not to be deemed a thing of—er—intrinsic or real value. . . . He'll understand. . .
A phony check! There MUST be a mistake. Nobody would do such a thing to me, would they, Danny? Not to old Honest John Snagg!
Not if they wanted to live—That's your phone ringing, Boss.

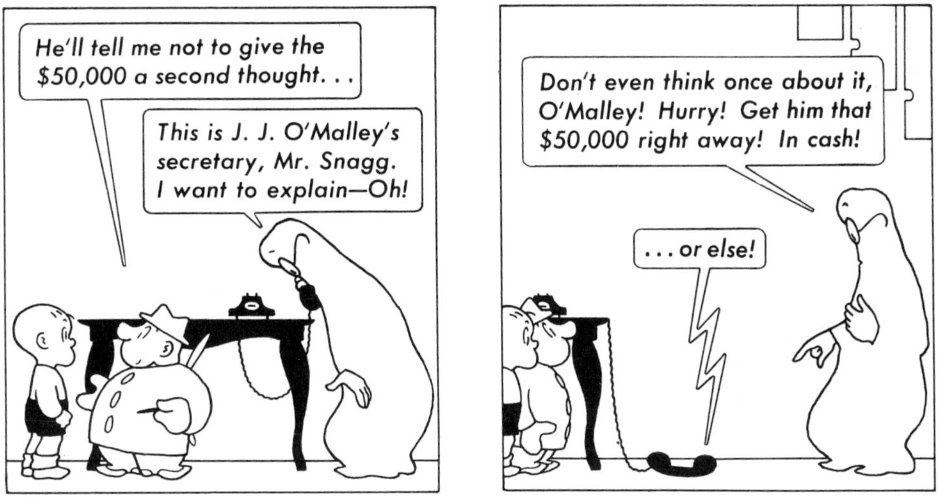
He'll tell me not to give the $50,000 a second thought. . .
This is J. J. O'Malley's secretary, Mr. Snagg. I want to explain—Oh!
Don't even think once about it, O'Malley! Hurry! Get him that $50,000 right away! In cash!
. . . or else!

THE NEXT DAY

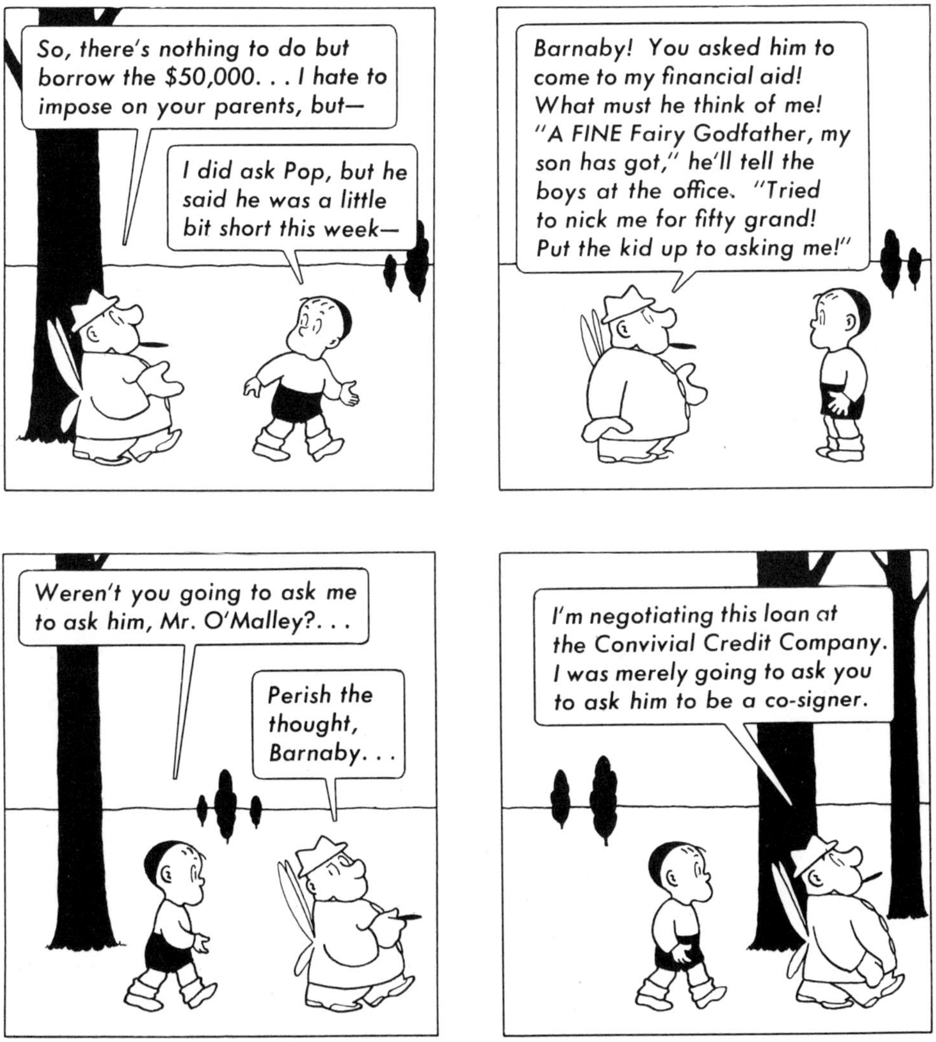
So, there's nothing to do but borrow the $50,000. . . I hate to impose on your parents, but—
I did ask Pop, but he said he was a little bit short this week—
Barnaby! You asked him to come to my financial aid! What must he think of me! "A FINE Fairy Godfather, my son has got," he'll tell the boys at the office. "Tried to nick me for fifty grand! Put the kid up to asking me!"
Weren't you going to ask me to ask him, Mr. O'Malley?. . .
Perish the thought, Barnaby. . .
I'm negotiating this loan at the Convivial Credit Company. I was merely going to ask you to ask him to be a co-signer.

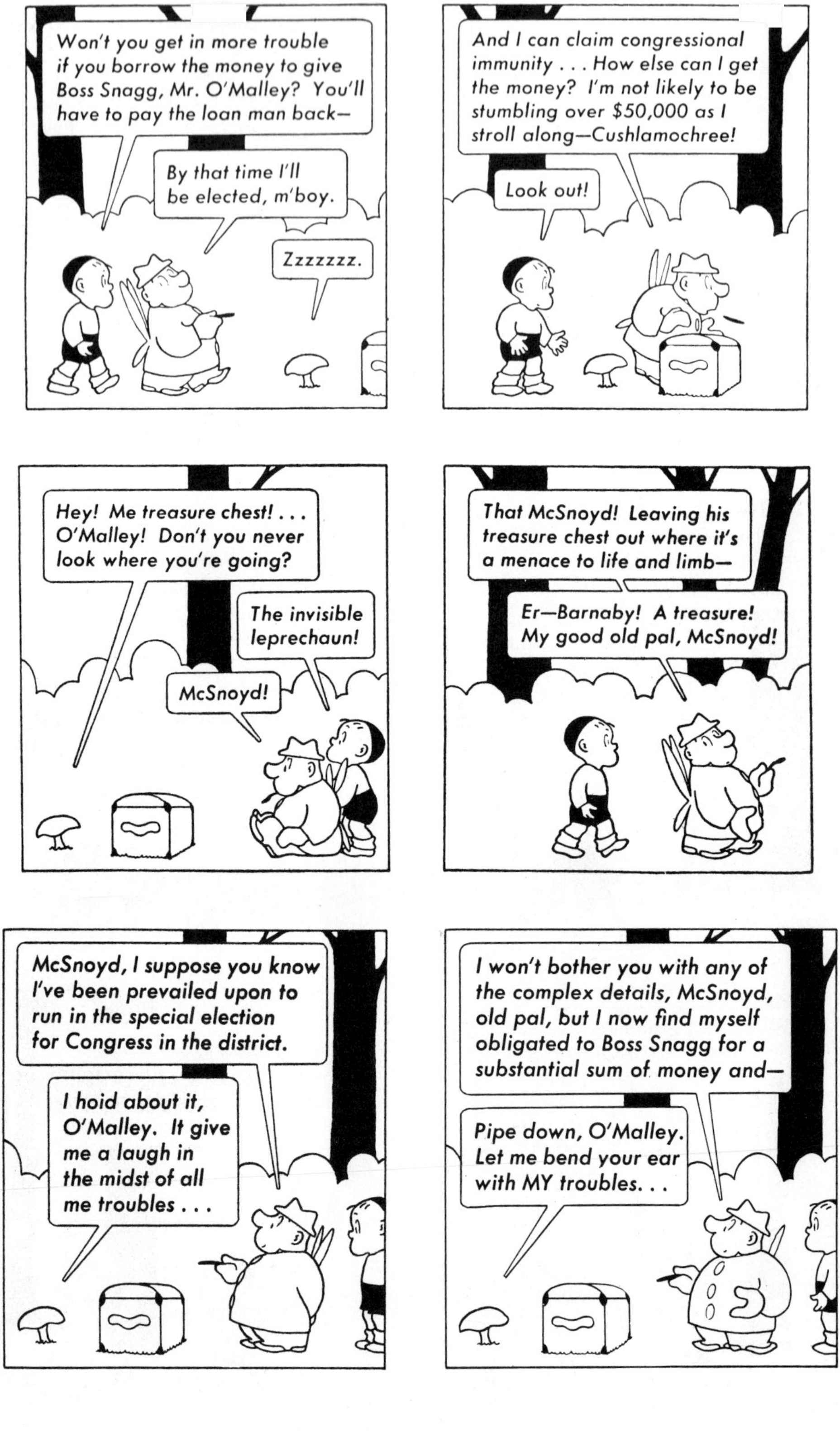
Won't you get in more trouble if you borrow the money to give Boss Snagg, Mr. O'Malley? You'll have to pay the loan man back—
By that time I'll be elected, m'boy.
Zzzzzzz.
And I can claim congressional immunity . . . How else can I get the money? I'm not likely to be stumbling over $50,000 as I stroll along—Cushlamochree!
Look out!
Hey! Me treasure chest! . . . O'Malley! Don't you never look where you're going?
The invisible leprechaun!
McSnoyd!
That McSnoyd! Leaving his treasure chest out where it's a menace to life and limb—
Er—Barnaby! A treasure! My good old pal, McSnoyd!
McSnoyd, I suppose you know I've been prevailed upon to run in the special election for Congress in the district.
I hoid about it, O'Malley. It give me a laugh in the midst of all me troubles . . .
I won't bother you with any of the complex details, McSnoyd, old pal, but I now find myself obligated to Boss Snagg for a substantial sum of money and—
Pipe down, O'Malley. Let me bend your ear with MY troubles. . .

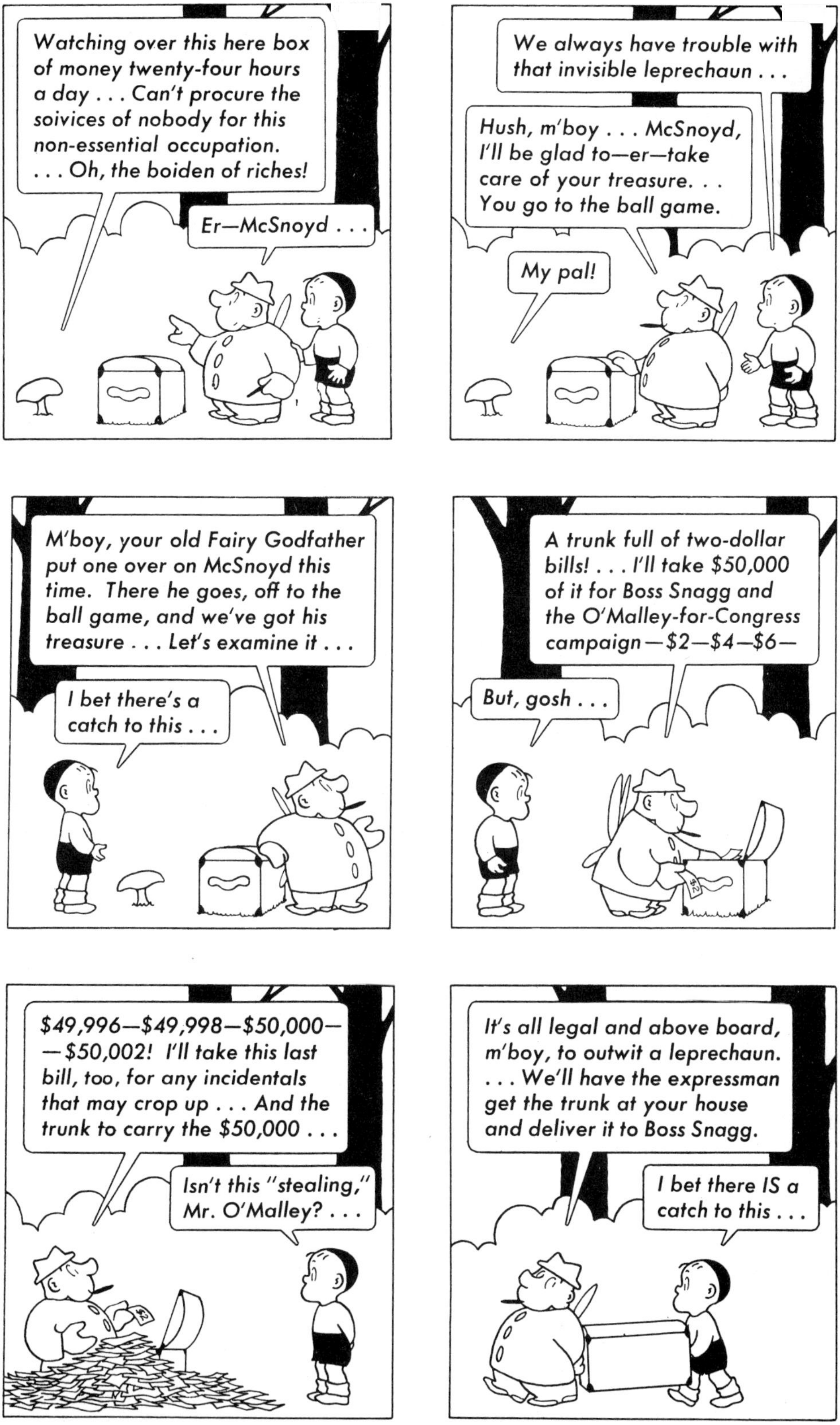
Watching over this here box of money twenty-four hours a day . . . Can't procure the soivices of nobody for this non-essential occupation. . . . Oh, the boiden of riches!
Er—McSnoyd . . .
We always have trouble with that invisible leprechaun . . .
Hush, m'boy . . . McSnoyd, I'll be glad to—er—take care of your treasure. . . You go to the ball game.
My pal!
M'boy, your old Fairy Godfather put one over on McSnoyd this time. There he goes, off to the ball game, and we've got his treasure . . . Let's examine it . . .
I bet there's a catch to this . . .
A trunk full of two-dollar bills! . . . I'll take $50,000 of it for Boss Snagg and the O'Malley-for-Congress campaign—$2—$4—$6—
But, gosh . . .
$49,996—$49,998—$50,000—
—$50,002! I'll take this last bill, too, for any incidentals that may crop up . . . And the trunk to carry the $50,000 . . .
Isn't this "stealing," Mr. O'Malley? . . .
It's all legal and above board, m'boy, to outwit a leprechaun. . . . We'll have the expressman get the trunk at your house and deliver it to Boss Snagg.
I bet there IS a catch to this . . .

Boss. The expressman left a trunk . . . $1.22, collect. I paid for it . . . But it's full of two-dollar bills! And—

O'Malley finally has kicked in with his "campaign" money!

You're our candidate for city treasurer, aren't you, Muggins? Can you count?

Sure, Boss. —One—Two— Three—Four—

Fine. Count those bills and see if there's $50,000 . . . Then put a thousand in the black bag in the safe to pay the boys on election day and lock the rest up in my safe deposit vault . . .

Okay, Boss. But . . .

But what, Muggins?

I was just going to say, ain't two-dollar bills kind of unlucky?

SOON AFTERWARD

Now that Boss Snagg and I are again on amicable terms he'll loose an avalanche of O'Malley-for-Congress ads, handbills, posters, banners—

Here's Jane . . .

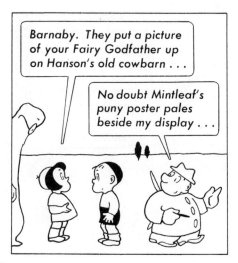

Barnaby. They put a picture of your Fairy Godfather up on Hanson's old cowbarn . . .

No doubt Mintleaf's puny poster pales beside my display . . .

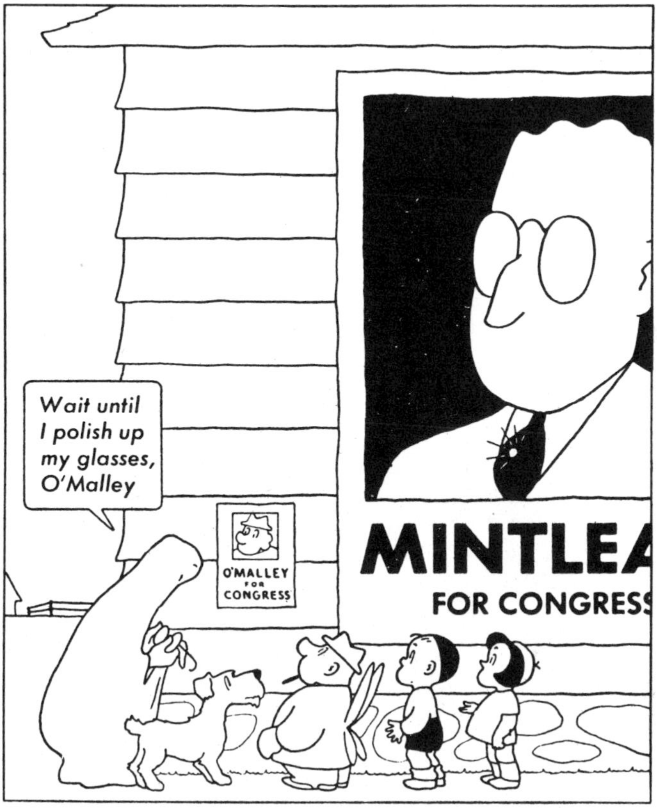
Wait until I polish up my glasses, O'Malley
O'MALLEY FOR CONGRESS
MINTLEA
FOR CONGRESS

EPISODE EIGHT

The Election

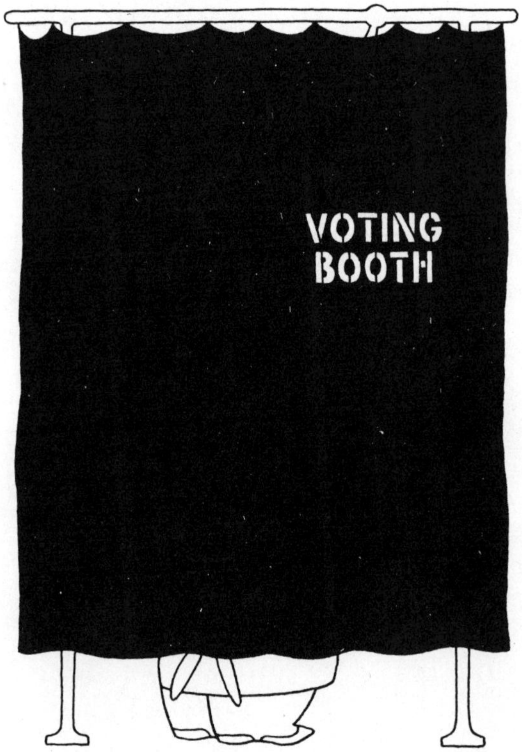
VOTING
BOOTH

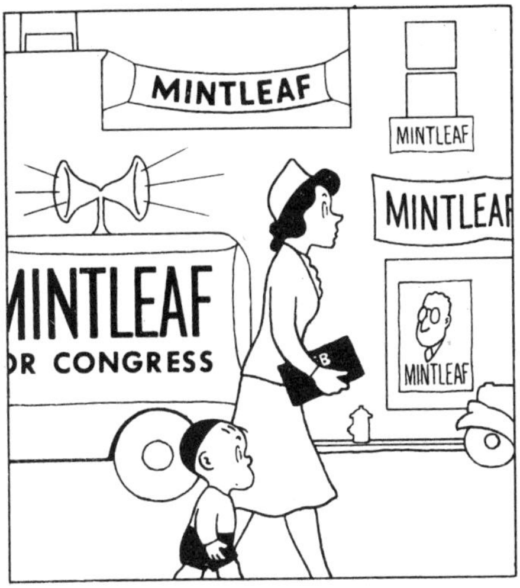
MINTLEAF
MINTLEAF
MINTLEAF
MINTLEAF
FOR CONGRESS
MINTLEAF
EB

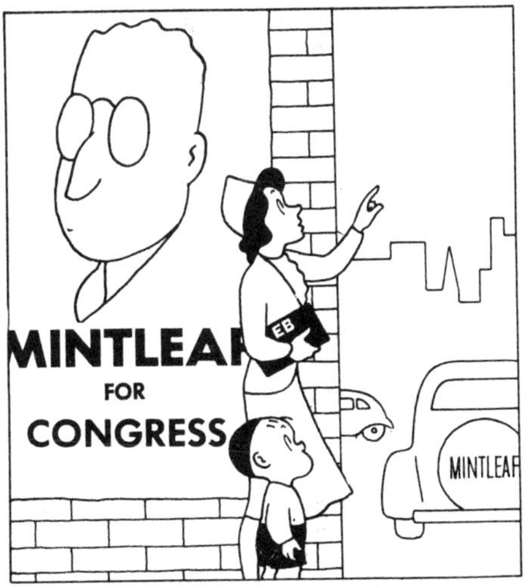
MINTLEAF
FOR
CONGRESS
EB
MINTLEAF

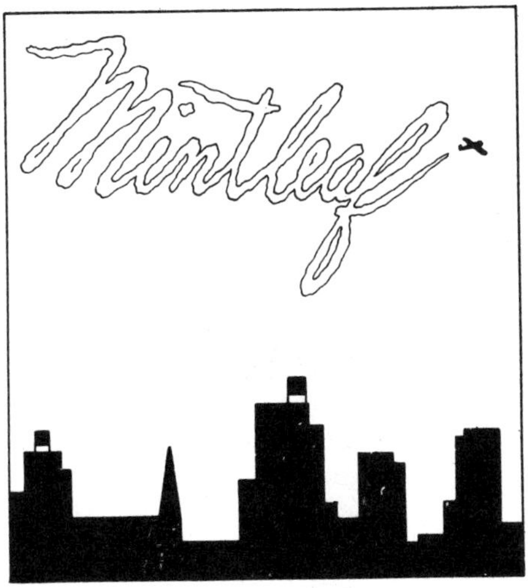
Mintleaf

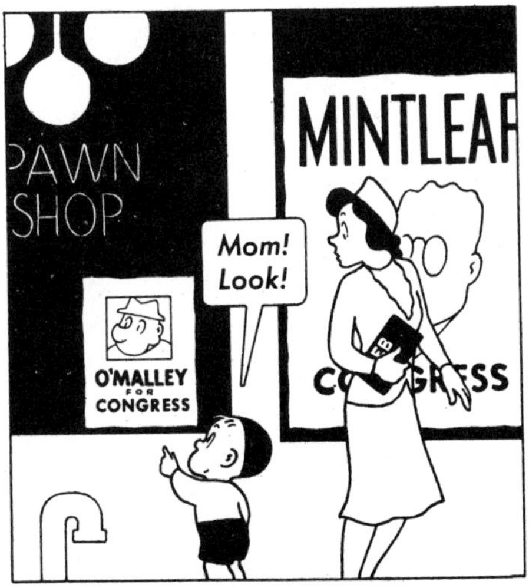
PAWN
SHOP
MINTLEAF
O'MALLEY
FOR
CONGRESS
Mom!
Look!
EB

ONE EVENING

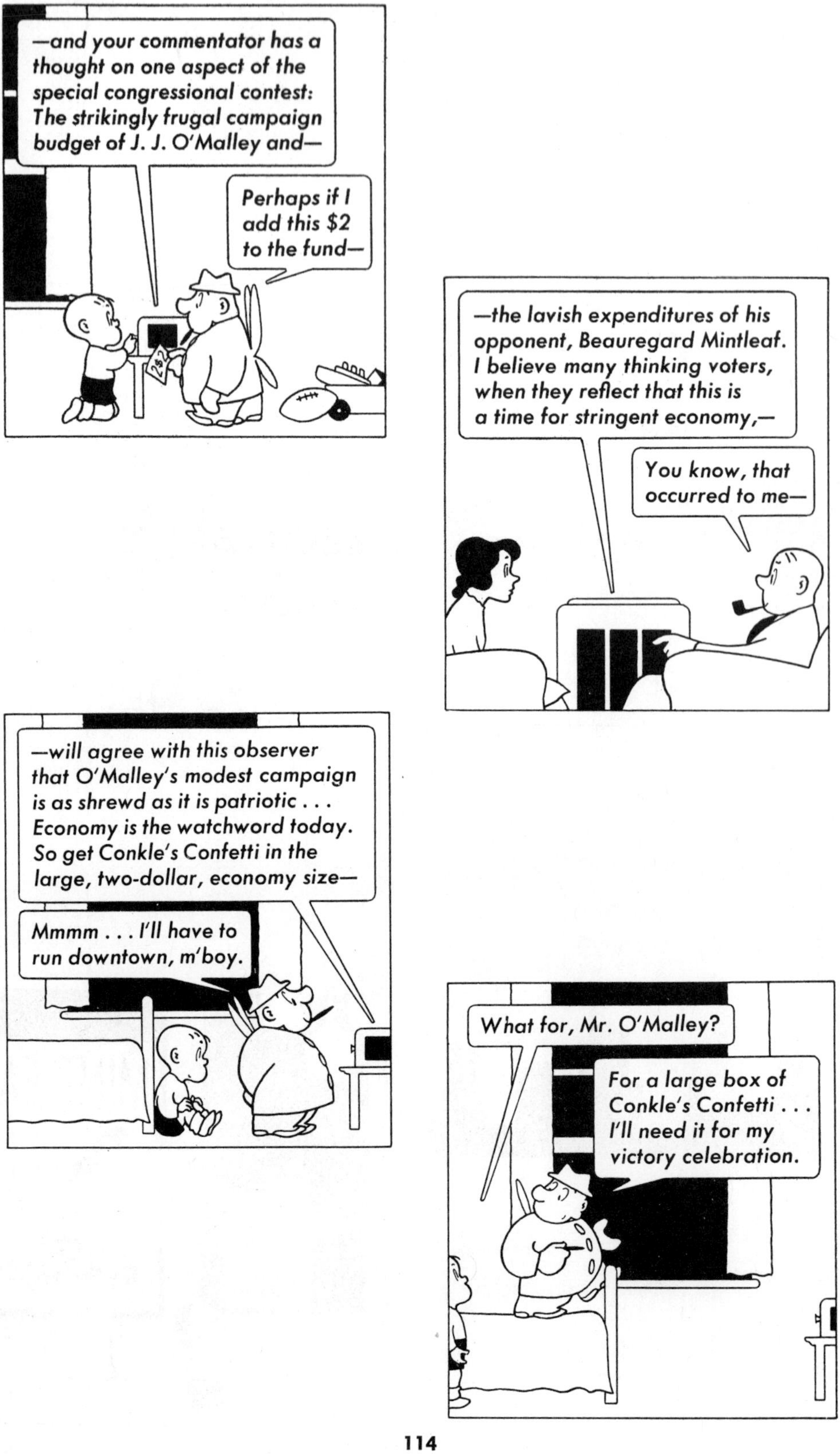
—and your commentator has a thought on one aspect of the special congressional contest: The strikingly frugal campaign budget of J. J. O'Malley and—
Perhaps if I add this $2 to the fund—
$2
—the lavish expenditures of his opponent, Beauregard Mintleaf. I believe many thinking voters, when they reflect that this is a time for stringent economy,—
You know, that occurred to me—
—will agree with this observer that O'Malley's modest campaign is as shrewd as it is patriotic . . . Economy is the watchword today. So get Conkle's Confetti in the large, two-dollar, economy size—
Mmmm . . . I'll have to run downtown, m'boy.
What for, Mr. O'Malley?
For a large box of Conkle's Confetti . . . I'll need it for my victory celebration.

THE NEXT NIGHT

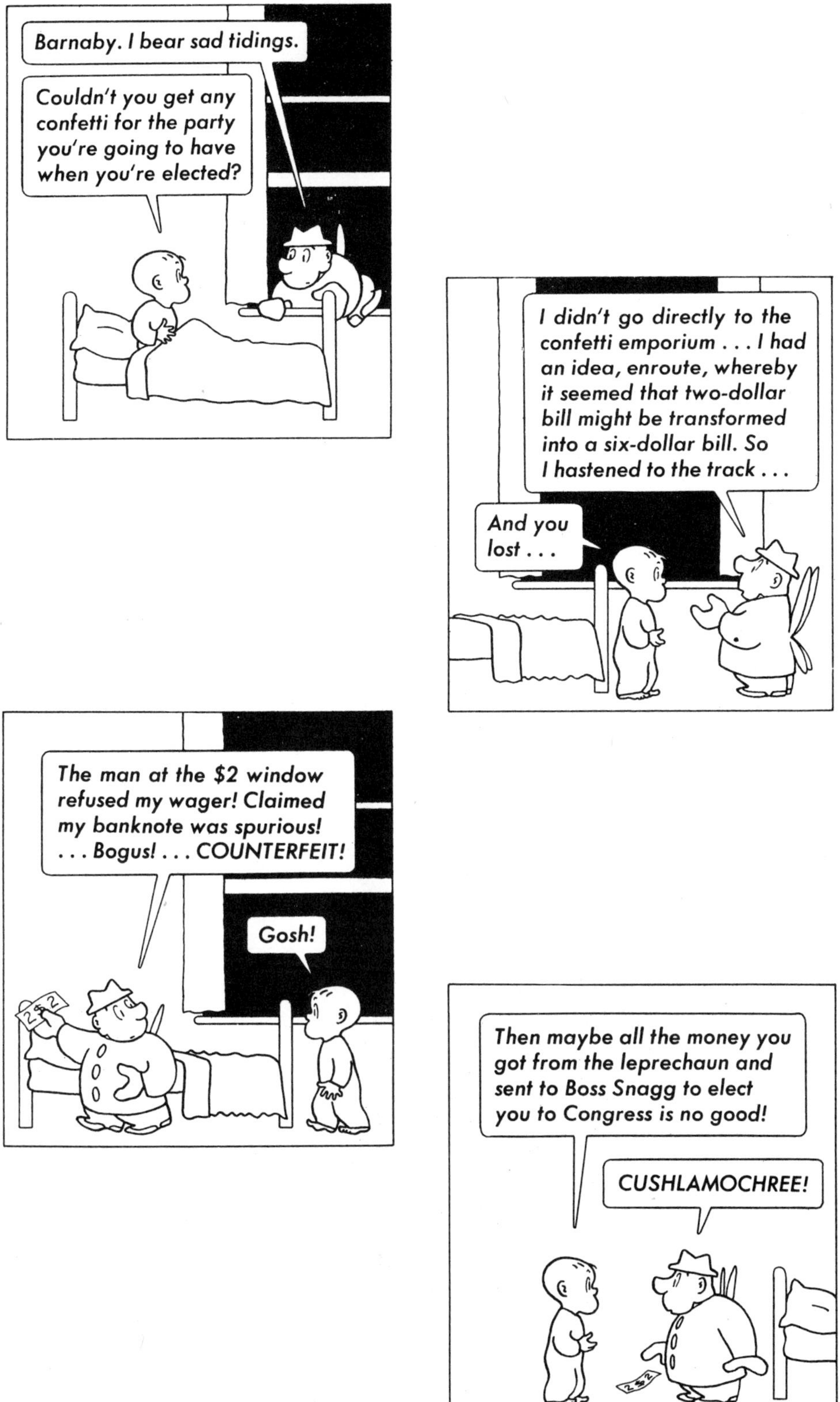
Barnaby. I bear sad tidings.
Couldn't you get any confetti for the party you're going to have when you're elected?
I didn't go directly to the confetti emporium . . . I had an idea, enroute, whereby it seemed that two-dollar bill might be transformed into a six-dollar bill. So I hastened to the track . . .
And you lost . . .
The man at the $2 window refused my wager! Claimed my banknote was spurious! . . . Bogus! . . . COUNTERFEIT!
Gosh!
Then maybe all the money you got from the leprechaun and sent to Boss Snagg to elect you to Congress is no good!
CUSHLAMOCHREE!

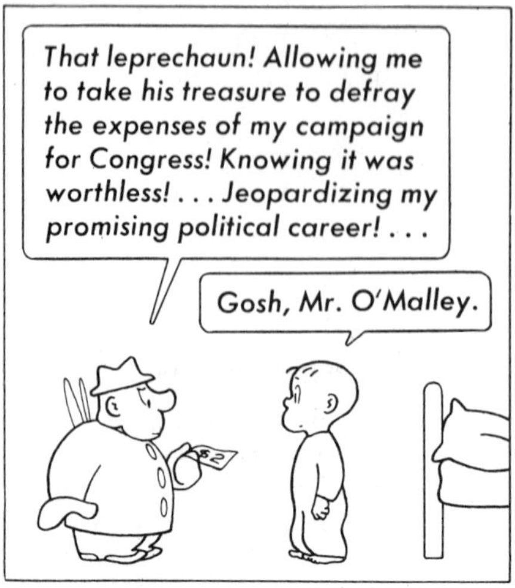
That leprechaun! Allowing me to take his treasure to defray the expenses of my campaign for Congress! Knowing it was worthless! . . . Jeopardizing my promising political career! . . .
Gosh, Mr. O'Malley.

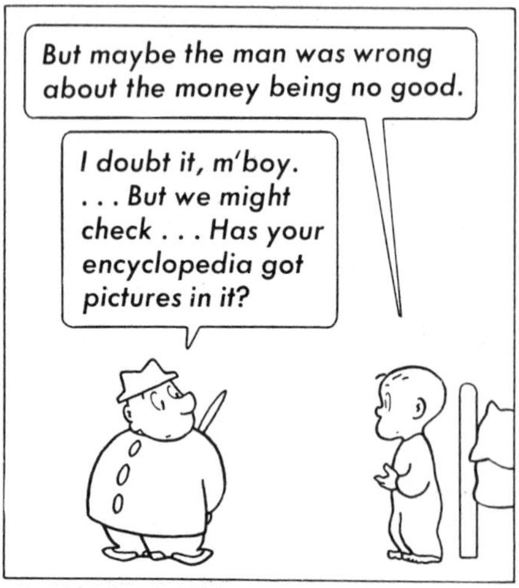
But maybe the man was wrong about the money being no good.
I doubt it, m'boy. . . . But we might check . . . Has your encyclopedia got pictures in it?

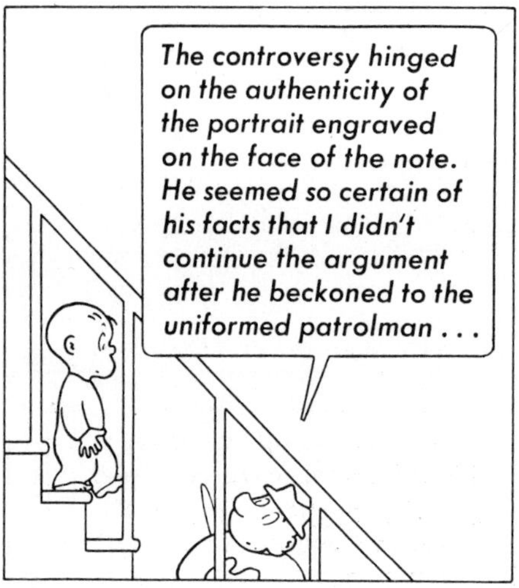
The controversy hinged on the authenticity of the portrait engraved on the face of the note. He seemed so certain of his facts that I didn't continue the argument after he beckoned to the uniformed patrolman . . .

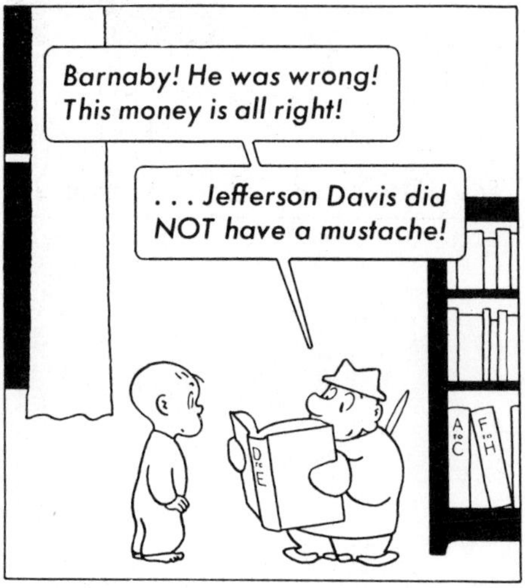
Barnaby! He was wrong! This money is all right!
. . . Jefferson Davis did NOT have a mustache!

E MORNING

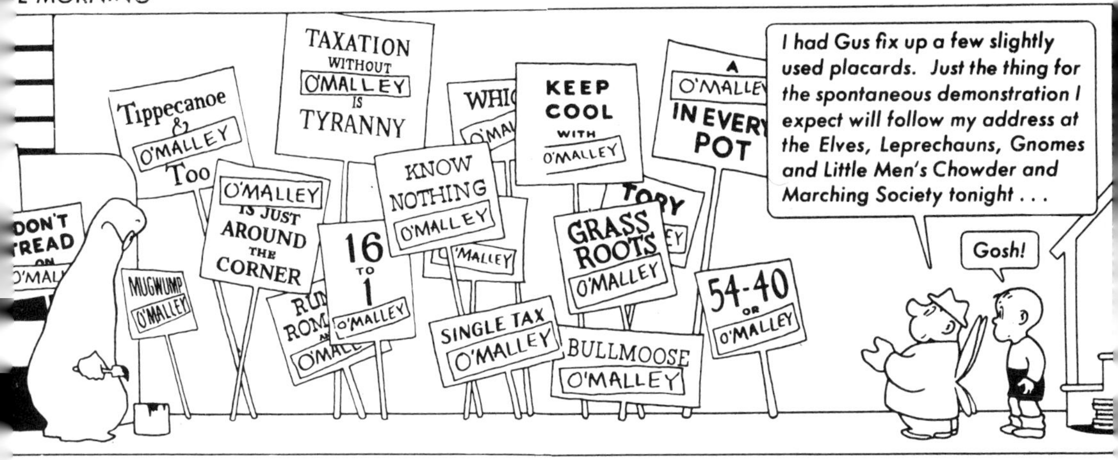
TAXATION WITHOUT O'MALLEY IS TYRANNY
Tippecanoe & O'MALLEY Too
KEEP COOL WITH O'MALLEY
KNOW NOTHING O'MALLEY
O'MALLEY IS JUST AROUND THE CORNER
MUGWUMP O'MALLEY
16 TO 1 O'MALLEY
GRASS ROOTS O'MALLEY
SINGLE TAX O'MALLEY
BULLMOOSE O'MALLEY
54-40 OR O'MALLEY
I had Gus fix up a few slightly used placards. Just the thing for the spontaneous demonstration I expect will follow my address at the Elves, Leprechauns, Gnomes and Little Men's Chowder and Marching Society tonight . . .
Gosh!

ONE AFTERNOON

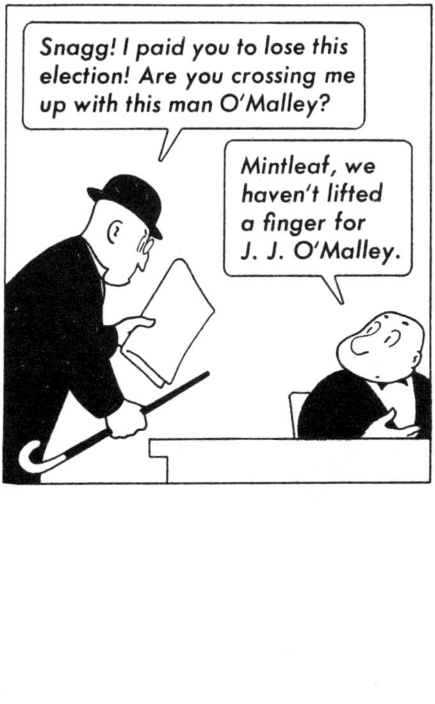
Snagg! I paid you to lose this election! Are you crossing me up with this man O'Malley?
Mintleaf, we haven't lifted a finger for J. J. O'Malley.

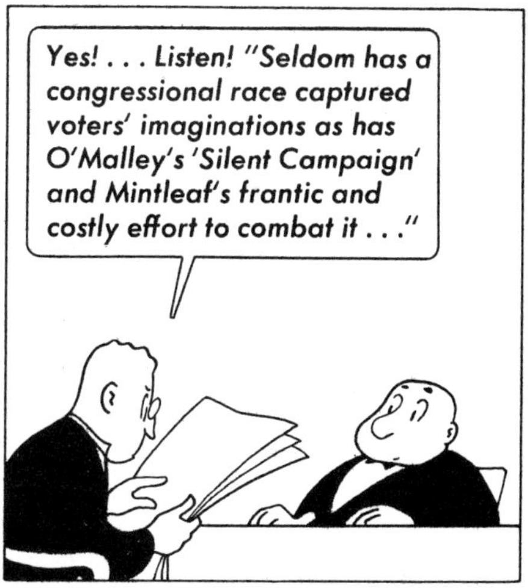
Yes! . . . Listen! "Seldom has a congressional race captured voters' imaginations as has O'Malley's 'Silent Campaign' and Mintleaf's frantic and costly effort to combat it . . ."

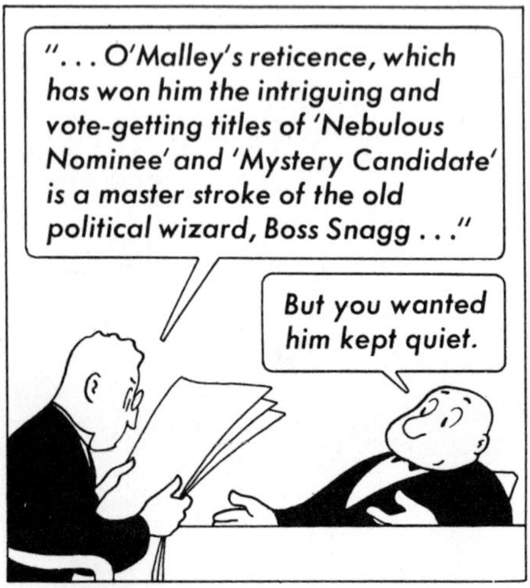
". . . O'Malley's reticence, which has won him the intriguing and vote-getting titles of 'Nebulous Nominee' and 'Mystery Candidate' is a master stroke of the old political wizard, Boss Snagg . . ."
But you wanted him kept quiet.

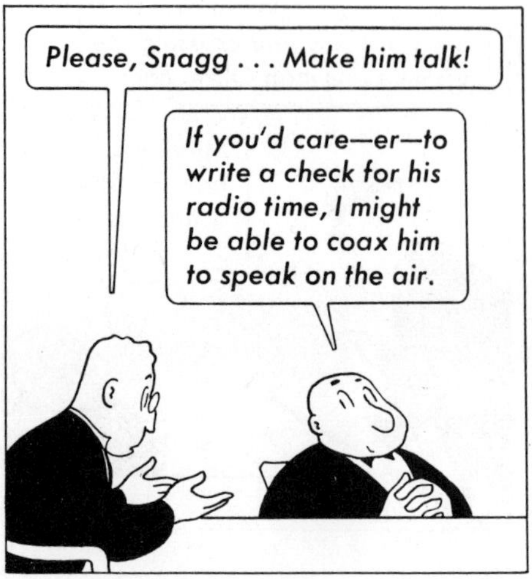
Please, Snagg . . . Make him talk!
If you'd care—er—to write a check for his radio time, I might be able to coax him to speak on the air.

THE NEXT MORNING

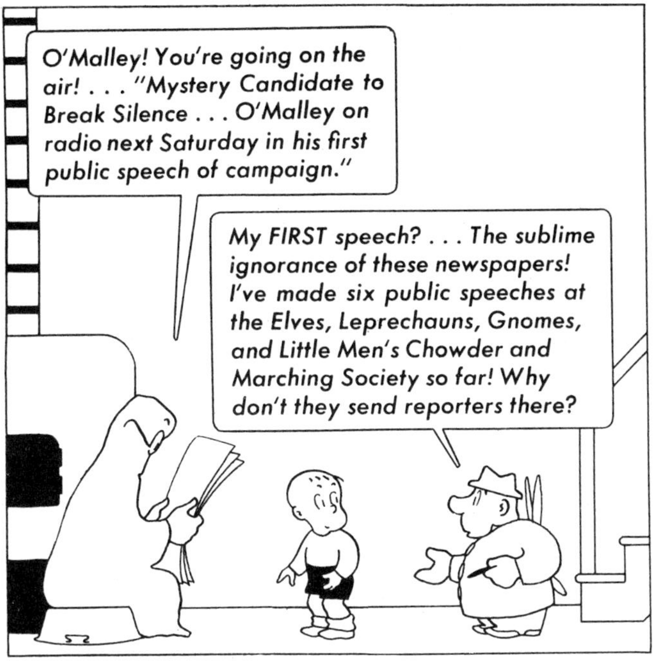
O'Malley! You're going on the air! . . . "Mystery Candidate to Break Silence . . . O'Malley on radio next Saturday in his first public speech of campaign."
My FIRST speech? . . . The sublime ignorance of these newspapers! I've made six public speeches at the Elves, Leprechauns, Gnomes, and Little Men's Chowder and Marching Society so far! Why don't they send reporters there?

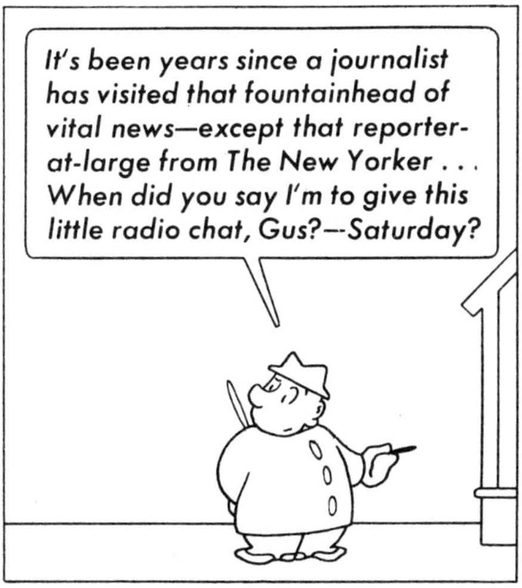
It's been years since a journalist has visited that fountainhead of vital news—except that reporter-at-large from The New Yorker . . . When did you say I'm to give this little radio chat, Gus?—Saturday?

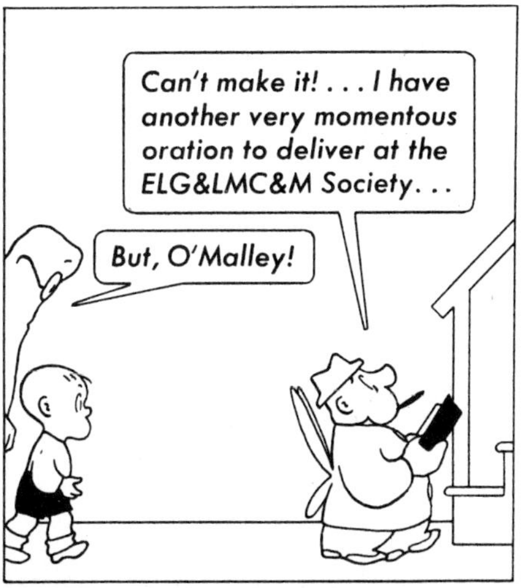
Can't make it! . . . I have another very momentous oration to deliver at the ELG&LMC&M Society. . .
But, O'Malley!

SOME TIME LATER

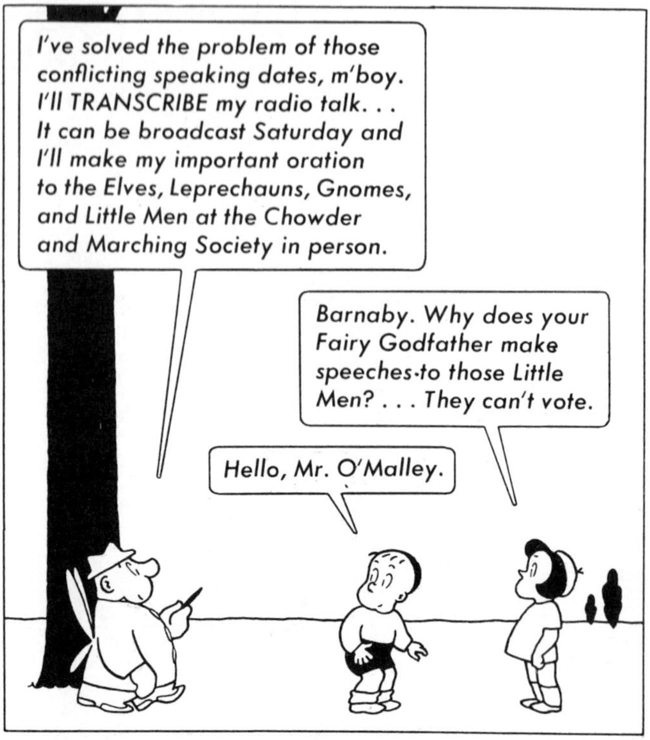
I've solved the problem of those conflicting speaking dates, m'boy. I'll TRANSCRIBE my radio talk. . . It can be broadcast Saturday and I'll make my important oration to the Elves, Leprechauns, Gnomes, and Little Men at the Chowder and Marching Society in person.
Hello, Mr. O'Malley.
Barnaby. Why does your Fairy Godfather make speeches to those Little Men? . . . They can't vote.

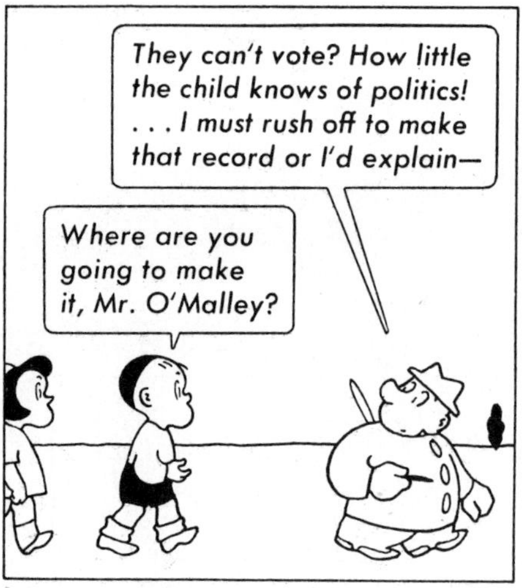
They can't vote? How little the child knows of politics! . . . I must rush off to make that record or I'd explain—
Where are you going to make it, Mr. O'Malley?

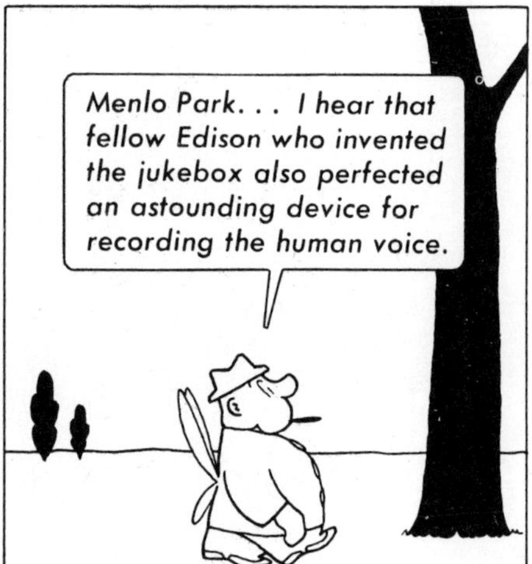
Menlo Park. . . I hear that fellow Edison who invented the jukebox also perfected an astounding device for recording the human voice.

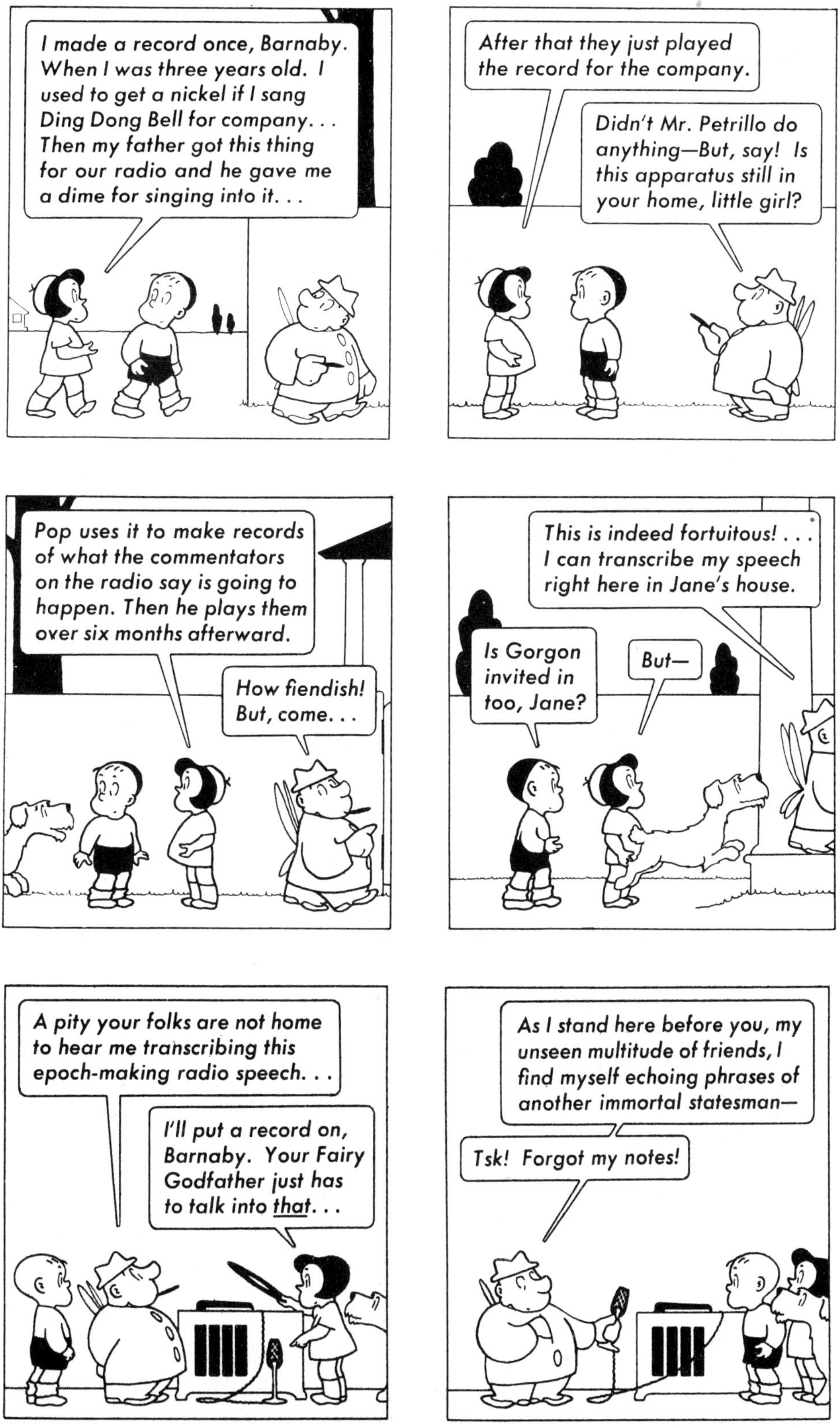
I made a record once, Barnaby. When I was three years old. I used to get a nickel if I sang Ding Dong Bell for company. . . Then my father got this thing for our radio and he gave me a dime for singing into it. . .
After that they just played the record for the company.
Didn't Mr. Petrillo do anything—But, say! Is this apparatus still in your home, little girl?
Pop uses it to make records of what the commentators on the radio say is going to happen. Then he plays them over six months afterward.
How fiendish! But, come. . .
This is indeed fortuitous! . . . I can transcribe my speech right here in Jane's house.
Is Gorgon invited in too, Jane?
But—
A pity your folks are not home to hear me transcribing this epoch-making radio speech. . .
I'll put a record on, Barnaby. Your Fairy Godfather just has to talk into that. . .
As I stand here before you, my unseen multitude of friends, I find myself echoing phrases of another immortal statesman—
Tsk! Forgot my notes!

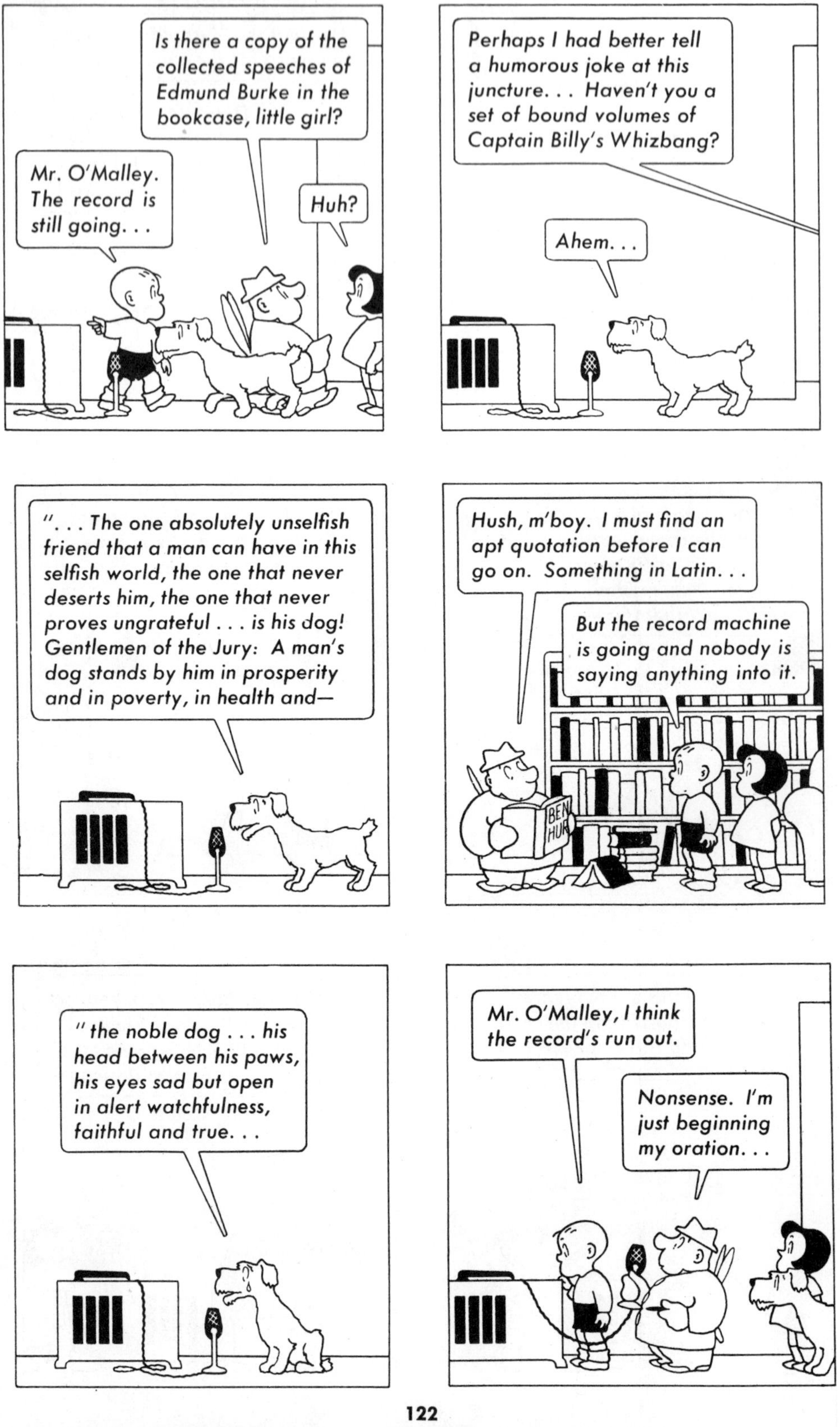
Is there a copy of the collected speeches of Edmund Burke in the bookcase, little girl?
Mr. O'Malley. The record is still going. . .
Huh?
Perhaps I had better tell a humorous joke at this juncture. . . Haven't you a set of bound volumes of Captain Billy's Whizbang?
Ahem. . .
". . . The one absolutely unselfish friend that a man can have in this selfish world, the one that never deserts him, the one that never proves ungrateful . . . is his dog! Gentlemen of the Jury: A man's dog stands by him in prosperity and in poverty, in health and—
Hush, m'boy. I must find an apt quotation before I can go on. Something in Latin. . .
But the record machine is going and nobody is saying anything into it.
BEN HUR
"the noble dog . . . his head between his paws, his eyes sad but open in alert watchfulness, faithful and true. . .
Mr. O'Malley, I think the record's run out.
Nonsense. I'm just beginning my oration. . .

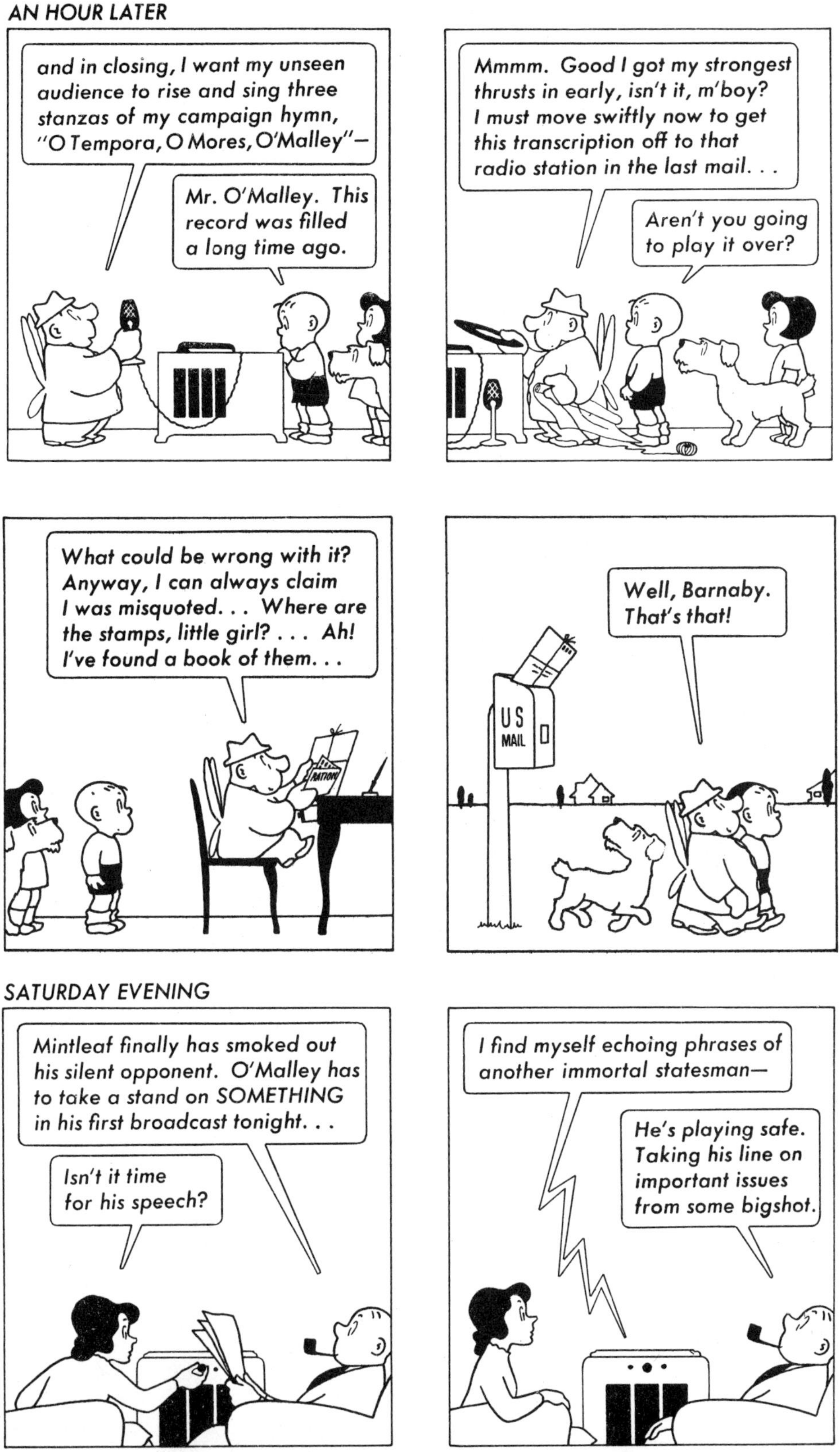
AN HOUR LATER
and in closing, I want my unseen audience to rise and sing three stanzas of my campaign hymn, "O Tempora, O Mores, O'Malley"—
Mr. O'Malley. This record was filled a long time ago.
Mmmm. Good I got my strongest thrusts in early, isn't it, m'boy? I must move swiftly now to get this transcription off to that radio station in the last mail. . .
Aren't you going to play it over?
What could be wrong with it? Anyway, I can always claim I was misquoted. . . Where are the stamps, little girl? . . . Ah! I've found a book of them. . .
RATION
Well, Barnaby. That's that!
US MAIL
SATURDAY EVENING
Mintleaf finally has smoked out his silent opponent. O'Malley has to take a stand on SOMETHING in his first broadcast tonight. . .
Isn't it time for his speech?
I find myself echoing phrases of another immortal statesman—
He's playing safe. Taking his line on important issues from some bigshot.

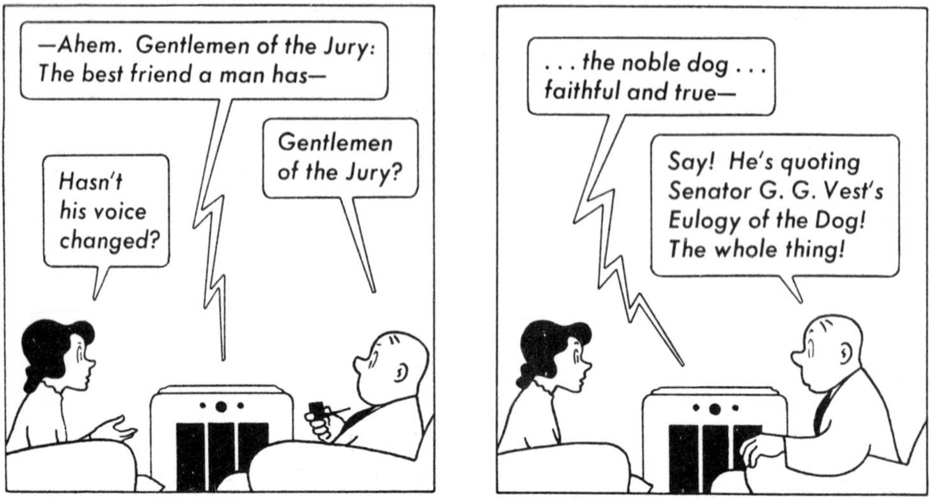
—Ahem. Gentlemen of the Jury: The best friend a man has—
Hasn't his voice changed?
Gentlemen of the Jury?
. . . the noble dog . . . faithful and true—
Say! He's quoting Senator G. G. Vest's Eulogy of the Dog! The whole thing!

THE NEXT DAY

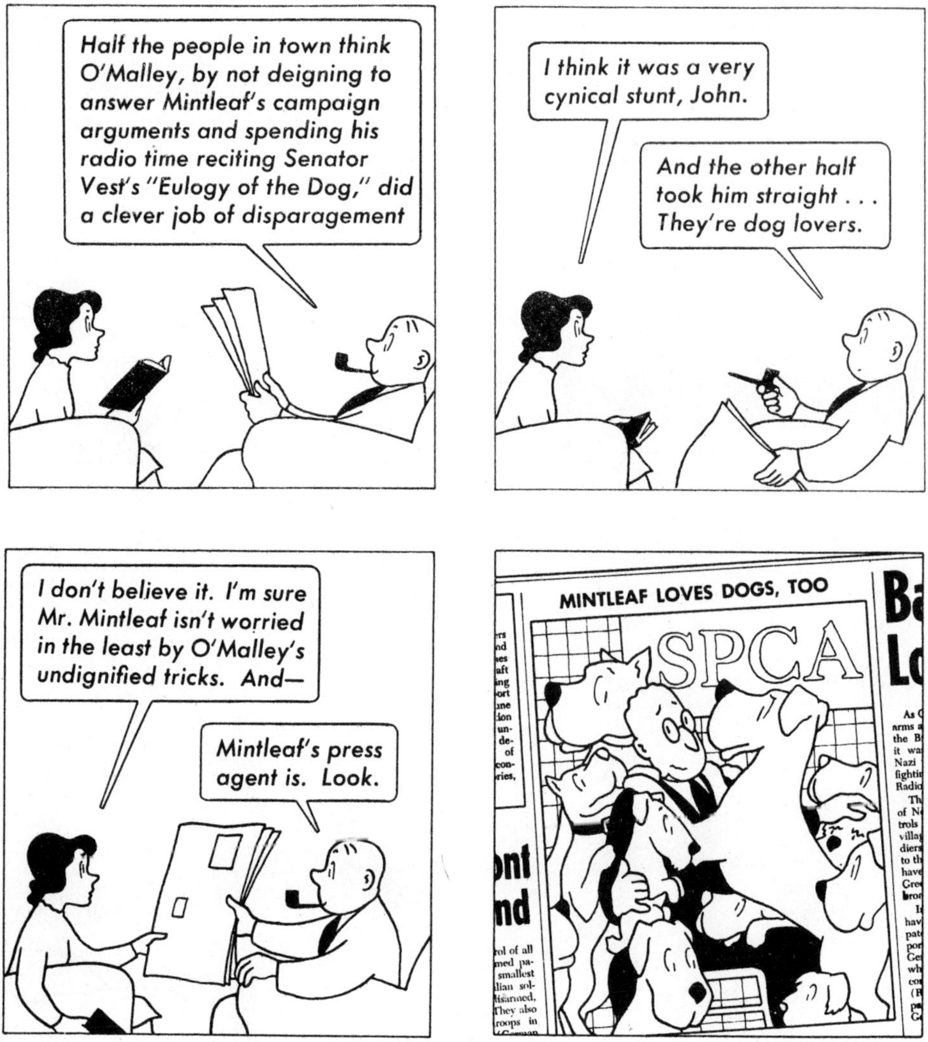
Half the people in town think O'Malley, by not deigning to answer Mintleaf's campaign arguments and spending his radio time reciting Senator Vest's "Eulogy of the Dog," did a clever job of disparagement
I think it was a very cynical stunt, John.
And the other half took him straight . . . They're dog lovers.
I don't believe it. I'm sure Mr. Mintleaf isn't worried in the least by O'Malley's undignified tricks. And—
Mintleaf's press agent is. Look.
MINTLEAF LOVES DOGS, TOO
SPCA

A DAY OR SO LATER

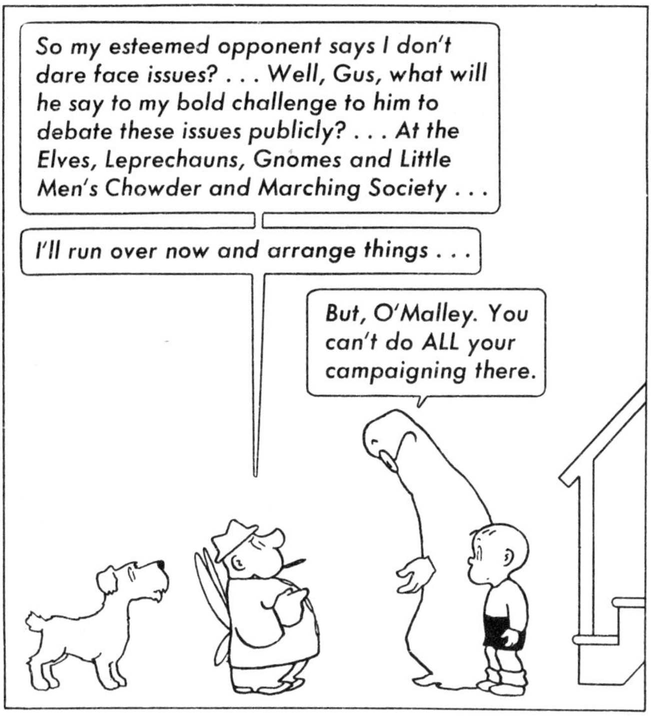
So my esteemed opponent says I don't dare face issues? . . . Well, Gus, what will he say to my bold challenge to him to debate these issues publicly? . . . At the Elves, Leprechauns, Gnomes and Little Men's Chowder and Marching Society . . .
I'll run over now and arrange things . . .
But, O'Malley. You can't do ALL your campaigning there.

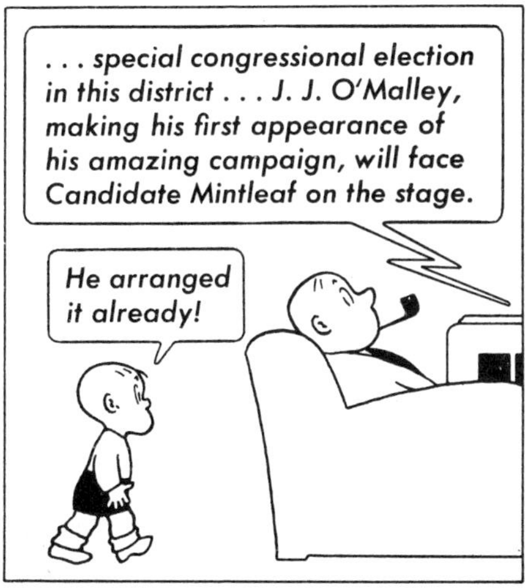
. . . special congressional election in this district . . . J. J. O'Malley, making his first appearance of his amazing campaign, will face Candidate Mintleaf on the stage.
He arranged it already!

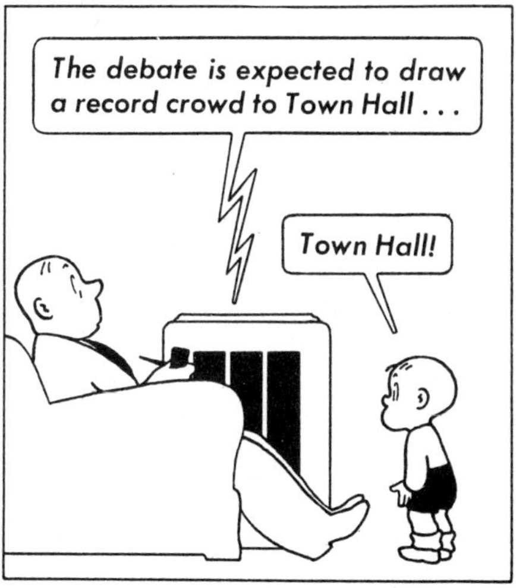
The debate is expected to draw a record crowd to Town Hall . . .
Town Hall!

But, Pop, Mr. O'Malley, my Fairy Godfather, said he was going to debate his esteemed opponent at the Little Men's Club . . . And—

Barnaby. The two candidates for Congress are having their debate at Town Hall! . . . And that imaginary pixie of yours is NOT one of the candidates!

There's one way to convince him, Ellen. Attend the debate!

Swell, Pop! But first I'll have to see Mr. O'Malley.

. . . And ask him how to get to the Little Men's Club.

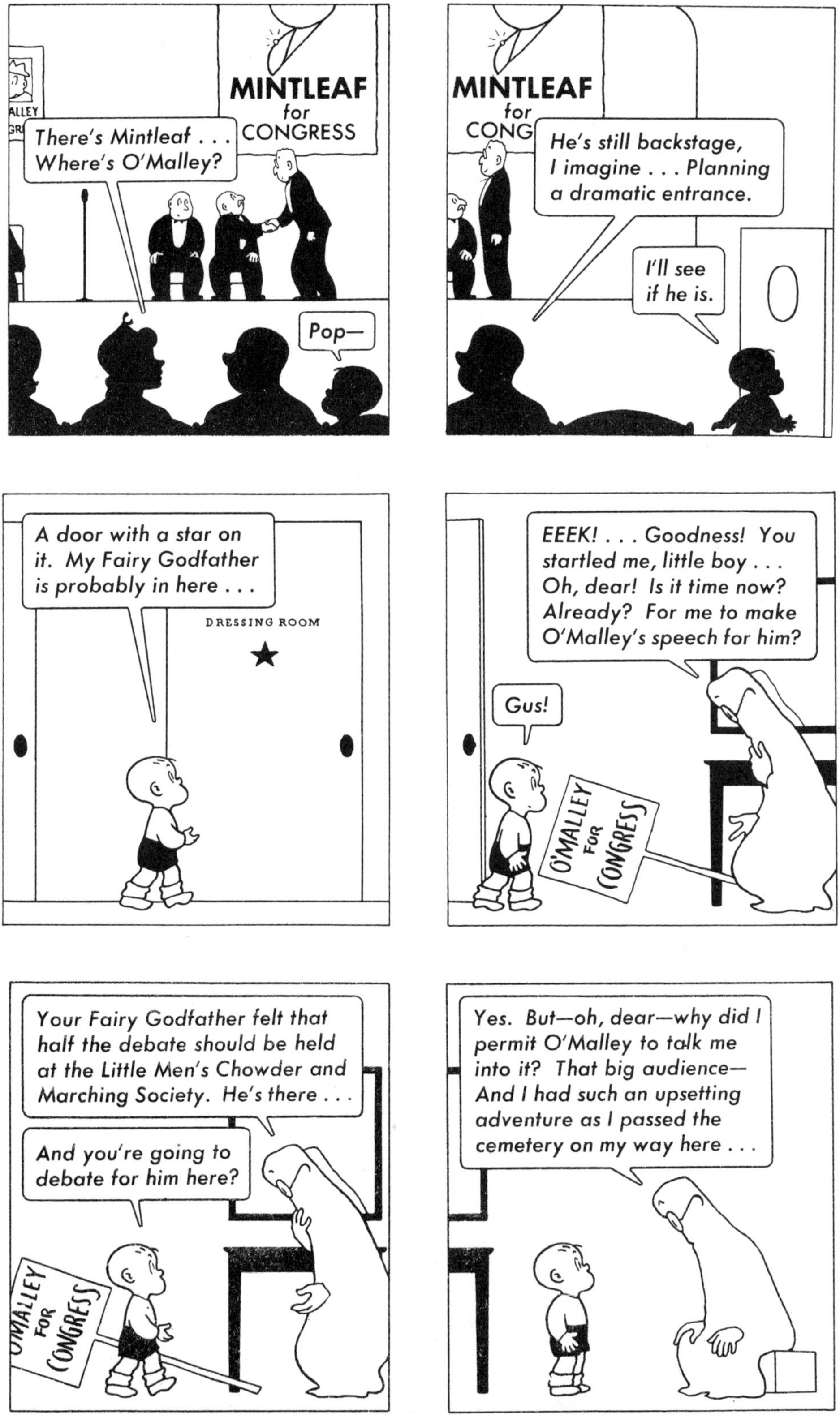
MINTLEAF
for
CONGRESS
There's Mintleaf . . .
Where's O'Malley?
Pop—
MINTLEAF
for
He's still backstage,
I imagine . . . Planning
a dramatic entrance.
I'll see
if he is.
A door with a star on
it. My Fairy Godfather
is probably in here . . .
DRESSING ROOM
EEEK! . . . Goodness! You
startled me, little boy . . .
Oh, dear! Is it time now?
Already? For me to make
O'Malley's speech for him?
Gus!
O'MALLEY
FOR
CONGRESS
Your Fairy Godfather felt that
half the debate should be held
at the Little Men's Chowder and
Marching Society. He's there . . .
And you're going to
debate for him here?
FOR
CONGRESS
Yes. But—oh, dear—why did I
permit O'Malley to talk me
into it? That big audience—
And I had such an upsetting
adventure as I passed the
cemetery on my way here . . .

Two ghoulish figures! Huddled up against the headstones and writing in big books the shape of voters' registers . . . Hideous creatures! Like Boss Snagg's ruffians! What an experience!

I can't face that audience out there tonight, little boy. I'm a bundle of nerves. I can't do it!

But, Gus, gosh! Somebody has to make a speech to get Mr. O'Malley elected!

. . . my opponent, J. J. O'Malley, has not dared come here tonight to refute my arguments because he CANNOT refute them! Nor can ANYONE refute them—

MINTLEAF for CONGRESS

Pardon. Is this seat taken? . . .

Huh?

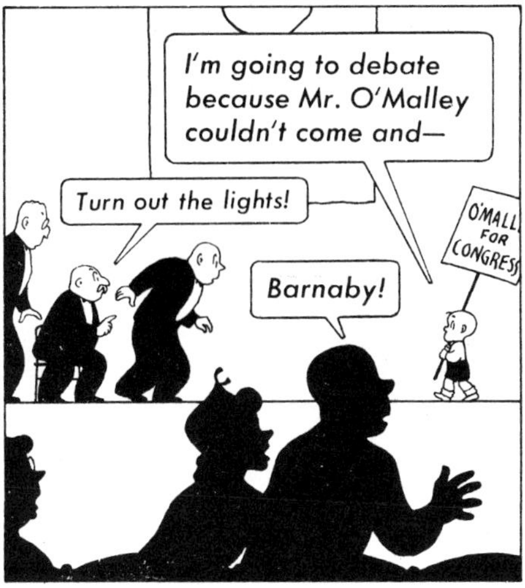
I'm going to debate because Mr. O'Malley couldn't come and—
Turn out the lights!
Barnaby!
O'MALL FOR CONGRESS

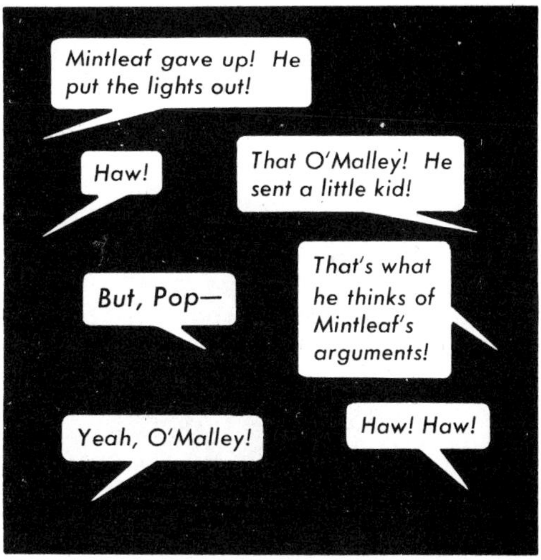
Mintleaf gave up! He put the lights out!
Haw!
That O'Malley! He sent a little kid!
But, Pop—
That's what he thinks of Mintleaf's arguments!
Yeah, O'Malley!
Haw! Haw!

JUST BEFORE ELECTION

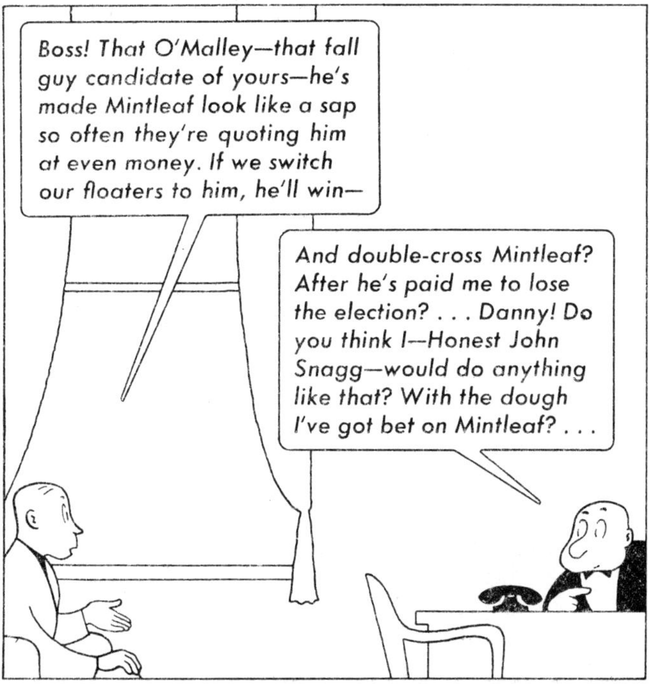
Boss! That O'Malley—that fall guy candidate of yours—he's made Mintleaf look like a sap so often they're quoting him at even money. If we switch our floaters to him, he'll win—
And double-cross Mintleaf? After he's paid me to lose the election? . . . Danny! Do you think I—Honest John Snagg—would do anything like that? With the dough I've got bet on Mintleaf? . . .

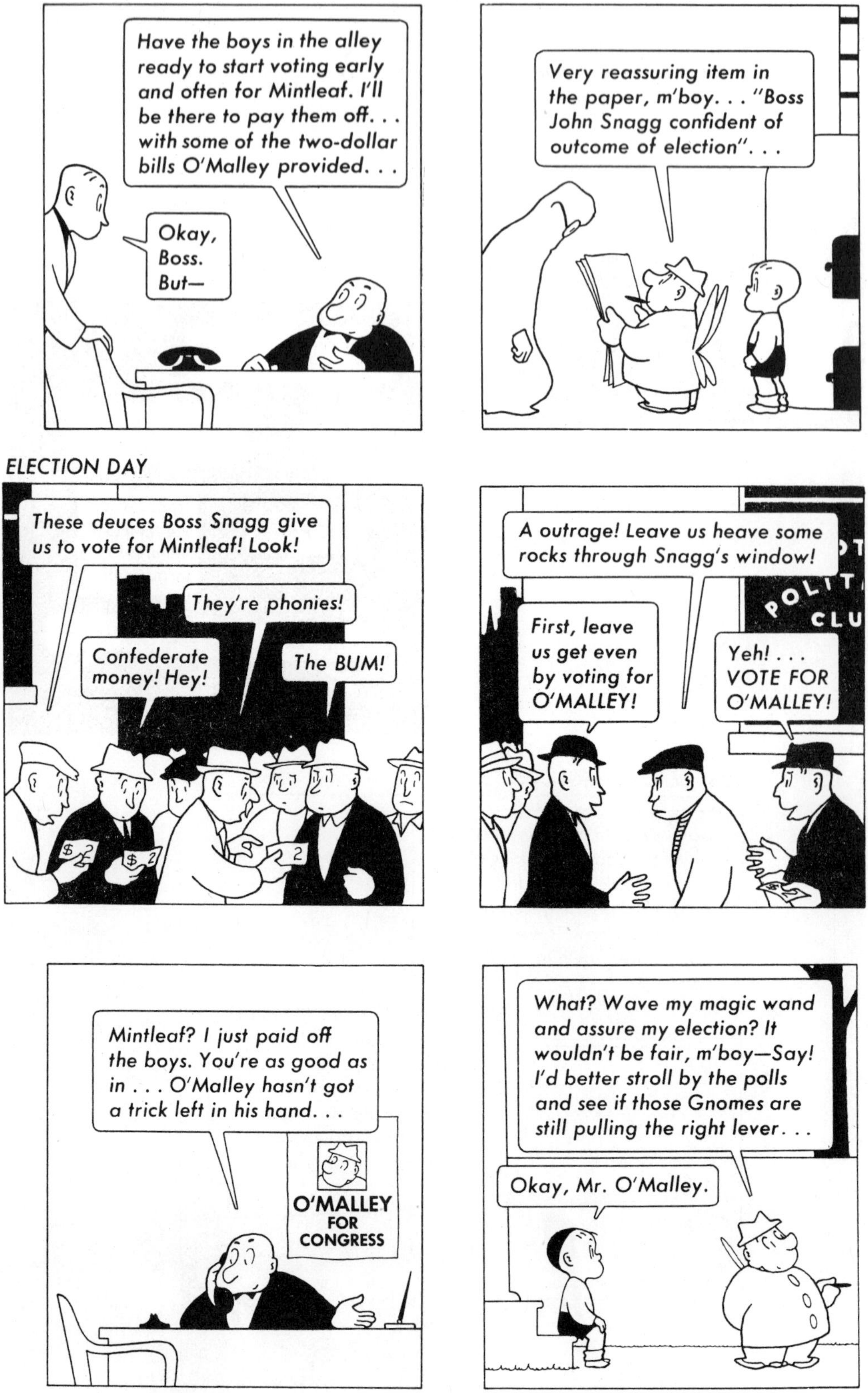
Have the boys in the alley ready to start voting early and often for Mintleaf. I'll be there to pay them off. . . with some of the two-dollar bills O'Malley provided. . .
Okay, Boss. But—
Very reassuring item in the paper, m'boy. . . "Boss John Snagg confident of outcome of election". . .
ELECTION DAY
These deuces Boss Snagg give us to vote for Mintleaf! Look!
They're phonies!
Confederate money! Hey!
The BUM!
A outrage! Leave us heave some rocks through Snagg's window!
First, leave us get even by voting for O'MALLEY!
Yeh! . . . VOTE FOR O'MALLEY!
Mintleaf? I just paid off the boys. You're as good as in . . . O'Malley hasn't got a trick left in his hand. . .
O'MALLEY FOR CONGRESS
What? Wave my magic wand and assure my election? It wouldn't be fair, m'boy—Say! I'd better stroll by the polls and see if those Gnomes are still pulling the right lever. . .
Okay, Mr. O'Malley.

THE MORNING AFTER

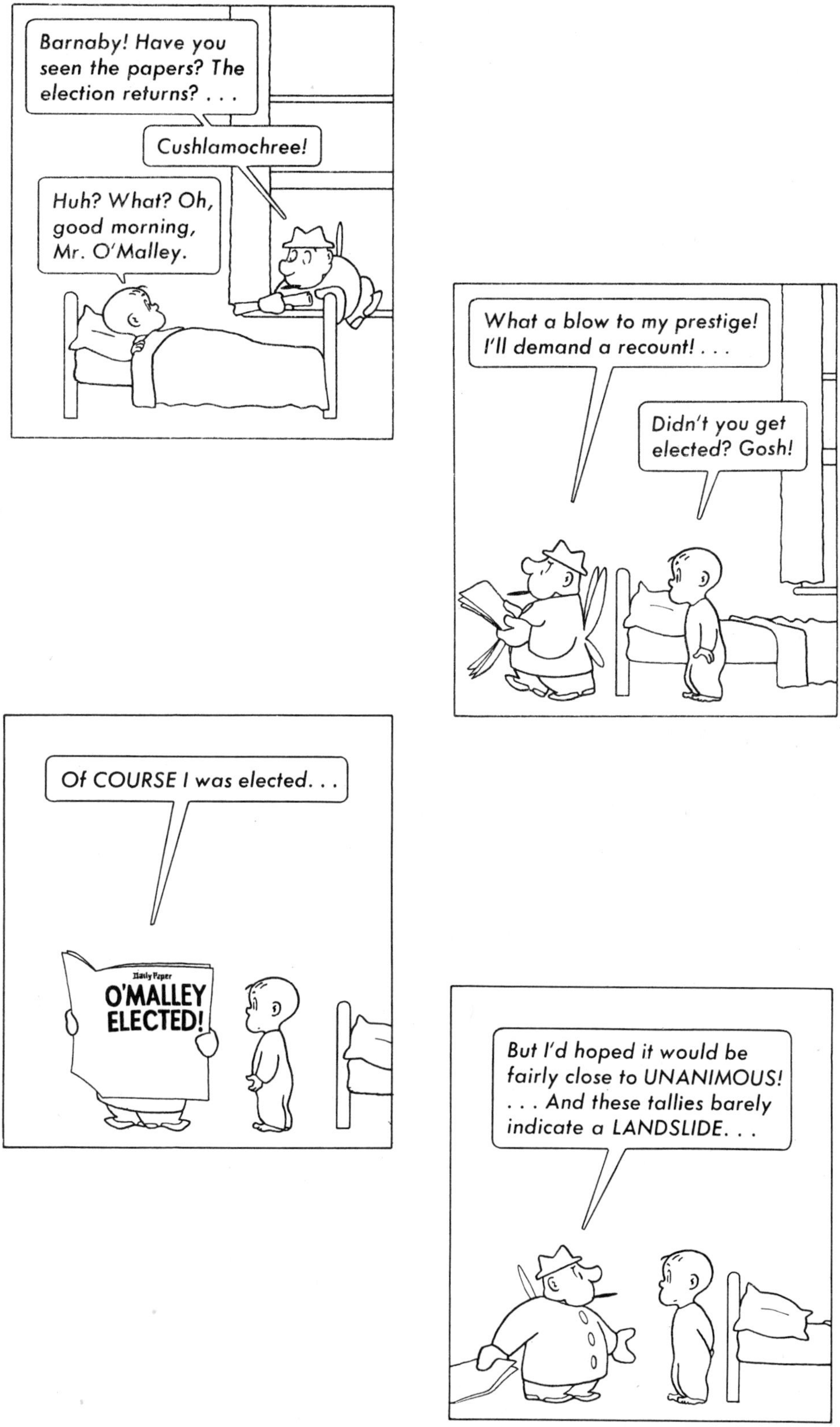
Barnaby! Have you seen the papers? The election returns? . . .
Cushlamochree!
Huh? What? Oh, good morning, Mr. O'Malley.
What a blow to my prestige! I'll demand a recount! . . .
Didn't you get elected? Gosh!
Of COURSE I was elected. . .
Daily Paper
O'MALLEY ELECTED!
But I'd hoped it would be fairly close to UNANIMOUS! . . . And these tallies barely indicate a LANDSLIDE. . .

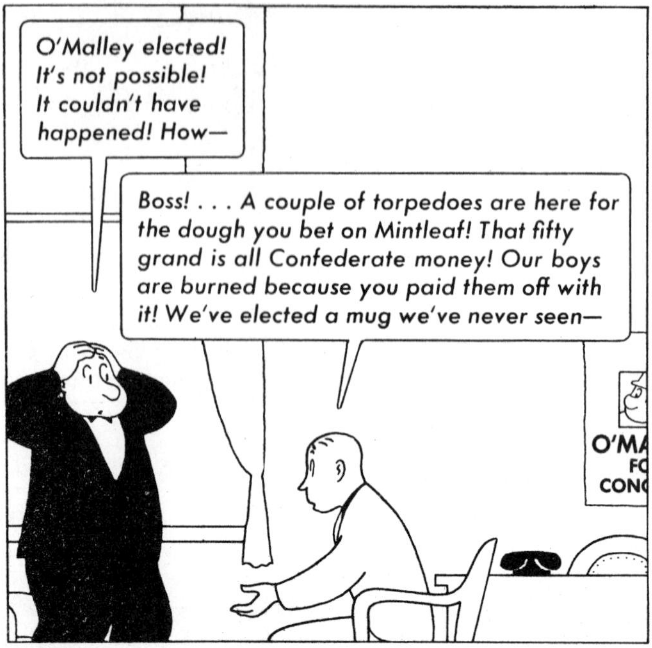
O'Malley elected! It's not possible! It couldn't have happened! How—
Boss! . . . A couple of torpedoes are here for the dough you bet on Mintleaf! That fifty grand is all Confederate money! Our boys are burned because you paid them off with it! We've elected a mug we've never seen—

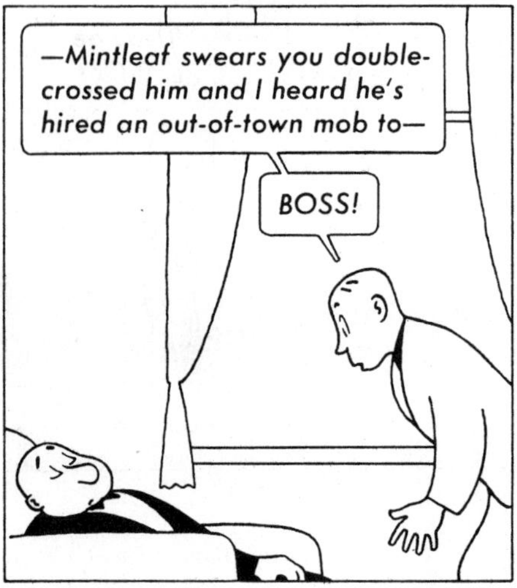
—Mintleaf swears you double-crossed him and I heard he's hired an out-of-town mob to—
BOSS!

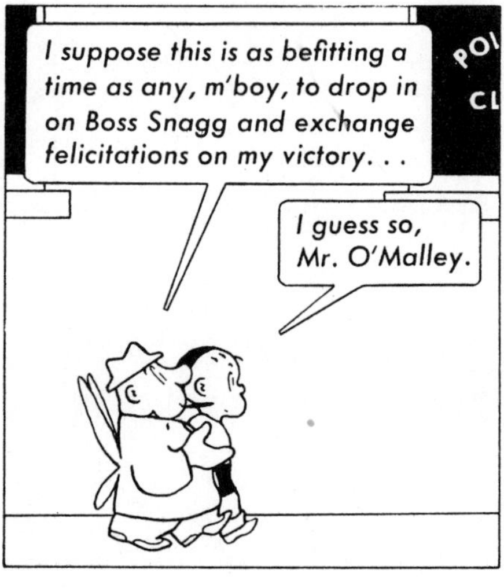
I suppose this is as befitting a time as any, m'boy, to drop in on Boss Snagg and exchange felicitations on my victory. . .
I guess so, Mr. O'Malley.

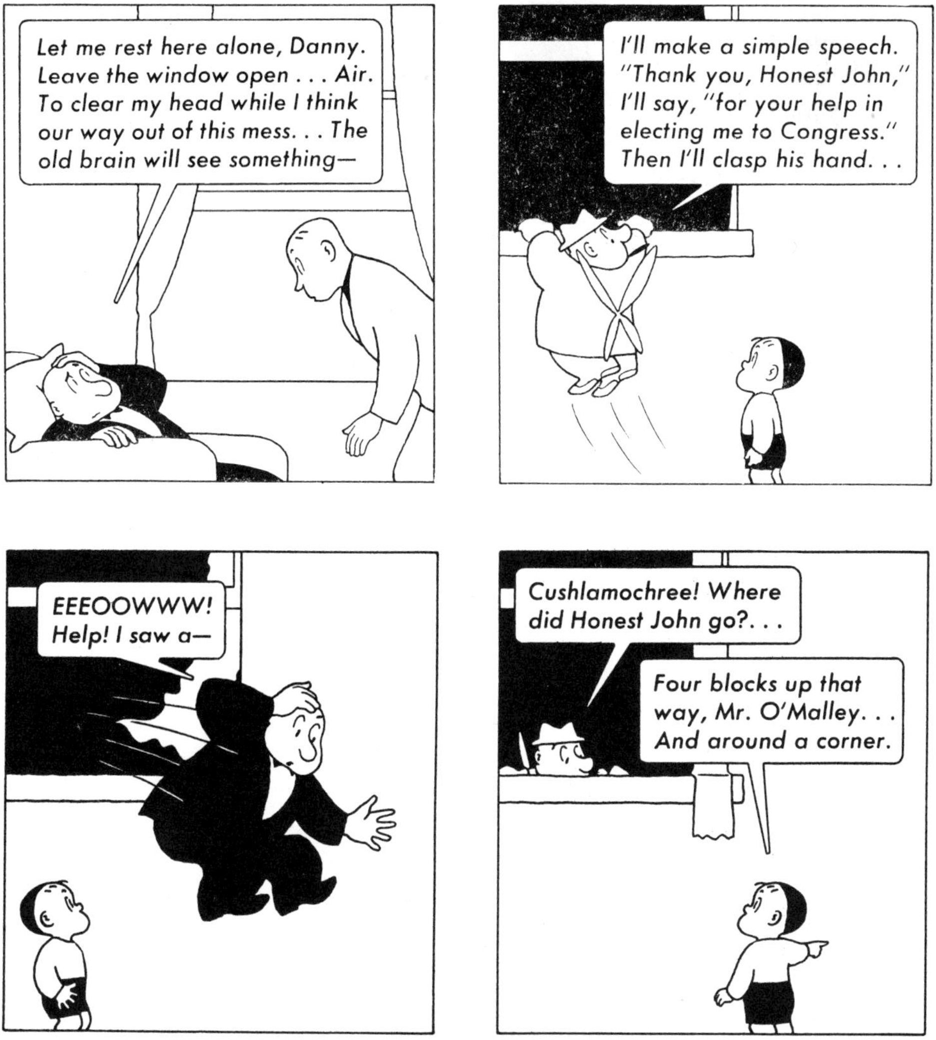
Let me rest here alone, Danny. Leave the window open . . . Air. To clear my head while I think our way out of this mess. . . The old brain will see something—
I'll make a simple speech. "Thank you, Honest John," I'll say, "for your help in electing me to Congress." Then I'll clasp his hand. . .
EEEOOWWW! Help! I saw a—
Cushlamochree! Where did Honest John go?. . .
Four blocks up that way, Mr. O'Malley. . . And around a corner.

THE NEXT DAY

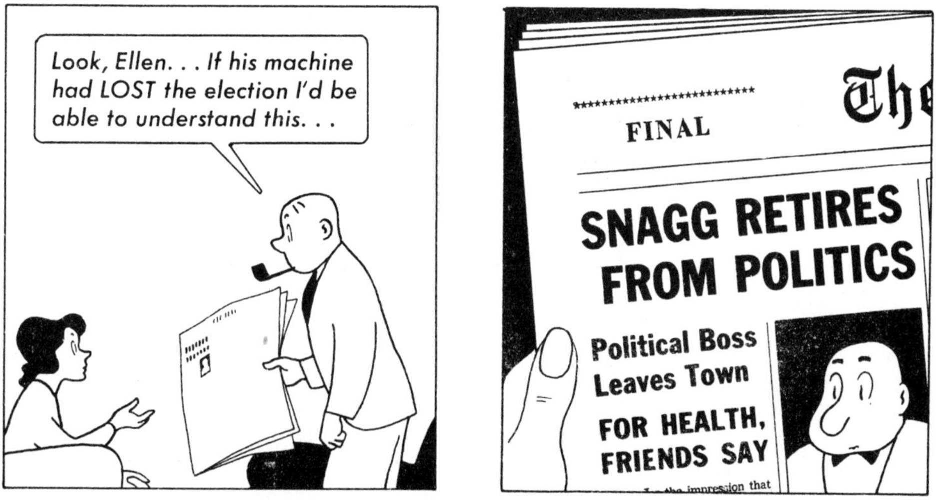
Look, Ellen. . . If his machine had LOST the election I'd be able to understand this. . .
FINAL
SNAGG RETIRES FROM POLITICS
Political Boss Leaves Town
FOR HEALTH, FRIENDS SAY

Yes. Boss Snagg's behavior yesterday was a bit odd. . . The responsibility of getting me elected was a strain. . . Well, Barnaby. It's time for me to leave for Congress . . .
Goodbye.
Take my word for it. . . There's an extraordinary story behind all that. . .
CROCKETT JOHNSON